Broken At A Crossroad

Roza Perry

Rackhouse Publishing
Read to Learn. Write to Remember

Copyright © 2021 Roza Perry
All rights reserved. No part of this manuscript may be reproduced, stored in a retrieval system or transmitted in any form, or by any means, electronic, mechanical, photocopying, recording or otherwise, without prior permission of the author.

ISBN-13: 978-1-7355350-4-3
ISBN-13: 978-1-7371987-0-3

For information about custom editions, special sales, premium and bulk purchases, please contact:
Rackhouse Publishing Inc.
904-530-6754
rackhousepublishing.com

NOTES

1 Explore All Countries-Senegal, The World Factbook, 8 June 2021, www.cia.gov/the-world-factbook/countries/senegal/
2 Wolof, Countries and Their Cultures, 2021, https://www.everyculture.com/wc/Rwanda-to-Syria/Wolof.html
3 Polygamy in Gambia, Gambia Information Site, 2021, http://www.accessgambia.com/information/polygamy.htm

First Edition
Printed in the U.S.A

To God Alone Be The Glory

A Dios Solo Sea La Gloria

A Dieu Seul Soit La Gloire

To my Lord & Savior Jesus Christ for all that you have done, are doing, and have yet to do. I stand in awe of you

CONTENTS

CHAPTER 1: THE LOVE I ONCE KNEW (1)

CHAPTER 2: A WHOLE NEW WORLD (29)

CHAPTER 3: MARRIAGE & MOTHERHOOD (45)

CHAPTER 4: LIES, HURT & BETRAYAL (59)

CHAPTER 5: A STRANGER FROM AMERICA (75)

CHAPTER 6: UNEXPECTED INTERRUPTIONS (85)

CHAPTER 7: UNFAMILIAR TERRITORY (105)

CHAPTER 8: BROKEN AT A CROSSROAD (125)

CHAPTER 9: 24 HOURS TO LIVE (145)

CHAPTER 10: THE GOD OF THE CHRISTIANS (157)

CHAPTER 11: THE POWER OF A NAME (167)

CHAPTER 12: HOSPITAL MIRACLES (183)

CHAPTER 13: TO GOD BE THE GLORY (213)

ACKNOWLEDGMENTS

Tatiana Alexandra Brooks
You are my one & only! My world, today, tomorrow and always!

Mark Singleton, my spiritual father, you took me under your wing & have shown me the love of Christ in ways that will impact my life forever.

The Cox family
My mom Kendaka Samba Cox
Awa, Abdul Isha, Sukai, Agi, Doudou & Mohammed Cox
Fatoumatta, and the rest of my family in Gambia & the UK.

Manor Park, London United Kingdom (my Prayer Warriors)
Jaynnes Mwaniki Wangari
Florence Mbelo
Caroline Mensah
Aunty Anita Raphael
Meisha Nontongo
Ngozi , Rosemary Agu
Kemi Fajoye
Jacky Raphael
Reita Sato Eby

Pastor Tony & Evelyn King
New Hope Revival Church International
Holiday Inn, Greenwich, London, United Kingdom SE10 OGD

Pastor John & Crista Bailey
Pastor Mat Pace
The Springs Church, 317 Blanding Blvd, Orange Park, Florida, 32073
United States

Mentions

Pamm Turner
Tut John Palmer
Tasha Harmon
Adji Ndiaye Souareh

LaTanya Peterson
Jhene Chula Rodriguez
LaTonya Rogers
Jamarra Mcgraw

Roza Perry

Ericka Sturdivant	Toni Scott
Rhonda Brown	Duncan Alan Wiggins
Maggie D (Derksen)	Katie Ethridge
April Varner Hare	Awa Wally Njie Guest

Thank you all for your love, friendship, prayers, and support. For walking with me in both the best and the darkest days of my life. For being there when I needed to talk or a shoulder to cry on.
God chose each and every one of you to play an important role in our journey this far; for that I am humbled and grateful. May He bless you all as you have been a blessing to us.

With Sincere Love and Gratitude,
Roza & Tatiana

In Loving Memory
My dad - Mohamed Mustapha Cox
My sister - Ya Lissong Cox
My best friend - Adeola Osinuga

Roza Perry

DEDICATION

To Tatiana Alexandra Brooks, my miracle child. You are fiercely loved with no reservations. As long as I breathe, you can count on me.

Always & Forever,

Mommy

1
The Love I Once Knew

I was born into a Muslim family and a polygamous home in Gambia, West Africa on the 8th of May in 1982. Gambia is a country in West Africa located on the Atlantic Coast and near the country of Senegal. It was colonized by the United Kingdom and is the birthplace of Kunta Kinte, one of the prominent slaves from the novel *Roots* by Alex Haley. Kunta was a warrior from the Mandingo tribe who was enslaved and voyaged across the world to start a new family in America. He had a voice, and he was going to use it. He refused to comply and do whatever they told him. He often challenged the slaves born in America to fight for their freedom and was later given the name Toby. It was meant to be his English name, which he refuted because he remembered that little African country where he was born with his family and where he was captured.

Like Kunta, the roots of my life run deep in the rich and resilient soil of my ancestors. Even though The Gambia is Africa's smallest non-island country, it is a big place that I could never forget.

I am the second of six kids; four girls and two boys. At the time of my birth, my mother said she and my father were extremely excited. Initially, she wished she was having a boy but still felt happy when I came along, because she already had my sister and had experience, even as a young mother. It wasn't as scary and daunting as it was the first time around for her. The only thing that intimidated her was my size. I was quite small so they would wrap me up in swaddles and baby blankets to keep me warm, as they do with premature babies. That was a challenge, but it was nothing that my mother couldn't handle.

My mother is the second of eight children and came from a very wealthy polygamous family. She is from a tribe called Wolof (a West African ethnic group found in northwestern Senegal, The Gambia, and southwestern coastal Mauritania.) In Senegal, the Wolof are the largest ethnic group, while elsewhere they are a minority.¹ Her dad (my grandpa) had several wives, and my grandma was the second or the third wife. My mom's family was a very religious Muslim family who was very well-known and respected in the community. They would pride themselves on their Islam faith. They were always respectful enough to follow all of the rules and regulations that went with it. In other words, their faith was the foundation of their being. That was the home my mom was born into and the way in which her life was governed as a child. Being born into a polygamous home was normal to her. Most Wolof people are Muslim, and in Gambia, polygamy is a widely accepted practice. Islamic tradition allows a man to marry up to four wives, and they are usually referred to as co-wives.³

My grandpa was a building contractor and he prided himself on being very fair. Back in those days, people didn't send their daughters to school. In fact, only about twenty percent of Wolof women were literate.² He wasn't very educated himself, but he knew the importance of it. My mother was the smartest out of all of her siblings and went on to pursue a career in teaching. By the time she married my dad, she had already embarked on her teaching career. She's one of the best teachers I have ever known, because she has that desire to impart knowledge to people. She is also one of the strongest women I know.

My mother didn't actually grow up with her mom and dad. She was brought up by a cousin of the family who couldn't have kids. This cousin was a good friend of my grandma, so my grandma decided to let her raise my mom. Her upbringing didn't impact her desire to live a good life; she had a decent education in the standards of those days and embarked on a career.

My dad was a foreigner in Gambia. His people came over from Angola, Mozambique, Lisbon in Portugal, and Cape Verde. His ancestors and his heritage ran deep in these countries. But somehow, they found themselves over in The Gambia. The story of how has always changed from year to year, but ultimately it all boils down to the fact that he landed in that country.

My mother was a beautiful woman—nearly six feet tall—when she was young. She was slim, dark, and very intelligent. Her and my dad together were the definition of vanilla and chocolate. Everyone says they made a beautiful couple in their day. I bet this played a role in them fighting for their love and contributed to my mom not caring that he was already married to another woman. My mom was his second wife and accepted him despite the fact that he already had a first wife and four children. That had to be love because many women back then would not have necessarily done the same—even though many didn't have a chance to choose, depending on their families. That must have been hard, but I believe their love made it easier. That is what real love does.

In Africa, back in those days, it was common for parents to choose their child's spouse. They sit down and arrange it. They do all the marital rites and traditions. If you aren't lucky, you're even told on your wedding day. Some very generous families will tell you who you will marry ahead of time. They do not ask you because it's already a done deal. They've sorted it out. They know what's best for you. They've mapped out your future. They trust that person to take very good care of you. All of these things were arranged back in those days when my mother was born. My mother and father wanted no part of an arranged marriage; they fell in love and often found themselves fighting to be together. There was disapproval on both sides of the family. My dad's side had their reservations for whatever reason, I suppose. Some welcomed my mother into the family, and some had their reasons not to. Either way, they were married and well on their way to building a family together.

My dad was mixed-race Portuguese so he has a very fair complexion. He is very tall, six foot six one to be exact. He has beautiful, soft, curly black hair and a well-shaped face with strong features. He worked out back then, so he had an impeccable physique. He had handsome features in general, but his smile was the icing on the cake. That smile is what got him in trouble. He had a pristine set of teeth with a jawline that seemed quite prominent in many of his photos. Overall, he had a masculine, strong, aura and presence about him. My father's family was Catholic, and he grew up in the church. My dad was actually one of the choir boys. He was one of the little boys walking with the candle behind the priest, and his family was very proud of their faith as well.

These two families were on opposite ends of the spectrum. And because my mom and dad fell in love with each other, history had to be written for the two of them. Not only was my father a foreigner, but he was also not a Muslim. They wanted him to convert, which he eventually did. They faced great hardship while fighting to be together: social discrimination, lack of financial stability, and her family's lack of confidence in my father. My parents took all of that into consideration; in the end, no matter who was for or against them, their love won.

Before they started a family, my dad joined the police force. He had to undergo rigorous training before he embarked on this career, which was interesting because he never really wanted to be a policeman in the first place. One day, his best friend, who had ambitions to be a police officer, convinced my dad to accompany him to the police academy. They both approached the recruiter, and my father's friend stepped forward and introduced himself as the interested participant.

The recruiting officer gave him a form, and then addressed my dad, "What about you? I'm sure you would make a fine young police officer."

At that moment my dad thought, *What the heck? What have I got to lose?* I'm not even sure if he was working at that point in time, but he applied and was accepted into The Gambia Police Academy. This was the start of him serving his country through a career in law enforcement. Even though he was a foreigner, he came to love the country he served and did his job with integrity and character.

Soon after this, he met my mom at a local disco that she attended with a friend. My dad was there with his friends, and they started talking. Soon after, they began dating; one thing led to another, and they fell for each other. They are the ultimate example of how complete opposites can attract. They were two totally different people with very different heritages and lifestyles until they were married. Once they were married, they were both bound by the Muslim faith. I don't think their families would have allowed them to marry if he was still a Christian. Back then, intermarriage of any kind was frowned upon, but especially when both people had a different faith.

To make things worse, my dad's family was very modest. They came from humble beginnings and didn't have much compared to my mom's family. It looked like all the odds were against them. In life, some people are lucky not to have to fight to be with the one they love. But there are very real situations where the start of a relationship is terrible, because you're fighting for your right to be together. To actually end up with the person that you wanted to spend the rest of your life with was a privilege afforded to few.

When you love someone, the need to be with them far outweighs any logical reason not to be with them. No one else understands the feelings you hold for that person except you and your partner. When I think about what they had to go through and all they've achieved in their respective careers together, both of them had no choice but to be hard-working. They never sat around at home. I had parents that left for work every morning. One was a police officer who donned a dapper uniform and served his community daily. The other, an amazing teacher who loved educating children and anything involving academics. The two of them were a power couple in their respective careers. They were both well respected. All you had to do was say my father or my mother's name, and everybody knew them. I was conceived out of love. My parents loved me. They fell in love, and my siblings and I are the tangible products of that love.

When I was born, they disagreed on names for me. My dad wanted to name me after his grandmother, Roza; this was a Christian name. My mom was not in agreement in the beginning, but she eventually gave up and agreed. So, I was named after my grandma who lived with us and nurtured me like I was her own child. The differences my parents had with their families before me seemed almost invisible because I was the apple of their eyes. I was something they all shared.

My grandma loved me. I was her namesake. My earliest memories of her are vague, because she died when I was still very young. My grandma lived with us until she passed. My dad's family is very small. My dad only has a sister and a brother, while my mother has so many siblings that I couldn't count them all if I tried. This is because her dad had about four or five wives. Growing up, we had both sides of the family, and I loved them both. However, they lived their lives in vastly different ways. My Muslim family members never cooked pork in the house, but there were no dietary restrictions when I would visit my Christian family. I could eat pretty much whatever I wanted, even though I wasn't supposed to according to my Muslim beliefs. It was nice to break the rules while I was there. My Portuguese family was a very integral part of my childhood.

When you're from a polygamous home, it's hard to make someone understand the challenges that come with it. For instance, my father's first wife gave birth to a girl exactly two days after I was born. It couldn't have been easy for him: having a baby by each wife so closely together and wanting to nurture them both fully. I imagine that he felt divided at moments because he couldn't always be a part of the ever-changing activities as the infant developed into a toddler. No one knows what went wrong, but not long after my birth, things started to fall apart for my dad and his first wife. When I was a newborn infant, they separated and finally divorced. Soon thereafter, my mother took in his first wife's four kids. In Gambia and most of Africa, it is the norm to take in your stepchildren and raise them as your own. It was expected of the wife and not frowned upon, so I guess my mom had to be okay with it as well. Our home grew from two to six, as well as the four others that she went on to have with my father.

My mother is an incredible woman. She's one of those women that are tougher than old boots. She's resilient and resourceful. She's especially kind to children, which I think is why she wanted to teach. She loved what she did, and it was very rewarding to her. I couldn't tell you how many people passed through my mother's doors. I don't know whether she was ready for the responsibility she took on, but I can tell you that she took it on with grace. She did a better job than most and I couldn't imagine having to take over a huge family at the tender age that she was with my dad. She had to master mothering and nurturing everyone, including a husband.

During all of this, my dad's career took off. He traveled in order to go up in the ranks in the police force, which meant he often had to leave his family. We also moved frequently. I think it's fair to say that each and every one of my siblings were born in a different town, city or region, because Dad was so hardworking. He went into the toughest areas that people didn't want to go: under-resourced food deserts, places with no electricity or no water. In other areas, they used the well as their water supply and grew a lot of their food. They were very self-sufficient.

On his journey to get to the top of the police force —his driving aspiration— my dad would go to the low-income places that nobody would volunteer to go to. He was very proud of his career, and that allowed him to travel out of the country. He went to London, Nigeria, and even South Africa in his training. He did whatever was available that could help him be the very best, that was what he always aimed for. There were times when he had to leave his family for long periods.

My mother had to hold the fort down for him. Of course, it wasn't easy, but my mother's career prepared her for the challenge. She was a disciplinarian and loved routines. She was very much the kind of wife that had a passion for cooking and nurturing her family. My mother had to rule with an iron fist. She was the one that would give you the beating of your life.

And my dad was the one that you would run to for cover, but he would only intervene and say, "That's enough," or, "I told you so, but you wouldn't listen. Now you're going to get the beating you deserve."

My mother implemented the punishments most of the time. The fact that Mom was the one at home with us the most, but Dad was more likely to give comfort and a shoulder to cry on was quite a travesty for me.

Broken at a Crossroad

It is the norm in Africa to have maids to help care for the house when you are at work. Nearly every home in Africa has them, and growing up, we've always had two. Even while having maids, my mom was a traditional wife. One would say she was educated, somewhat independent, and somewhat modernized, but it didn't matter. Saturday and Sunday and some days in the week when she finished early, my mom was at home cooking and getting things ready for my father. That was the kind of mother I saw. She was a great cook, who knew my dad's favorites. My mom nurtured us all and waited on my father well. All the same, when my dad was in training in another country, I missed him terribly when I was alone with my mom and my siblings. I was a daddy's girl. He loved me and I knew it, too.

I'm not saying my mother didn't love me; of course she loved me. I just had this special bond with my dad. And the fact that I was named after his grandma, whom he loved so much, held a special place in his heart and mine.

My dad was my hero. He was that person that could look up and tell me the sky was yellow and I would have believed him. I felt so secure in his love for me. I treasured the moments in which I played with his hair and asked him questions about why he was so light while I was so dark. I remember asking questions about his people, where they came from and the places he visited. I was that little African girl who had a father who was seeing the world; I was seeing through his eyes and traveling the world vicariously through his stories. My siblings and I were always in for a good story time. There was always something to tell and there was never a dull moment.

Big families have their perks. One of them is you will not be lonely if you do not want to be, as there is always someone there. During the times that my dad was gone, I was glad to have my siblings. I can't remember the time that I realized that some of them were my full siblings and some of them were only my half siblings —my father's children. Even though she didn't give birth to all of us, my mom didn't like it when people segregated the kids or asked her questions about their mother. She had made the decision to be their mother and that was exactly what she did. If something had to be done, she did it yesterday. That was the kind of person she was. Even though my dad was gone, overwhelming as it must've been, she made it look quite efficient because she put us all into a routine.

We all woke up at the same time. One by one, we would shower and get ready for school. I remember the driver waiting to take us to school. We didn't take public transport, as there was no school bus. My dad always had a driver who would drive us to school and pick us up right after school as well, or sometimes he would do it himself. We all knew exactly what to do and where to wait for the driver after school. When we arrived home, we didn't have to be told what to do. We would always do our homework while lunch was prepared; then we would eat lunch. After that, it would be study time. My mom had all kinds of study books for us to read. She taught math, English, literature, and social studies; she was very versatile. Whatever my mom taught at school, we had an overdose of it at home. These were subjects she expected us to excel at. Can you imagine teaching other people's children and your own failing at the same subjects? That would have been very embarrassing.

So my siblings and I would file into the house after school, have our lunch, and get into our books for the rest of the day. We would only have just a couple of hours to play outside with other kids and be a child before it grew dark. A routine worked for her, but there were a lot of other things she had to learn along the way because after my father agreed to move his family and receive another promotion in another remote region of the country, his bride and his family had to go with him. This was a huge adjustment since my mom was born into a different lifestyle. I think it humbled her a lot, and I think it made her want to be one of those people that changed the narrative. She believed in building a career for herself and in her own ability to deliver her work well. My mother loved what she did to the point that she was taking in other people's kids and tutoring them after school for free. There were kids that she saw had a unique ability in some areas, slow maybe in others or even in certain cases absolutely brilliant with photographic memories. They weren't able to have the extra help after school to help them with the subjects that they struggled with because of the financial conditions of their family. I saw my mom taking all those kids and teaching them term after term, one kid after another.

Can you imagine the pressure we were under as the kids of a teacher? There was no room for failure. Where other kids are told it's okay to bring a "B" home. A "B" was a downgrade, because your mother expects you to know more than everybody else. She was the one imparting knowledge, and as her child, you should somehow have that ability automatically to ace every subject, especially the ones that she taught. She was a mother raising kids. We weren't the type of children who were being raised by the "nannies" or "the help." She was very hands on and wanted to know what was going on with each and every one of us. It still puzzles me how she was able to keep a tab on that many children, but she did.

Whenever my dad came home, it would be like a celebration in the house. The man of the house was home. Some of my most memorable and loving moments of my childhood were during the times when my dad returned home from being away, because then you wanted to just hold him and not let go. In my mind, I believed that if I let go, he would be gone again since it happened so often. I just wanted to be by his side and savor every moment because I knew the drill.

In the West, it was almost the same as army brats. Everybody jokes about how army brats are used to change and being shipped from one place to another, following the head of the family as they pursue that career in law enforcement, in protecting the freedom of the people in the country. It was basically the same concept when he was away. I was strong-willed and stubborn with a smart mouth, very sensitive and emotional. I was the type of child that would get into trouble very easily. You can imagine the punishment I had to go through while my dad was away. By the time he returned, it was time to go have some daddy-daughter time. I was like his shadow; wherever my dad was, I wasn't too far behind. I'm not saying I was the only one he loved, as he loved all of my siblings. I'm quite sure of that, but I know I was his favorite. So when my mom would lay complaints of all that had happened in his absence, I knew my dad would be more merciful and understanding. There is nothing more beautiful to children than to know that they're loved, wanted, and valued. I felt that knowledge from my dad very early on. Even though there were a lot of us, I had somehow found home in my dad's heart and he in mine. I think my siblings, family, friends, everybody knew it as well.

My dad was more likely to comfort you rather than to whoop you. It was in his nature to come up with the kindest words that he could find to chastise us. He always balanced things out. Wherever there were lots of children, there would always be drama or some kind of discord. This was the case in our family, there were older kids that were half siblings of the younger ones and my mother was raising us all. It was challenging. Sometimes the kids would fight amongst themselves; or when they weren't in one accord and unified, they would talk back to my mother. There were times when they overstepped the rules clearly knowing they wouldn't have done that if my dad was present. All these hardships of a polygamous home are real, while the lessons learned in a big family can also be useful for life if applied properly. You get used to not getting your way; you become very patient, because you have to learn to wait your turn. You become very good at sharing, because everything is split between you all. You're good with people because you're used to dealing with all of these different personalities. And there are so many other benefits of coming from a big family.

But when the family's big *and* polygamous, there can be some very explosive moments. At some point at a young age, I came to realize that there was a difference in the family. A polygamous home is very competitive, and you learn to hold your own very early. You learn not to let anyone else outshine you, so you are not in the shadows all the time. You learn to step up and be seen and heard, because otherwise you'll just be forgotten. There is so much going on.

Everyone in the home has a need, and every need is urgent.

When my father came home, after my mother finished reporting her complaints about the kids and what went wrong in his absence, it was time for us to tell him what we had been doing. I lived for these moments, because I had been keeping a dialogue in my head of all the things I wanted to tell him. I let everyone go before me; gave them time to ask all of the questions they wanted; to jump on his lap; do whatever it was all good. I knew when he had time, it would be all the more special. My favorite times are those of my dad laying on the carpet in the living room with his head on my lap while we watched TV. I was in heaven there braiding and playing with his curly hair. These were the most tender memories of my father. I would take the comb and yank out a tangle.

He would dramatically cry, "Be careful with that, that's lethal!"

I would giggle and say sorry.

My dad would say something like, "You make a lousy hairdresser anyway."

I loved playing with his hair; I loved the way it curled upwards. His hair was very soft and curly because of his heritage, as were most mixed-race people's hair. I didn't understand why his was that way and mine was so hard. I had the typical African hard, tough Afro.

And very soon, I would inquire, "Why is your hair so soft?"

And he would say, "Well, that's because I'm biracial."

When I asked questions, he always took the time to break things down into layman's terms. One of his parents was white, the other was mixed race. He would explain it right down to his generation. He was lighter than my mom and that would trigger another question.

"So, because my mom is dark and you're very light, that's why I'm kind of brown and chocolatey?"

He would laugh, "There's no such thing as brown or chocolatey, Roza. We're all black."

Later on, I realized my dad was very comfortable with the black culture and way of life, because of the surroundings he was exposed to. He did acknowledge the fact that he had a heritage that was different. One that we maybe didn't understand, because the elders of his family lineage all passed on before we were born. But he tried to explain to us that his heritage was different; whereas I was from a fully black bloodline. His bloodline was not, as he had Caucasian blood in his bloodline. He would tell me stories about how one of his maternal aunties had blonde hair and blue eyes. He also shared that his mother had very beautiful, silky, soft hair, and very light-colored eyes like a Caucasian's. All of these things triggered the conversations I had with him.

After all of that, we would move on to his travels, what he did and who he met. I couldn't believe the stories that he told me. One specific memory that stuck with my dad was the story he told me about the royal family. He told me how there was a queen in England who lived in a palace. My first lesson about the royal family was mentioned by my dad. I remember it very clearly; he would tell me about the servants and people guarding over her house every single day and how it's very cold over there. He mentioned the different foods and did his best to give me an insight into how different the West was. He would tell me the tales of how he had to board an airplane, high in the sky, to get to each of these magical destinations.

For a small African child, all of these questions are lodged in your head and in your heart; you're just waiting for an adult to answer them. For me, my dad was my person. My question-answerer. I could bring my every inquiry to him. I was a very curious child, because my dad had traveled a lot. I was more interested in a world outside of my own. From a very young age, I was fascinated by airplanes and by the fact that there's another world so far beyond our reach. My dad told me how Europe and especially London were very cold and so different from our Gambian traditions.

My dad could see the awe and wonder within me. I was just different. While my siblings were more interested in other things, I was so fascinated by his stories. I couldn't wait for his arrival so I could barrage him with various queries about his struggles while abroad.

I absolutely adored my dad. He was a very intelligent man; he was quiet with a self-assured spirit that made him stand out.

He once admonished me, "Roza, there is a big world out there. And one day…one day when you're grown, you will have the opportunity to travel the world, to make something better of yourself. Go and give the world what you were born to…"

As I was combing his hair, he fell asleep halfway through that sentence, but I loved it. That was my perfect time with my dad. That was our thing. These are the moments that I keep in my heart.

When all this was taking place, Gambia was under the presidency of the first President of the Republic of Gambia. The country gained independence from the United Kingdom in 1965; then, the first President of the Republic of Gambia was elected. His name was Sir Dawda Kairaba Jawara. He was in that role when my dad was working as one of the top police officers in the region. He was actually the second in command in the whole country; that was how hard he worked for his career.

We kept moving until the final move during which my dad and my mother built a beautiful six-bedroom house in Knifing Estate, which is about a twenty five-minute drive from the capital city Banjul. By then, my dad decided that he was going to stay put in the city. All the other provinces are where most people really don't desire to take families. He was working on his career, and we were very proud of him. Him and my mother were able to buy a piece of land in a newly industrialized area that was not yet built up. We were among the second or the third family in that area in 1990. They built a beautiful home, and they moved their family into it.

At this point, the members of the family consisted of the four kids from Dad's first marriage and my mother's six biological children. So in our home there were ten kids, my father, my mother, the driver, the maid and the garden boy. Everybody lived in the house. It was a big family compound that accommodated everybody. I had to share a room with my sisters, and I learned how to appreciate things there. Because my parents couldn't always afford to buy all ten children brand new items, we could rest assured that we were going to get someone else's hand-me-downs. I remember always getting gently used clothing and toys that previously belonged to my older siblings. We weren't wealthy, but were doing a whole lot better than most people. We had never gone to bed hungry, and we never had to be naked. We had lots of clothes and shoes. We went to school and never had issues affording school fees.

I was a very intelligent kid. But the pride of the family —the one that everybody knew was going to really make something of himself— was my brother. He was the one after me, and he almost had a photographic memory. My mother made sure she quickly nurtured it and that the boy concentrated more on his studies than anything else. I would come home with A's and B's, and didn't apply myself as much as he did. My other sisters were doing well also, but the pride of my family really was my brother.

He went on to study and graduate from London School of Hygiene and Tropical Medicine. He is now a doctor in Melbourne, Australia.

THE TURNING POINT

We had been living in our new home soon after it was finished, and life was good. We lived twenty-five minutes from the city. My dad's office wasn't very far. I could walk over to the police station to see my dad and ask for money, food, or whatever it was that I wanted. Living in that house felt like we were finally settled. We felt like our family was finally home. The stability of our family home was beautiful. It was awesome to know that we weren't going anywhere else and that my dad and my mom had finally found a place to raise their large family.

We were blissfully happy for a very short while, because very soon the fights started. My mom and dad were having problems. We could hear them shouting at each other. We could hear him screaming. Sometimes I could hear my mom sobbing in her bedroom, but I didn't understand what was going on. My dad would pick up his car keys and leave during nearly every fight or disagreement. He was not just leaving my mom; he was leaving all of us. I wanted him home. I wanted him to stay. For a while, I didn't understand why my mom was driving him away from the family.

In my head, I wanted to tell her, *Stop arguing with him, so he won't have to go. If you don't argue with him, he will stay home where he belongs, with his family.*

That was my logic at that point in childhood. All I saw was that whenever my mom had a complaint, my dad would listen, but he wasn't ready to come clean about what was happening.

We were young, but we weren't stupid. Hearing things through the grapevine and witnessing some of it ourselves, we started talking about it. Everybody in the area realized what was going on, before us. My dad was getting ready to take another wife. She was going to be the first and my dad was going to bring a younger woman into the fold. My mother heard the rumors, and it hurt her deeply.

Being older, I now understand it from a different perspective.

At that point in time, she was thinking, *I have stood by you through everything. When your marriage to your first wife didn't work out, I took on your kids.*

She was given more than she bargained for. It must have been the ultimate betrayal to have him start looking for another wife. Just when they were getting settled. Just when things were starting to become normal. Just when the family was enjoying having one big house for everyone to live in.

In a polygamous home, each family member has his or her own perspective, and this is mine. I can only assume that my mother's perspective was very painful. She felt betrayed. She felt traded in for a younger model. The woman my dad was about to marry was a whole lot younger than my mother, and no woman wants to be replaced with a younger version of herself. Nonetheless, it happened.

My father's disappearances became more and more frequent. Eventually, he was nowhere to be found, and my mom was left wondering where he was. After she finally found out where he was, I will never *ever* forget that fight that ensued in our home.

None of us understood exactly what my mom was going through. We just saw the outside reactions to the drama. My dad hated drama. My dad hated strife and toxic situations; at the slightest sign of conflict, he would pick up his car keys and flee for hours on end.

In the Muslim religion, they are allowed to marry up to four or five wives. Now, I didn't know what the agreement between my dad and my mom was. I don't know whether she actually realized that my dad was going to be marrying more women or whether he made a promise in private that he wasn't going to. Either way, my mom was absolutely devastated when she found out. I remember that day very well.

My mom got a phone call from a friend of hers who told her that my dad had just sent out the preliminary traditional kola nut rites. This is what a groom would send to the bride's family for an introduction to ask for a woman's hand in marriage. I remember my mom questioning her friend on the phone. We were all sitting in the living room watching TV. When she finished with the phone call, she went into her room. I could hear my mother sobbing. Not only was she weeping for herself, but she was weeping for us.

This was the unknown that we were stepping into once again. She didn't know the woman very well, but she knew another woman was about to be her husband's second wife. My dad was oblivious to everything that had just happened in the house. My siblings and I were petrified; the older ones were talking about it and immediately silenced when the younger ones came in. Everybody was trying to find out as much intel as they possibly could.

I overheard two of my siblings conjecturing, "He's taken a new wife, he's got another wife now."

Learning this news coupled with hearing my mother crying, I knew in my heart that it was true. To this day, I still cannot explain my feelings. Behind closed doors, a man can make a lot of promises to a woman; whether he'll keep it or not is all up to him. But we were devastated. I was devastated. I couldn't believe my dad was going for another woman.

I can imagine my mother thinking, *You've got enough responsibility here at home, we need you here. Why are you trying to make another family elsewhere?*

Money was tight. There were now so many people to feed. I can understand right now exactly how my mom felt back then. But at that point in time, I was too young to understand all of the dynamics of the situation. No woman wants to feel like she is not good enough, like that's why her husband found another woman. My mother was a brilliant wife and an amazing mother. She was one of those strong women that you knew would face whatever came her way with the tenacity and a made up mind to give it her all.

That day when my dad came home, all the kids at this point had known. We had all heard my mother's conversation, and we were eavesdropping on it. In Africa, there is no such thing as privacy; whatever they wanted to say was left out in the open. When they argued indoors, the last thing on their minds was the fact that the kids were listening or that those kids were going to be affected by whatever was going on. It was a very different way of dealing with things. Children had to literally be shielded from situations that could affect them. But we were already in mourning.

I snuck out and went back to our room. I was an avid reader. The books got me out of my situation; the books got me out of the monotony of family dysfunction; the books got me out of Africa. All that I was reading about the world made it much more pertinent for me to get out of Africa, to travel the world, and see what it had to offer. I didn't want to be caged in the four corners of what Gambia was. My dad had opened my eyes through his stories. He had sown a seed in me that grew into a desire for something so different from what I was born into. I remember lying in bed and feeling so unwanted. My mom felt her own feelings and emotions based on whatever had broken between her and my dad. My mom's heart was shattered. I don't think they realized that us kids had our own score to settle. We all had our own pain. We all had questions that needed answers, none of which were a priority.

I remember lying in bed feeling rejected and abandoned as I wondered, *Why was he doing this? Why did he want another woman? Weren't we enough? I mean, he has so many children. Aren't we the family that he's always wanted? If I behaved right; if I loved him some more; if I stopped being naughty; if I got into less trouble; would it have made a difference? Did we push him away? Did my mother push him away?*

All these questions plagued my mind as I lay in bed, crying myself to sleep. I cried so much. But I was trying so hard not to let my other siblings see me, because they would have made a mockery of what I felt. I was a very emotional child. I was very sensitive. I was a child that had lots of emotions. Even though I didn't say it, they were still in there. I had no one to talk to about how I felt, no adults to actually run to and ask questions.

It was more like the kids were seen and not heard, very much like that. As I lay in bed, I had this strong feeling that our lives were about to take a different path, that things were never going to be the same. Everything was about to come crashing down. My mom didn't even realize that her children — especially me— were also mourning the loss of the man she loved. I was so angry at what he was doing. For the first time, I was angry at *him*. Because no matter how bad things were, my mom was the one who was going to be home with us now, while he would have to make time to spend with his other family.

In the Muslim faith and tradition, when a man has two or more wives, he divides his time between them. He spends two days with each, depending on the arrangement. But he's meant to spend equal time with both wives and families. This lady wasn't coming into our home. There was no space or room for another woman in our home. I knew that for a fact, after hearing all these arguments for months and knowing how my mom felt. It all made sense now, but she was not coming to our home. At least that was the light at the end of the tunnel in the situation. It was one thing for my dad to be married to another woman, but it was another for her to have to move into our home and change the whole family dynamic.

But the way it sounded and the way my mom reacted to it, it seemed like my dad was going to get another home for this woman and move her in it. I laid there crying for my dad. Wanting him to come home. Wanting him to come and hold me. Wanting him to tell me everything was going to be okay, to tell me it was all a lie or a bad dream. I would have given anything for anyone to step into my reality and tell me this wasn't happening. It was a mistake. It was somebody else. It wasn't my dad.

I cried with anger boiling inside of me. I couldn't wait for him to come home. I remember one of my sisters actually coming into the room, not realizing I was laying on the bed. She was having a conversation with my brother. And she literally told him it happened. He's done it. He has got another woman that's going to be his wife and so the confirmation again was there as I look back into our lives with my dad being there full time, I knew we'd like I knew I was Roza, nothing was going to be the same.

As I fell asleep, the darkness consumed my mind and my heart. Anger took over, as I sobbed myself to sleep. I must have slept for hours, because I woke up to the sound of my dad. Normally, I wanted my dad; I ran to him, flinging myself on him, and I would hold his hand. But this evening when he came home, there was a somber mood in the house, as if someone had died. Everybody was subdued, quiet, and contemplating. Everyone had their questions that they wanted him to answer.

But most of all, my mother was waiting. It was one encounter I would never forget. He came into the house not knowing that this was the calm before the storm. Inside there was a broken-hearted woman to whom he had once promised unconditional love, honor and care. Now, that same vow would be given to another woman. I moved solemnly from the bed, and I walked over to meet him. I didn't run to him this time. I was angry. I didn't want him to just hold me, I needed to know why he had done it. But then in Africa, you didn't question your elders; you did as you were told. You're not brought up with the freedom to express yourself.

As he came in through the hallway to go into the living room. He saw me standing there looking at him. This was not how we usually greeted each other. Something had changed. He looked at me, and I looked at him. But he quickly averted his gaze. My dad knew what I'd been told and that the news had reached his other children as well. I looked at him, and I felt betrayed. I felt traded in. I knew we had the best relationship. My dad and I were always very close, closer than most of my siblings, to be honest with you. And so I felt like he owed me an explanation. Isn't it amazing? When you have that love connection with somebody, it's almost as if you expect them to naturally have your back. You expect for them to be the one to come in when you're going through hard times and be understanding. I wanted him to tell me. I didn't want to hear it from my mother.

My mother was angry. My mother was very sad. My mother had her own score to settle, which was very different from the children's.

I wanted my dad to love me enough to say, "Let's have this conversation."

This was what was going on in my head as I looked at him, *Tell me, just tell me, tell me the truth!*

It was as if I wanted to be his confidant. Maybe he couldn't tell anybody else or my mom. But I almost wanted him to know that he could trust me, that he could tell me and reassure me. He could comfort me and tell me everything was going to be okay. My mom was going to be staying put; it was him that was going to be leaving. I needed reassurance from him more than anybody else. I stood there looking at him, watching him clearly feeling uncomfortable. That wasn't my dad; I was watching him act in a very strange way. He knew something had happened. He knew from everybody's reaction, but God, he didn't know exactly what he was stepping into. Then he went into the living room.

My mother, having heard him come in, also came into the living room. There were a few whispers, and they headed towards their bedroom. My mother was briskly walking towards the bedroom. You could tell she had a lot on her chest. You could tell she had been crying. You could tell my dad was going to get the brunt of her mood. They went into the room and closed the door. I was right outside, and I wasn't about to miss anything. I watched my siblings. They were waiting in line for my mom and dad to go into the room. As I walked quietly towards their bedroom door, two of my siblings came out of nowhere and wanted to know exactly what was going on behind those closed doors.

The first thing I heard was my mom saying, "How could you?"

The raw emotion with which those words came out was staggering, "How could you? How could you do this? Haven't we got enough responsibility with all these kids, with all these mouths to feed, the school fees, and the living expenses?"

As she was talking, my dad became very angry. I guess he didn't appreciate being put in a position that didn't allow him to choose the time or the place to have this conversation. Followers of Islam are to tell their first wife that they plan on taking in a second to have her blessing or consent before Muslim men marry the new wife. None of that had happened in my mother's case. She literally heard the gossip out on the streets through somebody else; that was how she found out. She deserved an explanation, and she was going to get it. Soon enough, they were arguing so badly that they were yelling at each other.

I could hear my dad defending himself, "I do not have to explain myself! How did you know?"

My mother ignored his question and said, "No wonder you have been going missing all this time. Never home, always disappearing, making us wonder where you are. How could you do this?"

My mom was sobbing by now. As for my dad, I don't know whether he felt guilty or justified because he was the man of the house. Perhaps to him, that gave him the right to do what he wanted to do without asking for my mother's consent. My siblings and I leaned in to hear every single word that was being spoken.

My dad literally told my mom that she needed to deal with it, because it had happened. He had met somebody else and was getting married to her very soon. All I heard was wailing. She cried for her family. She cried for the man she loved. She cried for the fact that life and our family dynamics were never going to be the same.

"I cannot deal with this right now. I cannot have another argument with you!" My dad shouted. The next minute, there was the turning of the keys to open the door at which we were stealthily eavesdropping..

We ran into a room. All of my siblings ran for cover, everybody hiding to avoid the consequences that came with intentionally overhearing your parent's conversation. I was under the bed when I heard my dad yank the door open and slam it so hard that I thought it was going to fall off its hinges.

"I am not doing this with you," he said one more time as he walked briskly out of the door.

"No, you will come and answer my questions. You owe me that much," my mom roared, following him, "You can't just do this, casually come in here, and expect everybody to be okay with it. I deserve some explanation. I deserve to know what is happening."

The level of his fury was almost perplexing. What did he have to be angry about? This was *his* doing. As I cowered under the bed, I heard him walking. You could hear his footsteps going down the hallway, out into the foyer, and into the compound. I couldn't believe this. Would you believe this situation if you were there? Why wouldn't he just sit all of us down and talk to us? Why was he treating my mother like this? So many questions!

I crawled out of the bed and I ran to him. I ran to him to see exactly what he was trying to do, and I saw him getting into his car as I came out. I had never seen my dad speed that quickly. He got into the car, slammed the door, and the next minute, he was leaving. I stood watching the dust rise as his car was racing down the street. My siblings and I watched him go. All we knew was that whatever had taken place couldn't be undone and that it was only a matter of time before we knew the full extent of what was going to happen to my mom and dad.

I was transfixed there, standing there watching my dad drive away until his car went out of view. I turned back and there were my siblings standing right there, witnessing everything, all of us confused not knowing what was going to happen. I slowly made my way back into the house and headed for my mother's room. When I went to my mother's, the door was closed but you could hear the weeping from inside. That woman was broken, and my heart went out to her. But part of my heart was also with my father, he had taken it wherever he was going. I was never going to be whole. Not with my father going to have another family.

I wanted him. I wanted my dad, a part of me wanted him to even turn that car around and come back for me. Maybe not for my siblings, because I was looking out for my own relationship with him.

I thought, *At least come for me. I know you love me. I know you want me. I've always been secure in your love. Why is this happening? Why is this happening?*

With resignation, I told myself, *There is nothing I can do for my mother.*

She needed her time to be by herself, so I walked away and went into our room to find a secret hiding place where I could let my feelings take over and allow myself to feel what I needed to feel. I went into the bedroom and cried my eyes out. My mother was crying in her room and I was crying in mine. All my other siblings handled their hurt in a different way.

I will never forget that evening, as it was the start of a different life, of a different world than what we had known. He was doing something that came with being a Muslim, he was doing something that his faith allowed him to. He felt entitled that as long as the religion was okay with it, why would anybody else have any problems? I bet that's how we saw it. He never realized how much we loved him, how much we needed him, or what his absence would mean for our lives. This would go on to affect all of our relationships. He should have known that for his children, things were never going to be the same again.

I think for the first time in my young little life, fear came into my heart. *What was going to happen, what was the future going to be like? How is he going to be with us this evening, are they going to divorce like the first wife?*

All kinds of questions were in my head.

You see, in the Muslim faith back then, divorce was unheard of. This was in the early nineties, and no matter how hard your marital status was, you sucked it up and did the best you could. But with these circumstances, you never knew how it was going to unfold. As I lay in the bed, I prayed that my dad wouldn't divorce my mom, that he wouldn't leave us permanently.

I prayed to Allah that he would change the whole situation, and allow my dad to come home and be with us. I couldn't understand how we were going to be celebrating everything now. Because with everything going on, my dad had always been the head of the home. He was gone in that respect. He was the head of another home. Now, everything would be different.

When it was time for dinner, my mom came out with swollen eyes and her face all distorted. She was having a hard time, but she had a family to feed, and she came out trying to put her best foot forward. She proceeded to make dinner for us, but we could all tell she was deeply hurt. As we sat down as a family that night to eat dinner, I couldn't look at my mom's face. She couldn't look us in the eye. We all knew what was happening, and as we ate our dinner, we were comforted by the fact that each and every one of us was there.

We took comfort in each other's company. The fact that we were there, even though my dad wasn't, gave us solace. So we had dinner, cleared the table, brushed our teeth, and went to bed. Nobody was interested in even hanging around to watch TV, as it just wasn't the same. Everybody just wanted to be on their own. My mom proceeded to go into her room. She closed the door, turned the lights off, and proceeded to go to sleep. We did the same and it was one of the longest nights of my life, because I couldn't sleep. Insomnia set in, my mind was racing and I couldn't shut it down. I lay there for hours and stared at the ceiling wishing I could sleep; wishing I was no longer craving for my father; wondering what he was doing and who he was with. Was he happy or was he as sad as we were?

The next morning, I was so tired, but still I had to go to school. I had such a troubled sleep that I wasn't functioning properly, and I think my mom realized this. Everything was different. You could cut the atmosphere with a knife; we were all so despondent and heartbroken. The ride to school was the longest I'd ever had because it wasn't my dad but the driver instead, and we weren't teasing each other. I could tell my siblings wanted to talk about it, as they were whispering. But for some reason, we didn't say it out loud.

We went to school, and I couldn't wait to get into the sanctuary of the school to see my friends to try to have a normal day. But what was normal? I went into class that day feeling so lethargic, my mind occupied with everything that was going on at home. Everybody, including the teacher, expected me to just get over it. School finished; it was a terrible day. The teachers and even my friends could tell I was not myself. My best friend kept asking what was wrong but I didn't have the heart to tell her the truth, because I didn't want to break down in front of everybody. I wasn't strong enough to share my feelings with other people yet, and I wasn't ready for that. I didn't know how to tell other people about what was going on. See, most people knew the relationship I had always had with my father. Family members would even tease that I was his favorite because I was named after his grandma.

Even still, I guess they forgot that I was going to feel his absence much more than everybody else. My other siblings were already having to live without their mother, who lived at least seven hours away from where we lived. They hardly saw her.

I don't remember ever seeing her come to visit. She wasn't permanent in our lives. How hard was it for them? Did they miss her as much as I was going to miss my dad being gone? Did they long for her? I think him leaving opened up the whole scenario for me where I started seeing things differently. They were still missing out on their mother and the fact that she wasn't there. Now, we would all miss out on the fact that my dad wouldn't be there all the time, as well. It was shared sorrow.

I couldn't share in the sorrow of them not having their real mom be involved in their lives. I didn't know how that felt; that was their own pain to carry and their story to tell. I didn't understand that or appreciate the feelings they felt.

But for the first time in my life, I knew a little bit of what they felt having had my dad leave. That day we got back home and did our best to keep up with the daily routine. I remember sitting at the table, eating, when I heard my dad's car. The sound was very special to me, as it signified what was coming next. Whenever I heard it, whatever I was doing wasn't good enough to hold me there. I wanted to be with my father, so I dropped the food and ran to the door. I watched him come down the path clearly, a shadow of who he once was. He wasn't the confident, loving or kind person that I knew. The man I saw wasn't the person that would walk into a room with confidence, he was different, more guarded. I suppose now that he was afraid. He didn't know how people in the house were going to respond to him, especially my mother. He came into the home knowing that his family was upset with him and that it could lead to another altercation. I went over to meet him. I said hello and just stood there looking at him. I didn't run to him; he didn't come for me. He walked into the house purposefully and went into the spare room where he kept most of his personal belongings. It was separate; the place where he put all his personal belongings and paperwork; the place where he kept his guns so we couldn't reach them.

He went into that room and I thought, *Why isn't he in the room that he shares with my mom?*

I heard some commotion in that room and wondered what he was doing, so I stood right there and waited for him.

Some time passed.

Then my dad opened the door with two big suitcases at his feet. I watched him carefully, wondering what was going through his mind at that moment. My mom came out and saw him with his two suitcases, and it was very evident what was happening. He was having to transport some of his belongings back to the house that he was going to be sharing with his new wife.

Sometimes, even though you know so many people have gone through a loss like this, it feels like you're the only person in the world who has had to watch someone you love walk away. No explanation, no conversation or apology. It makes you feel almost like you're worthless.

He went in, had something to eat, and finished his packing without saying a word to anyone. He didn't speak to us and we didn't talk to him. We all waited to see what he was going to do. He went back into his room a final time, got a few bags, dragged those suitcases out to the car, threw them in the trunk, and slammed it shut. He turned around and looked at me from where I was standing. I was looking at him, and I don't know what I saw in his eyes. Pain. Happiness. Joy. It was hard to tell because he had this poker face that was very hard to read.

Then my dad looked at us one more time, got into his car and sped off. This was the final straw, because he was actually dividing his belongings between two households. Next would be his love and attention.

My whole world came crashing down.

But there was another person who was hurting more than I was: my mom. She knew this was going to happen, there was no way he was going to buy brand new things to take to the other house. No, he would come for his old stuff. Whatever he used to bring into the house would be cut short. As I watched my dad drive away I stood there, and I wished to God that he would come save my family. I prayed to Allah to come and help my mother, as she was never going to be the same again.

Before this, she was happy and joyful. My mother didn't suffer fools lightly and was a very smart woman. She was not as emotional or as sensitive as my father, but something in her head and heart had been broken. I walked back to the house, and I went and joined my siblings in the living room. We all knew what had just happened, and as we sat there playing on the carpet and watching TV, we took consolation in all knowing that it was the start of the unknown. We were going to have to maneuver it in our own way to make the best of the situation.

That was my first heartbreak, my first feeling of rejection, abandonment, and the cause of my low self-esteem.

If I loved him enough, he wouldn't have gone. This was the thought that birthed my low self-worth. *If he loved me enough, he wouldn't have left.* Even at that age, wanting to sort all the things out, wanting to fix the problems that my family were having. The only person who could fix it had literally just packed his bags and left us.

The months that followed after that were hard. There was a change coming that we didn't have any control over, and we needed to do the best that we could. It was the start of another life, one full of strife and pain. We were trying to change the dynamics of the home to accommodate the fact that he would be away half of the time. With the arrival of this new woman, the feelings and the hurt were deeper. The peace was yanked out of our home, because my dad (in his love for this woman) sometimes wouldn't come home as planned.

You see, the woman was allocated two days with my dad and another two days according to the usual polygamy arrangement. So, it would be Monday and Tuesday for my mother, Wednesday and Thursday for her, Friday and Saturday for my mom.

It didn't happen like that. In the beginning, I think my dad was trying so much to avoid drama and anguish at our home that he would choose to stay with her longer than he was supposed to. This caused a lot more hurt. This woman had turned our family upside down. I was so angry with her, because she could have had any other man with no kids and no wife to make a family of her own. But no, out of all the men in Gambia she had chosen my father. She chose to destroy what took years for them to build. I was angry with her. Those were the first feelings of anger that I had ever known in my life.

Everything was a first at that point. There was so much confusion and drama. My mom saw people walk away from her; people that were always loyal to her now paid their allegiance to this new woman. The betrayal she was going through was immense and as the months unfolded, there was more hurt and pain with people taking sides and turning their backs on her. She had done nothing wrong. My mom wasn't going to be healed for a very long time. As she maneuvered this new state of affairs in our home, she was sitting watching not only her marriage disintegrate but also having to say goodbye to some friends she had looked out for.

This woman was young, beautiful, and tall. She was everything a man would have wanted. My dad had fallen hard, regardless of how anybody felt about it. That was the start of the dysfunction in my home and even though my mom and dad never got divorced, I don't think their marriage ever recovered from that. My dad proceeded to have kids with this lady; they had two girls.

My mother had another son, who was their last one. I guess it was a case of wanting to have a piece of him and not waiting on another woman. We were all very happy when my last brother came, as he was the second boy.

All of a sudden, out of nowhere, my dad fell ill. He had this sore on his foot, it started out being a little wound that was just itchy to start with. But soon, it was oozing and the wound had turned septic. He had to go to the hospital. My dad was the kind of person that would go to his health checkups. He had never had a weight problem, and being a police officer, he was actually very fit. He always took care of his body. No one expected what was about to unfold.

He went to the hospital after becoming concerned that the wound wasn't healing. He had been to the doctor, and he was putting ointments on it. However, it continued to make him feel ill and nauseated. He was on antibiotics and even started using a cane to help him walk. He was in intense pain and when he finally went to the hospital, they realized that he had diabetes. That was the reason why the wound wasn't healing. They admitted him to the hospital but the wound wasn't getting any better. If anything, it was just getting worse to the point that his whole foot was a greenish black color.

At this point, my relationship with my dad wasn't the same as it was when I was younger. I still loved him but he had broken my heart without even knowing it, so I had walls up to protect myself. Things that I couldn't understand, I filled in with my own perspective of what was going on. As I watched him lying on that hospital bed watching him get weaker by the hour, it didn't come as a surprise when the doctor said they had to amputate his right leg because it had become so bad. There was no way they were going to save it, so they amputated it just above the knee. I didn't know how my dad was going to live as an amputee. No one saw that coming, and we were devastated. By this time he was working less and less, and we wondered if he would have to stay at home? We didn't know what was going to happen. How would he get over this? This would affect his life, his livelihood, and his ability to earn for this huge family. We were worried about all of those things, but little did we know that something worse was about to happen. Allah had other plans. We were praying for his recovery and praying that he would find a way to get on with life, given the fact that he had just lost one of his legs.

That was the least of our problems, because they were doing his medical paperwork to send him to England for treatment. They filled in the paperwork because the doctors knew things were going to be really bad, and they were looking for ways to get him out of the country for him to get better medical treatment. But that never came to pass, because a few days after it was amputated, my father died. I was fourteen years old.

I will never forget the day when we got the phone call, it was early in the morning, about five a.m. My wonderful, handsome, loving, compassionate father was gone. He had left his world to rest in the arms of God. He left this world and I wasn't sure where I fit into his heart. I felt like I was kicked out of it when the woman came in, and so it was very hard. I mourned him, and I was broken. The first man who ever showed me compassion, love, and kindness was gone. The man that showed me for a very long time how to be treated in a relationship was gone. He would never get to see me graduate. He wouldn't get to see me get married. He would never get to meet my children. His firstborn, my half-sister, was married and heavily pregnant when my dad died, so he had missed out on seeing his first grandchild. My world was never going to be the same.

I couldn't wait to embark on my own life. I couldn't wait to get out of what I knew; I wanted out. I didn't want this kind of marriage for myself . I made a promise that I was never going to marry a polygamous man. In fact, whatever man I married would have to promise me and put it on paper that he would never marry another woman. I had been brought up in dysfunction with so many hurts, pains, and insecurities that would shape the rest of my life. I didn't have a choice, I didn't ask for it, but I knew I wasn't going to put my children through that.

As time went on after my dad passed, a lot of things transpired. The head of the family was gone. That voice that literally made everything happen was gone, and there was a hole in all of our hearts. There was a hole in our family, one that would never be filled ever again.

Roza Perry

2
A WHOLE NEW WORLD

Eventually, my sister and I left Africa to move to England. She went on to live with my aunt in London.

I went to live with my brother, his wife, and kid in Brighton. Even with all those talks that I had shared with my dad, never did I think that one day I would be living in a country that he had traveled to. He had told me stories of the queen, the monarchy, and everything else. And here I was.

The difference between London and Africa is like day and night. Not only the difference in the people, but the food, the culture and the way of life. Everything was totally alien to anything I had been used to even down to the weather. The weather was just so different; Africa is so hot with temperatures going into the nineties and hundreds. And here I was now living in London, and the weather was colder than anything I'd ever experienced. Living in Brighton near the beach in Hove, we felt the brunt of the weather so much more than those living in London. I had visited my family in London, and I absolutely loved the city. The bright lights were calling me. London was exciting. There was a buzz in the air and it was a much faster pace than Brighton. I had visited and gone to the carnival, which happened in the summer in August. It was the Notting Hill carnival. Just being in the midst of different cultures, different races, different experiences, food and interactions was exciting.

Brighton was more of a suburb; it was quieter and more of a laid-back type of pace. I just felt like it wasn't for me. In my heart, I felt London calling. I felt the lights beckoning my name. I felt like the city was exactly where I needed to be. I couldn't wait to leave. Whenever I visited my sister, it took all of me to go back home to Brighton, because I didn't like it there at all. I was waiting for an opportunity to leave. My new world was so different for me. Emotionally, I didn't even know exactly how I felt. The change was so drastic.

Eventually, after living in Brighton for so many years, the opportunity came when a friend of mine came over to London. We were going to London for the carnival; but I knew I wasn't coming back, because I had planned it. I had worked and saved some money, and I wasn't going to go destitute in London. I knew it was quite expensive there so I had planned it, worked, and saved up. And so when this friend of mine came, I knew I was never coming back. And that's exactly how I left Brighton. When we boarded that train, I anticipated the idea that I was entering a new chapter of my life. I knew I could survive in London. I was actually working very hard in a hotel before I left, earning good money. I had never been afraid of a hard day's labor and worked quite hard, because I knew I wanted to leave. I knew I had to put a plan in action, and that's exactly what I did. So with that gusto and confidence in myself, I knew that as long as I worked hard, I would make it through. That was the confidence that I went to London with, like this little city just couldn't contain me.

And so as we boarded that train heading for London, I felt free for the first time in a long time. I was stepping into another dimension of my life. I didn't know how it was going to pan out, but I knew this was going to happen. We reached London, and the first thing I did was rent a flat with my friend and another girl that I had gone to school with back home in the Gambia. We enrolled in college, and our lives started. It was work in college, but I wasn't consistent because all I wanted to do was work, earn money and get the things that I wanted. I would skip classes, because my education wasn't a priority in my life. My work was and I worked extremely hard.

After years in London, something happened I will never forget. I lived very close to a nightclub called Legends. I was working just down the street in a hairdresser's shop. I was the youngest hairdresser in the salon, and I had just embarked on that career after giving up. I was still going to college at that point, but my heart wasn't in it. I knew I was about to give it up. I just didn't want to do that without knowing what else to get into.

One particular night, there were some celebrations going on at the club. I was invited by a friend who was leaving work; they were having a celebratory night for it. At that point in time, I was always partying and going out after work. I had so much strength left over after twelve hour shifts because I was young, beautiful, and very sociable. Overall, I enjoyed my life. I went out and I met a lot of people through my work; so I was invited to parties, nightclubs, weddings, and engagements. You name it, I was there. It was a miracle that I actually had strength left to go out then wake up early in the morning to go to work. I worked six days a week if I wasn't going to college. I was supposed to be in college three times on three days of the week, which never really satisfied me. I just felt like something was missing. Truth be told, my education was not a priority at the age of nineteen going on twenty. A new need had entered my heart.

I didn't just come to London for a better life. I came to London to find my soulmate as well. I had read enough books to know that one day I wanted to meet this amazing man who would be the love of my life and be my knight in shining armor.

You see, when you come from a polygamous home, you develop this need to love and be loved. People don't understand how desire can take over your life. I knew I wasn't going to finish college. I just needed a reason to leave, because what really was in my heart was to fall in love, get married, and have babies. The idea that I was going to one day have not only this man, but our children who would love me unconditionally, was so much more alluring to me than the idea of going to college, getting my degree, and starting a career. Yes, I was hardworking but that wasn't where my heart was. I saw myself not only as a wonderful wife, but a mother. I wanted to feel that love. I was still looking for it, not only in a man, but in my future child that I would be blessed with.

I did date a few men, but I was very ruthless at that point. When I felt like there was no connection, or I really didn't feel any attraction or chemistry with that person, there would never be a second date. I wasn't going to settle for less. I believe in love wholeheartedly. I believe in meeting somebody who would change your whole life by the way you felt for them and how they felt right back. I was looking for that, I wanted that in my life. It felt like I was looking for all the love that I didn't get in my childhood. Because at that age, it's like a journey towards yourself. You're trying to find the things that are important to you, the things you want to do, a career, and a man. You are being led into this journey where huge choices and decisions are going to be made. And as much as I partied, I was still on the lookout for that amazing guy that I was going to date.

I took very great care of my appearance. Being a hairstylist, it automatically came with the territory. I got a lot of attention from the opposite sex. Wherever I went, I got enough attention from men to be able to choose who I wanted to dance with or who I wanted to have a drink with or whatever. I was confident in who I was, even though underneath it all, I was an insecure young girl who had issues that came from my upbringing. Nobody gets to choose their journey.

Nothing else was going to stop me from pursuing that. I had fallen in love with books at a very early age, especially Mills & Boon and Silhouette romantic novels. It so happened that the more I fell in love with reading those books, the more I knew that I wanted one of those love stories. At a very early age, I had dreams of meeting this person, dreams of my wedding day, dreams of what my kids were going to be like. All because a huge part of me had the need to love someone and be loved right back.

I wasn't one for casual relationships or meaningless liaisons and acquaintances. I am a passionate person. I felt like there was so much love in me to give to the right person. I wasn't about to throw it to any Tom, Dick, or Harry that came my way. When I met other girls who just wanted to party and have fun, not thinking about tomorrow, I joined the crowd and partied with them.

But I don't think any of them thought that if they met the man of their dreams, that they would actually give it all up to be a wife and a mother, That wasn't a part of their plans. We all talked about the future. I remember them always coming up with traveling the world and doing all these different things, because that was their need. My needs were different. With that knowledge tucked in my heart as I partied, I was on the lookout for somebody that was going to fit that role. Somebody that I would fall helplessly in love with.

It hadn't happened until that night I went to the club, Legend's. I walked in. My friend had already gotten dressed and arrived before me, because I had to work late. I had to go home, shower, change, get dolled up, and then come over to the club to meet her. I will never forget what I wore and how I looked. It was one of those times when you dress up, and you look good. You know you look good, because you've made the effort. It was one of those nights. On the outside, I carried myself with so much confidence. I walked with my shoulders held high, and I'd enter a room and get all the attention that I wanted because of the way I looked. I carried myself in a way that from the outside, anybody would think I was the most confident, secure, valued woman who believed in herself. Little did they know, underneath it all was an insecure young girl who was really just trying to find her way in life. That was safely tucked under all the beauty and bravado. It was as if fate made me understand in an unspoken way that that was going to be one of the most important nights in my life. And that that night was going to impact my life in an amazing way; it was absolutely surreal. I'd heard people talking about instant attraction, love at first sight, lust, chemistry, or whatever word you like. It was happening to me at once, and there was nothing I could do about it.

"Let's go to the other side of the room," my friend said, but I didn't want to move, as I didn't want to lose this total stranger that had captured my attention. I tried to deter my friend, but it was too late and she was already walking away from the bar. I had no choice but to follow her, but not before turning around and looking in the direction of this stranger to see that he was actually staring back at me. We found a table, put the drinks down, and stood there, swaying to the music. The club was known for having some of the best DJs in the area. I mean, it was an R&B contemporary club that played the latest music on the charts. Saturday night was the busiest night, and the place was absolutely packed.

Soon enough, my friend found all these other people that she knew in the club who had come to celebrate an event. The area we sat in was packed with so many women; and clearly wherever beautiful women were, the men weren't too far behind. They were just loitering around, standing super close and while chatting with one of them, I looked up to meet the gaze of this stranger again. He had moved from the bar this time and was standing in a corner that gave him direct access to where we were sitting. He was just staring at me and I looked at him again. This time I saw him nodding in my direction as he was talking to one of his friends who followed his gaze and saw me. They started whispering to each other, and I knew they were talking about me. I pretended like I wasn't looking or even interested in what they were doing, but I definitely was. It was as if he purposely moved to go stand in that corner with his friend just to show him who had captured his attention.

Eventually my friend decided she wanted to dance and grabbed my hand. We went to the dance floor and started dancing, having a great time singing along to the lyrics of the song. We were so into the music and dancing that I didn't even realize that he and his friends had also moved to the dance floor. They were dancing very close to us. I looked up, and again he was just staring at me; this time my friend noticed.

She asked, "What's up with you and that guy just looking at each other? I'm not stupid. I can see it."

I asked her if she knew him; she said no. She in turn asked if I knew him, and I responded no as well. So again, she inquired about why we were staring at each other.

"I have no idea what you're talking about," I lied with veiled eagerness in my voice. We continued dancing, and he checked me out. I'm very confident when I'm on the dance floor; it's all about me and my moves. I love to dance and show off. But all of a sudden, I was so self-conscious as he watched me. He was a couple of feet away dancing and swaying, but his eyes were on me. The people in his party were realizing that he was barely dancing; he was just holding his drink and swaying.

His eyes wouldn't leave me. My friend decided that she wanted to go to the bar to get another drink, so again, we left the dance floor and headed to the bar. It was like we were playing cat and mouse games with each other all night, because wherever I was, he followed. Our friends were clearly coming to the knowledge that there was something going on here because they watched us very closely.

We danced, we chatted, we had drinks and it was a wonderful night. Soon enough, although too soon for my liking (because I would have loved the night to go on a whole lot longer) I had the opportunity to watch him dance and interact with his friends. But eventually, the lights came on in the club which meant it was time to go home. Reluctantly, people had to put their drinks down and start filing towards the door. He was very close to me as we were exiting. But for some reason, he didn't approach me. I was used to men vying for my attention directly, but this stranger was just looking at me. He didn't come to me even though he had been checking me out all night. As we filed out of the club, I was very conscious of him being nearby. He and his friends made it to the door before we did, and they stood outside.

As we came in through the door, I looked up and there he was again. This time our eyes locked, and he smiled at me. I smiled right back; I couldn't help myself. I was excited. I was giddy. I felt this lightness of the heart, which was pumping so fast in my chest. It was just a really lovely feeling.

And then my friend said, "See, I told you. I knew this was happening. I'm not stupid. Come on, let's go. I'm parked around the corner."

I didn't know if she was being protective or she just didn't want me to talk to him, but she grabbed my arm and started walking me out to the car. She had a man at home so her going out had nothing to do with catching a man. I was single, but she was living with a guy she'd been with for years. So we didn't go out man-hunting. We were just going out to have fun, going out to dance the night away, have a few drinks, and then come home. Her man didn't mind her doing that, because he trusted her. I, on the other hand, was a free agent. I had no one to answer to and no one to tell what I was doing or not doing. It was absolutely amazing, and we would go out a whole lot. Some weekends we'd go out twice in a row, or we would hang out if I wasn't hanging out with my other friends. She was always having a good time.

As we walked to the car, she begged me to tell her if I knew him, and I assured her that I didn't. I told her she would have known if I did. We partied there enough, and I had never seen him in this place. Or maybe if I did, I never really noticed him.

I was trying to make sense of this myself. And here she was wanting me to admit that I liked this total stranger who made my heartbeat that much faster. A man who made me so self-conscious that my knees were practically buckling under me. I wasn't going to have that, so I played it very defensive and coy. As we got into the car, she invited me back to her house for some time before she dropped me home because her mate would still be up. I agreed, and it was probably about five or six in the morning. We walked in the door and her partner started his usual conversation, asking how I was doing and if we were hungry.

While he was cooking, I went into the kitchen to get a drink and my friend told her man about the guy from tonight and how we were checking each other out.

She told him, "It was kind of creepy 'cause all night they just circled each other. I bet you he's going to be coming back, so we should go back next week. Did you hear the announcement? This DJ is coming into town, and he's going to be playing for a couple of hours. Maybe we should go."

We all laughed, and they continued on with the banter. I was just looking at them thinking, *Oh my God, as much as they have their problems, they're a lovely couple.*

When I finished eating, we proceeded to the living room. By now, it was nearing seven o'clock in the morning. I called a cab; as I waited for my cab, we talked about the next week. She promised to pop into my work so we could go have lunch. She was just one of those friends that was so fun and so loving. We would go shopping during my lunch break and everything.

My cab got there and called her phone upon arrival. I started putting my shoes on to leave.

Before I walked out the door, her man called my name and said, "By the way, you look absolutely stunning tonight."

"Well. thank you," I said.

My friend chimed, "I know! And that's why that guy couldn't take his eyes off her."

I modestly brushed her off with a chuckle, "Girl, you're crazy. You're really crazy."

But I knew exactly what she was talking about. I jumped into my cab; on the way home, I was able to just lean back in the seat and think about exactly what had happened in that club. I didn't have any explanation for it. All I knew was that I liked this stranger, someone whose name I didn't even know. This was something I read in books and now it was happening to me. I didn't know how much that stranger would come to mean to me and how much of an impact he was going to make in my life.

My week started again. I was back in class on Tuesday. Then, I finished early, met up with a friend for lunch, and we went shopping. We went shopping just to find something amazing to wear for the special night. The week was very uneventful, but soon enough it was Saturday. I worked on my clients rigorously so I was able to finish early and take extra care of my appearance. Something just told me he wasn't done with me, that he would be there. I was hoping and praying that he would turn up.

Finally, we made it to the club. I walked in; my eyes were like scanners scoping out of the room, checking to see if he was there. Disappointment washed over me. He wasn't there. As we picked up our drinks and were walking away to go find a spot to sit down, it was as if on cue, somebody told me to turn around.

There he was. He was just as good-looking as he had been last week. He looked absolutely handsome in a white shirt, blue jeans, and dress shoes. I could feel this energy, this chemistry, pulling me in and tugging at my senses.

My heart started racing, and I announced, "He's here," abruptly to my friend.

She said, "I know, all I had to do was look at you. And I could tell that he was there."

He nodded in my direction. I smiled, and I quickly turned my eyes away. I was a lady, and I wasn't going to chase after any man. A gentleman approaches a lady and makes his intentions known; that wasn't going to change, no matter how much I liked him.

Tonight, I thought to myself, *We shall see what's going to happen. It will be an interesting night.*

Soon enough, his friends joined him from where he was staring all over again. We just couldn't take our eyes off of each other; it was even more intense. Something just told me tonight, he wasn't just going to let me go like that. I had a feeling tonight, I was going to find out his name. We played the same cat and mouse game as our first encounter; halfway through the night my friend and I were dancing.

Finally, I heard someone say, "Hello, beautiful."

I turned around to look, and there he was. Before I even turned, I think my heart knew it was him. I looked right into these eyes, and he had the longest lashes and the most beautiful dark brown eyes. I found myself staring at him, unable to tear my gaze away. My brain was telling me to say something instead of just standing there looking stupid.

I snapped out of it, and quickly said, "Hi, how are you?" doing my best to sound more confident than I felt.

He looked at me one more time and he smiled. And then his friend approached him and said something about going to the bar. He reluctantly walked away; I didn't even get an introduction. That was so annoying. I wanted to know what his name was; I wanted to know *him*. I suppose I would just have to be patient.

Later as the night went on, we were sitting down at a table laughing and talking. Then all of a sudden, he was beside me.

He started the conversation by saying, "It looks like it's absolutely impossible to speak to you. There's always people around."

I turned to him and responded with an icy yet accessible demeanor, "Well, if you really wanted to talk to me, you would find a way, wouldn't you?"

He laughed, glancing down so as to regather his composure, "You're right, I'm taking my opportunity now to introduce myself."

He told me his name, and I told him mine I couldn't tear my gaze from him, and he clearly felt it as he extended his hand, "Would you like to dance with me?"

I was excited and replied enthusiastically, "Yes."

I had danced with men I felt less for simply because I wanted to dance. But with this stranger, it was different. Not only did I want to dance, I wanted to dance with him. He led me to the dance floor, and the music was a very fast paced beat so we were dancing apart for a few minutes. All of a sudden, as if on cue, the DJ switched it to a very slow number. All I felt was his hand on the lowest part of my back, pulling me closer to him. As we neared each other, I moved closer. He smelled amazing. My nostrils were filled with this beautiful cologne and this masculine scent of him. Sweat, perfume, testosterone, everything juiced up together. I was pretty sure he could smell my perfume as well. He didn't know me; we hadn't shared many words. He was holding me and dancing with me so protectively as if I belonged to him, as if I was his woman. I didn't want to talk; words were overrated. Sometimes you just have to go with the flow of what you are feeling. We held onto each other like that. Time stood still, I was in the arms of this total stranger, and it felt absolutely phenomenal.

All of a sudden, I heard him whispering in my ear, "By the way, you look absolutely stunning tonight."

He broke right into my thoughts that were everywhere and anywhere.

"Thank you," I said, blushing.

"So you didn't realize I was checking you out?"

"Well, I think the whole club realized."

He started laughing and said, "I'm sorry, I couldn't help myself. I mean, you know, you would think at my age that I would have mastered the art of controlling my emotions. But there's something about you that just draws me in."

He was speaking so softly in my ear. There could have been beating drums in that club, and I wouldn't have heard it. All I heard was his voice in my ear as he held me tight and we danced.

At the height of this beautiful flow of energy that was going on, my friend interrupted the moment by sarcastically probing, "You guys are having fun aren't you?"

I could have throttled her right then and there. I was having a wonderful time, and she just had to interrupt us. I reluctantly pulled away from him and introduced her to the stranger who had captivated me. I continued my dance with him and declined his offer to buy me a drink, because I felt like I had drunk enough.

The music queued up again, and this time when we started dancing, he inched very close and he said, "Can I have your number? I would definitely like to talk to you. I was trying to get it from your friend, but she didn't want to give it to me."

I said, "Well, that's good, I'm glad she didn't. Cause then it's up to me to give it to you."

Flirting with this guy was so easy.

"So are you going to give it to me? Or are you going to make me work for it?"

"Well, that's for me to know and for you to find out, we'll see."

When I said that, he laughed out loud, pulled me close to him, and we started dancing. I fell right back into his arms, and we must've danced for hours there. His friend had gone back to the bar, got some drinks, came over, offered it to him, but we didn't want to drink.

It was beautiful, there were a few moments where I would catch him just looking at me so intently. It was more than just lust or chemistry, there was something about him that told me he wasn't going to let me go and that was a beautiful feeling.

He pulled out his phone just before the lights came on and persistently entreated me again, "Can I have your number now?"

"I think after that dance, you have earned it."

Again, he burst out laughing. He was so handsome. I gave him my number, put it in his phone, and we continued dancing. Soon after the lights came on and my friend resurrected from nowhere again, it was time to go home. There was no way she was going to let me leave with this stranger. I guessed she would have preferred it if I was just her party companion who was always available for her. It was different this time, as I had met someone that ignited some feelings in me that were alien to anything I had ever felt. It was one thing to like someone because they looked good, but it was another for your whole being to be so attracted to someone at first sight. It was absolutely ridiculous.

I wanted to be with my own thoughts and reminisce over the night; so instead of our normal routine, I jumped in a cab and headed home. I knew that he was going to text me. I just knew it. I knew he wasn't going to wait till tomorrow to talk to me.

The very next minute I got a text to my phone, which read, "Please get home safely. I can't get you out of my mind. I can't wait to speak to you tomorrow."

In my mind I said, *Why wait till tomorrow? The night is still young!*

But I didn't say that to him, instead I kept playing hard to get. I responded, and I said I was on my way home. We engaged in small talk, both agreeing that we had a great time. He ended the dialogue by requesting that I text him when I arrived home. He insisted that I let him know when I was safely indoors. I wasn't used to that, as most other men never really cared if you made it home safely. His concern resonated with me, and I liked the fact that he cared about my safety.

I got home, and texted him as he had requested, and his response was exciting to me, "I look forward to talking to you tomorrow, more than you know. Good night."

I went to sleep with a huge grin on my face.

I didn't know what this was, but I liked every bit of how it felt. I went to sleep with this handsome stranger on my mind. The next morning, I woke up at about seven thirty to a text from him.

This time he asked me to let him know when I was ready to talk, and I thought, *Let me get ready and I can talk to him on my way to work.*

The phone rang, and I greeted him, "Hello."

He said, "Hello, beautiful."

I mean, he wasn't the first guy that had called me that, but somehow, I knew he meant it. I felt my heart becoming giddy and everything. I wasn't working that day, but I had some errands to run as it was a Sunday.

He said to me, "Do you think you have time for lunch with me today?"

I clarified, "Are you asking me out?"

He said, "Yes, I absolutely am asking you out."

I could feel my heart racing, and every part of me was thrilled at the possibility of going out with this man. He lived about forty five minutes away from me in a place called Pecker.

I thought to myself, *If I wanted to know more about him, I'd rather do it in person than over the phone*, so I agreed to meet up that afternoon. I hurried home and got dressed again and met him at this little fish and chips place, a small restaurant that was very close to the club where we met. I walked in, and he was already there sitting at the table. I approached him. He was just taking in my whole form from the moment I walked in through the doors.

I made it to the table, and he stood up and said, "Hello darling," he then pulled out the seat for me.

I sat down. I was nervous, because I liked him. He also made me very uncomfortable, because I knew he was checking me out intently. But at least he was very easy to talk to.

We started talking and he said, "I know you're single."

"Yes. Are you?"

"I'm going to be very honest with you."

I instantly replied with a skeptical, "Yep, I would appreciate that."

When he said that, my heart thought, *Is he married? Cause I definitely don't want a married man.*

I mean, I had morals. I had standards. I wasn't going to share my man with anyone. The polygamy in my home growing up was enough. So when he said that I was taken aback.

I could tell he was choosing his words very carefully, "I was seeing this young lady; we've been seeing each other on and off. But since I met you last week and I kind of got the impression that you liked me—"

Before he could finish the sentence I interrupted, "Well, who told you I liked you?"

"I can tell. Just like it was obvious to each and every person in that club that I wanted you, and that you wanted me, too."

I nodded in agreement with excitement flowing from the roots of my extensions right down to my toes.

He went on to say, "I have told her about you. It was nothing serious that we shared. I have stayed over at hers, and I've been spending a lot of time with her; but I don't want that anymore. What I feel for you, I really want to see where it goes. It's not a problem for me to let her go so we can see what we've got here. It's not every day that this happens to me where I'm absolutely infatuated with a young woman who has me thinking about her all day."

I was happy to hear that he liked me that much, but there was also a bit of apprehension at the fact that he was too handsome not to have somebody waiting in the wings, a partner, or a wife. He went on to tell me how he was divorced and he had two kids. He explained that he was very wary of jumping into anything, because he had been hurt. After our conversation, I knew that whatever he had with this woman really wasn't enough for him

When he finished, I took a breath knowing it was my time to talk.

I looked him straight in the eye and unabashedly said, "I do like you, but I must be very careful. There are things that I have been through in my own life that I will not feel again. I will under no circumstances ever share my man with another woman. I don't have to. I like you, so I will give you the opportunity to do right. So this is what I suggest. We're not going to proceed with whatever's going on here until you go and end that relationship. I am not going to see you with that ongoing."

I didn't know how I was able to put my feelings aside and speak from my heart, but I meant every word of that. I wasn't going to be played. I wasn't going to be anyone's second option or left on the back burner.

When I said that, he looked at me, a smile breaking across his mouth.

He responded, "I respect that. And I'll do exactly that."

I was happy. We had shared an understanding.

With this in mind, we went back to a beautiful lunch. We chatted, and I learned that he was an only child. His mother was Indian, and his father was Italian. He was mixed-race like me. It was two different nationalities coming together to create such a beautiful specimen of God's creation. It was just amazing as we got to know each other. I asked questions. He was curious about me, just like I was about him. Time flew by; we must have spent at least three or four hours just talking.

Eventually, I had to go, and he had a forty five minute drive all the way down to his part of town. We talked about literally everything. Nothing was off limits, but it was nothing sexual, that is what I liked. He was interested in me, and he wanted to know me. He didn't make any improper advances or make it about lust. He was a gentleman and I absolutely loved that. When we finished, he offered to take me home since I had come to meet him by train. The train was just so fast compared to the traffic you have to deal with if you're driving. I found myself agreeing, which was very rare. Normally I wouldn't even want a guy that I didn't know very well to know where I live. I felt comfortable enough to let him and soon enough we were outside my door and he asked to see me again.

I said, "Do you remember what I said back there?"

"Absolutely. I am going to do that. After it's done, can I see you again?"

"Of course. I do want to see you again."

He leaned over and dropped a quick kiss on my cheek. It took all the self-control I had not to turn my face deliberately and have his lips meet mine. I had to act like a lady so I bid him farewell and exited the car. As I made my way to the entrance, he drove a little bit towards the door where I was standing.

He rolled down his window and said, "I had a wonderful time today."

"So did I."

"I'll see you soon, beautiful. Look after yourself."

And then he sped off. I was standing there watching this car drive off, and I was thinking, *Did he just kiss my cheek?*

I was standing there, holding onto the moment.

I was at home daydreaming about him. I had even called my friend to tell her all about it. As I was sharing my excitement with her about this stranger, he was wrapping things up with this other woman.

Later that evening he texted me saying, "It is done."

He called shortly after sending this message.

I said to him, "What do you mean it's done? That quickly?"

"Yep, When I left you, I went straight to her, sat her down, and we talked about it. I apologized for this happening. I really didn't realize that she had such strong feelings for me. I had the opportunity to get my stuff out."

I think the woman had kids as well, and I think the kids were used to him. I got the impression that it wasn't as easy as he thought it was going to be.

"So how can I know that this is really over?"

His response was very certain, "I've got nothing to hide. I have proof of it on my phone. To see it you will have to see me again."

When he finished this sentence, I burst out laughing before saying, "Are you asking me out again?"

So, we arranged to meet again the next evening after work. And we had left it in the air where we were going to meet. We texted in between. He would text me sweet little nothings with pictures of a heart saying, "I just needed you to know I'm thinking about you." It was absolutely beautiful. We met up the next day, and he showed me the interaction between him and the lady on his phone.

I was so happy to see that the other side of him wasn't belligerent and ugly, because in the messages he apologized profusely for wanting more than whatever it was that they had. He didn't realize that she felt that much for him, while he was very casual about it.

He ended their correspondence by saying, "You deserve better; you deserve somebody who's going to be totally crazy about you. Not only wanting to be with you, but somebody who wants a future with you and your children. Someone who is going to be permanent."

I was very impressed to see evidence to show me that he wasn't lying.

After a while of reading, I handed him the phone and he asked, "Are you happy? Do you believe me now?"

"Yes, I do."

I think at that point something was solidified. We had come to a mutual agreement, and this was him signing his part of the deal. When we finished we went back to my house to talk, because I wanted to know more about him. I wanted to know more about this stranger. He was a floor contractor; no wonder his physique was so on point. His job was very laborious and manly, and his physique showed it. He had very strong shoulders, very defined muscles and biceps, and he had a nice body.

When we left the restaurant, he reached for my hand. We got into the car, and we went home. He was very much a gentleman and didn't try to push anything. We chatted. I loved hearing him laugh. I had a roommate. We shared the living room and the kitchen, but both had our own rooms. I didn't want to sit in the living room and have my roommate walk in; I wanted total privacy.

I invited him over to my room and he walked in and he sat down on the bed.

I remember looking at him saying, "My roommate might be coming home soon, and she's very loud. I'm just going to warn you right now, you're going to meet her, and you will love her; she's amazing. Trust me when she gets home, you will know."

We laughed and continued our conversation a bit before I went in to take my shoes off. I asked if he wanted a drink.

When I came back, I found that he had taken off his shoes and made himself comfortable on my bed. As I gave him the drink, he grabbed my hand and pulled me close to him. He sat on the bed with his legs spread apart, and I was sitting right in between them. He laid my head back on his shoulders and just held me.

His cheek was on mine as he said, "I didn't want you to think that just because I'm in your bedroom that we have to do anything. I want to get to know you, and I want you to be comfortable. If you're not, all you have to do is tell me; even if you feel like I'm moving way too fast, just let me know."

We didn't have to talk again. We laid there with him just holding me. It dawned on me just how dangerous this whole scenario was. We were at home, my flat mate was not, and we were on my bed. But for some reason, I felt safe. I believed he wouldn't pressure me or do anything that I didn't want to. We were so happy just holding each other, and I liked feeling his arms around me.

After some time, I thought I heard somebody at the door so I excused myself. I went down and found that it was my neighbor looking for my flat mate.

As I came back, literally with a drink in hand, he met me halfway. He took the drink from me and pulled me onto him. There was no music, there was nothing. He just held me very affectionately, and I loved it. He pulled me to him.

We swayed for a little while before he looked at me in my eyes as if searching, to say, "I'm about to do something, just let me know if you're not comfortable."

I guess my gaze back at him told him I was absolutely ready for it, because he leaned in closer. I could feel his head getting closer...closer...closer... until his lips met mine.

Time stood still.

I had wanted that from the moment I laid eyes on him. It felt like everything that was in my mind and in my heart culminated in the kiss. It was absolutely wonderful. I think right then and there, I knew this man was going to mean so much to me. I had known him only for a few days, but that much was evident. The kiss deepened so that we had to pull away. I respected him so much for pulling away.

He didn't force it or push me to do anything and said, "This will happen when you want it to happen. But you know, right now, I don't think it's the time. I don't think you're ready."

And he was right, I wasn't ready. I wasn't one to just sleep around. I had too many issues to just trust anybody and bring them to my bed. I think he could sense that.

And then he said, "You know what, I've got to go. If I do not go now I will get us both in trouble."

I laughed and he pulled me closer for another kiss. He had an appointment that he had mentioned with a client earlier on during the day. But I think we both knew if we stayed longer, we wouldn't have been able to take control and stop right there. Before he left he hugged me again, I rested my head on his chest and just smelt him and heard his heartbeat. It was all happening right in the middle of my bedroom, and we still managed to stop. I loved that about him. I didn't even have the opportunity to walk him out. I listened to his footsteps going down the stairs. Everything in my mind, heart, and my body told me that he was mine and I was his in all its entirety. There are a few moments in my life that I will never forget and this was one of them. He was sincere and just wanted to hold me close, not even fondle or touch or grope. I had found in him someone that was going to change my life forever. And that was exactly what happened.

After that day, it was like the dates just merged together. I saw him nearly every day. He would drive nearly an hour to come take me out for lunch, then go back to work and drive back down in the evening. He wanted to spend all this free time with me, not to mention the text messages. I would wake up each morning with texts and calls throughout the day, checking up on me. I never had anything like this. It was something I used to see in movies, in magazines, and in Mills and Boon books. But now, it was happening to me. Truth be told, that first day when he kissed me, in my bedroom, I had fallen irrevocably head over heels with this stranger. I'd only known him for a few days and we spent all our time together. I saw him at least every single day or maybe every couple of days, if he was busy. We spoke constantly on the phone. We went out to eat. We went out dancing. We went out to the movies. I'd even met his dog, who was one of the joys of his life. He absolutely adored that dog.

During this short time, it was the whirlwind type of relationship that took away your senses, your sanity, and everything that went with it.

Less than six months later, he proposed.

With what I felt for him, it would have been foolish for me to even contemplate letting him go. I had given my whole heart to this stranger. I loved everything about him; when he wasn't with me, I missed him. And I knew he felt the same. Thoughts of him occupied my mind. As I went through my day, when I was about to see him, it felt like my whole world was made right by his presence. I had never had a love like this; it was beautiful because it was reciprocated. He made me feel loved, wanted, and prioritized like I was the best thing that had ever happened to him. Like I was the one thing in his day that he couldn't be without. So, when he proposed, it was a yes, without having to think about it at all. I had introduced him to my friends, and he introduced me to his. I'd even met his mom. He met some of my family, came to my job, met all my employers and some of my employees. It was moving at a rapid pace by the time he proposed. That might not have been a long time to some people, but it was to me. I was ready. He was ready.

We got married less than six months later. I know there were people that thought we were moving very fast. We were engaged within a year of our meeting and about to take this journey to fuse our lives together in Holy matrimony. I knew beyond a shadow of a doubt that this man was absolutely helplessly in love with me, as I was with him. This was because of some of the things he did with and for me. I would wake up from sleeping and there he was just sitting there, stroking my head, staring at me. He wouldn't let me sleep on my side of the bed. If he wasn't touching me, he was in close proximity, holding my hand or cuddling me. I loved every minute of that. His love helped with my issues of rejection, abandonment, being overlooked, and all that I had gone through in my childhood.

It truly did feel that I had come home. I was going to spend the rest of my life with this beautiful stranger that crashed into my world. I was going to have his babies, and we were going to grow old and decrepit together.

3
Marriage & Motherhood

There is nothing more beautiful, more fulfilling and rewarding than being married to the person you love. A man who not only shares your everyday events, but the present and the future as well. A marriage is sacred because it joins two people in a way that only God can. You see, to not only live for yourself but for that person, your heart beats for that person that is made of perfection, yet also flawed. It is a joining of two people's soul and spirit in a supernatural way beyond human comprehension. When you get married, it's like a renewal of the mind; you seem to not just think about yourself.

As we settled into married life. it was blissful; it was wonderful; it was passionate. You know the butterflies that people talk about? It is real. You miss this person when they are away from you. It felt like my soul had found this other person coming from a broken place with all kinds of issues like rejection, feeling unworthy, overlooked, and all these things that I had brought along from my childhood. I couldn't tell you how much this man meant to me and most of all, our marriage.

To be very honest with you, we were two souls from different ends of the spectrum. He was from a Jewish family, with an Italian father and an Indian mother. His faith as a Jew meant so much to him. I couldn't see him ever changing into another faith because of the fact that he wanted to be with me. From very early on, even before we got married, we talked about it. He would hang onto his faith as a Jew, and I did the same with mine.

When we met, we knew we would have challenges and that not everybody would understand. It was as if I was living in my own version of my parent's' romance without the polygamy. Just like them, we knew that people would have their own perception of right and wrong, but none of it mattered to us. He wasn't a very spiritual man. He didn't go to the synagogue to pray and all that. I don't even think he owned a Torah to be honest with you, because we lived in a society that glorifies the self. It was all about us and what made us happy. And I was the same as him, to be perfectly honest. Even though I was born from a Muslim family, I wasn't spiritual at all. It wasn't part of what I did. I never prayed five times a day, as per the law of the Muslim faith. I prayed sometimes, but most of the time I didn't. I didn't even own the Quran, and I never read it or governed my life by it.

So, when it came to being married, we agreed that in the future, we wouldn't fully decide what faith to raise our family or what faith to base our beliefs on. It was all left to the unknown, and we would cross that bridge when we came to it. People didn't seem to understand that these things should be talked about because you can't base the most beautiful thing in your life on the unknown. God gave his wisdom for all of us to be able to discern from right and wrong, to make plans, to not just live for today like it is the last day. We should actually have something valuable and substantial. For the first time in my life, I felt like I'd found a home in him.

There was just something missing. There were the questions that were never answered. So to me, the gratification of my own self, enjoying my life, and living as I saw fit was more important. We enjoyed our life, we partied, we traveled; we had so much fun. It was all about us and being cocooned in that love, where nothing else took precedence. There were no rules or boundaries, so we just loved each other the best as we could.

Our families had a lot to say because of the difference in spirituality, culture, tradition, creed, race. Everybody had their say and their opinion on it. The first few months passed by blissfully. I concentrated on my career and getting my qualifications. He was instrumental in pushing me to my potential, because I had dreams of being an entrepreneur and owning my own business in the beauty world. He wasn't afraid of a hard day's work and neither was I. So we embarked on our married life with the aim of working hard to be financially stable, so that we could enjoy our love for traveling together.

He was fourteen years older than me and already a father of two, so of course he had much more experience, culture, and knowledge of the world. I looked up to him more than anyone else in my life. He was the moving factor —the one that my whole existence was based on— so whatever he said, I believed. He had never lied to me or told me something that I later found out to be wrong. He showed me that he had my best interests at heart. His intentions with me were pure, so I knew our present was secured and our future even more so. We both wanted that, and we had dreams of a future full of promises, hope, love, acceptance and companionship. All of these things are in their purest form in the start of a relationship or marriage.

Months flew by. I watched him become a great father to his children, especially the son who came from his previous marriage. He would talk about him with so much love and care, even though it was hard for him to see his child, because his ex was making it so much harder. He never relented; he proceeded.

A troop of wild horses couldn't stop him from seeing his child or taking care of him, even though he wasn't in a relationship with the child's mother. He wanted to be a great father, having grown up without one. We would have the kid on weekends, and the more I saw of their relationship, the more I wanted to have a family with him. I wanted to look upon the face of a child that we had created together in our love for each other. It is a dream that I think most women have at a very early age. You start dreaming about how your kid is going to look, about how you will look at her. I wanted a girl desperately for him. We chose a name for a girl; we had dreams about what she was going to be like, her complexion, and her hair being of a mixed biracial heritage. We had dreams; it was just so beautiful.

We embarked on making that happen, and our sex life was beautiful. We barely could have enough of each other. We were always so happy knowing that it could happen at any time. It was those words that I was dying to hear from a doctor, and so we talked about it. We would even talk about where we were going to take our kids on the holidays; introducing them to both our cultures; introducing them to both religions.

There's something very special about seeing a man wanting to be the best of himself, not only for himself but for his family. I loved seeing this through watching him interact with his child. At that point, his son was very young, and we would pick him up from his mother's house. He would spend the whole day with him, do things that he liked, and bond with him.

A few months into our marriage, nothing happened. Four, five, six months without protection, nothing had changed. We knew it wasn't for lack of trying; so by the sixth month mark, I started getting worried. I became pensive.

He already had two kids, so clearly the problem wasn't with him. I told him that I would feel so much better if we visited a doctor and found out exactly what was going on. He didn't think it was time to do that, he thought we had more time to let it happen naturally. After seeing the state I was in and how upset I was, every month when my menstrual period arrived he indulged me and eventually we went to get help. We visited a fertility clinic and discussed our concerns with the OBGYN. The following week, we started my treatments. We and the doctors assumed that he was okay, and that the brunt was going to be with me. That was okay; I just needed answers. Everybody around me was falling pregnant and seeing babies would touch the deepest part of me. The fact is that when you get married, it's not only about you. I became emotional looking at other kids because in Africa, we were taught from a very early age that marriage came hand in hand with babies. When you get married, your first duty to your husband is to provide babies for him.

    Coming from a big family, having a child for my husband was a duty unto itself before anything else. And so, I had my own dreams of having my own family. It was ingrained in me from birth because of the society I was born in. In Africa, a man would literally divorce his wife on the grounds that she couldn't bear kids. That could even be the reason why he took on other wives, have an heir for himself and preserve the legacy and family name.

    I had heard so many stories from people about the misery of a married childless woman: how she was looked over and marked; how she went through so much heartache and pain. Rarely did people seem to remember that a child comes from God. But this society I was born in made it seem as if the ability to conceive and bear a child was on the woman. When we started this investigation into the reason why I wasn't conceiving, I had peace of mind knowing I was on the right path and that soon our dreams would be realized. Little did I know that this would be one of the most difficult times of my life. But the saving grace through it all was my husband. We had a very intimate close bond with each other, in which I wasn't afraid to tell him how I felt.

    He was an emotional man and very in touch with his feelings. I would explain to him just how much I felt like less of a woman and less of a wife, even though I knew I was a good wife to him. I cleaned, I cooked, he had a hot meal on the table nearly every night of the week. I nurtured him. I took care of him. I shared in his dreams. I loved his children, but there was something missing. Something that meant the world to me that I had to share with him. We make the mistake of thinking if we are vulnerable and let a person into the most sacred vulnerable part of us, that we will either get hurt, manipulated, or used. For me, with this amazing Italian hunk of mine, there was no room for dealing with something on my own.

Little by little, I opened up to him, and he understood from a very good place that this meant a lot to me. We both made the appointments, and he was there every time. He was very supportive. When we got good news, he was there at my side. When we had the bad news, he was there encouraging me. He told me stories of how other women have been in my situation, how they persevered, and eventually they'd have their babies. Looking back, I was appreciative of that support, of that love, of that camaraderie. Knowing I could tell him anything; knowing I could rely on him; knowing that when my own feelings of inadequacy hit he was there to reassure me of how much he loved me with or without a child was everything. The desperation slowly waned, and I started taking better care of myself. I was eating well, watching my weight, and doing things that the doctors told me to do. I remember one time we were in hospital, and I was having a very invasive treatment done. Any woman who's gone through fertility treatment will tell you that the most invasive treatments are those where you feel like a guinea pig, vulnerable, and exposed.

I remember lying on the table as they did this procedure on me called a dye test. I had to lay there while they inserted this dark blue liquid into my fallopian tubes; they watched it on the screen to make sure there was no blockage to make sure everything was working in order. Reclining there, I was just so disheartened with all these things I had to go through to be a mother while other women just conceived with no problems, not having to go through what I was going through. I remember lying on the bed there and I just burst into tears; that was one of my most prominent memories of how this whole thing was taking a toll on me and eventually, on my marriage. I burst out crying, and he rushed over to my side.

Between sobs, I said, "I just want to give you a baby, to give you a child is all I want. This is just so much harder than I thought it was going to be."

He took my hand, and he looked deep into my eyes, and he said, "With or without a baby, I will always love you."

I looked into those deep brown eyes, and I knew that he meant it. I knew that it was coming from a very beautiful place. I knew that what he said was true. The words that he spoke weren't merely to comfort me. I knew they were coming from a very deep place in him, as I watched the tears roll down his face.

He held my hand and kissed my forehead, reassuring me, "Even if you can't give me a child, I will not think any less of you. I love you. You need to believe that."

When he said that, a calmness came over me. That was what I needed to hear because I had so many fears in my heart that no one would understand unless you were born in the same heritage, tradition and culture. I was scared of disappointing him, of failing him, of not being enough. Him reassuring me without knowing what was going through my head was one of the most beautiful moments during my fertility treatments that I can remember.

Writing this now, nearly fifteen years later, I become emotional when I think back to that moment. It takes me to a very beautiful place where my heart is full of expectation and promises to be fulfilled. A future that couldn't bring anything we couldn't withstand; our love was strong enough to withstand everything.

We cuddled each other that day on the bed in the hospital; this nurse was even feeling the pain of what we were going through. The nurse felt she had to say something and was very supportive.

She said something to the effect of, "We see this all the time. After the investigations, you will have the answers you seek; then you can decide what route to take. If God blesses you with a child, it will happen. And even if it doesn't happen naturally, there are other ways you can fulfill this dream."

That was one of the most poignant times that I remember in my fertility treatment. Afterwards we went home, and we talked about it. He did everything he could trying to make me feel good and put my doubts to rest.

Eventually, the relationship took a turn and the lack of a child did take its toll on the marriage. There were intimate times, and our need for our growing family bonded us together in a way that was absolutely special. But infertility was another strain, another hurdle —one that started making the relationship and our sex lives feel like a chore. Our feelings for each other hadn't changed, but the investigation involved me finding out the days of my ovulation through a machine. I remember taking that home, and I thought to myself, *our sex life is about to end.*

Before the device, we couldn't have enough of each other; we genuinely enjoyed each other. I had to find out through this machine exactly when my ovulation dates were and work around those to make sure our chances of conceiving were higher. If anybody has gone through this, they will tell you how it takes every bit of spontaneity out of a sexual relationship. I didn't like it. It did put a strain on the relationship, as much as I tried to make light of it.

I would call him and say, "Today is the day. So whatever you're doing, you better just know today is today."

He would drop whatever he was doing to make sure he was with me. He was selfless; he wanted to please me, and he wanted to love not only my mind, but my body. It was as if he wanted his touch to remain with me when he wasn't there. I resented that machine. I couldn't stand it, but I had no choice. And I would have done anything that the doctors wanted me to.

We continued on with the treatments and every time I would see a mother, I said a silent prayer to God. I prayed that one day I would feel the joy in that woman's heart. I would go to baby shops just to walk around and see what I would buy eventually, when I got the good news that we wanted. It was all I could think of; it felt like everywhere I looked there were mothers and babies, families with their children. Only God knew how much it affected my heart and mind. It's amazing in life, how we concentrate on the things we don't have, rather than the blessings that were right in front of us. I did appreciate and love him greatly, but there was also a need in me that made me feel vulnerable, helpless, and like a failure.

I know my desperation affected him. It was such a shame that so soon in the marriage; it overcame our lives. It became that elephant in the room that couldn't be moved. Right in the middle of my fertility treatments, my oldest sister, who lived about forty-five minutes away from where we lived, fell pregnant with her first child. I remember the day she called me and said, "I am pregnant." I was genuinely happy for her, because I knew she was experiencing something that was a part of the culture in my heritage. I knew what it meant to her. I was so ecstatic, because in the midst of my need and my pain, there was a blessing in my family. I remember after I put the phone down, I cried tears of joy and tears of sorrow at the same time.

In the midst of the joy, I asked Allah why my journey was taking so long.

I had cried out to God, "What did I do wrong? Why is this happening to me? Why does my life always have to be different from everybody else's?"

Eventually, I lay on the bed, feeling somber and numb. It's very shocking, the feeling of being happy for somebody because you know they deserve it. Then at the same time, it brings home your inability to fully share in their happiness. I wasn't jealous of my sister, because she was fulfilling a need for her own life and her own marriage.

I embarked on it again with a vigor that I was going to be a mother. On the day my sister gave birth to a beautiful baby girl, I was at her side. I held her hand through her labor pains as she screamed and bellowed in pain. I was thinking, *One day this will be me.*

Even while thinking about my own dreams I focused my attention on her and reminded her, "She'll be here soon and then all of this pain will go away."

It was a very difficult and long labor. And as I watched her belly, literally moving with life, I couldn't tell you how it made me feel. It was so surreal and one of the best experiences of my life. I wanted to be there. I wanted to see it. I knew that when it was my turn, that joy would have been multiplied immensely. When she was in the last minutes of labor, they decided the baby was too distressed to be delivered naturally. So, the doctors came into the room. I was praying to Allah again, *Let her be okay, and let the baby be okay.* I remember as they wheeled her into the operating theatre, I stood back, praying that she would be well. I was praying for God to preserve the new life of my unborn niece. I had taken everything on board, as if it was my own experience. I pleaded with Allah right there and then to save her.

When I heard my niece crying for the first time, only God knows how I felt. Something overtook my feelings; the most vulnerable part of my heart was awakened. I fell in love with my niece the moment I set my eyes on her. I took in the tiny hands, the small features, and the way she squinted. I was infatuated, I was in love. This little human being was tugging at the strings of my heart. As I watched my sister reach for her breast to feed her child her first meal outside the womb, I was in awe as she latched onto her mother's breast. Her mother radiated an air of protectiveness, a fierce love, and a shining bright joy as she looked down upon this beautiful baby girl that she and her husband had created. I knew she felt complete.

That was a blessing to me. I remember driving home that day feeling so overwhelmed by the whole experience and crying my eyes out. At one point, I stopped to throw my hands up in the air in thankfulness and in pain. I was thanking Allah for this new wonderful blessing in our family even as my heart ached at my reality. I started praying that Allah would remember me and bless me with a child too. I couldn't stop talking about this baby. I couldn't stop talking about the experience of what I saw, and my husband was so indulgent. He asked questions; he shared his experience of being a father the first and second times. It was a conversation that meant so much to me because he was opening up his true feelings. He actually explained his deepest fears; he went through the motions, the love, the protectiveness, and the need to do right by the child. He said it was one of the most surreal moments of his life. Listening to him talking about how he felt as a father and knowing what I saw that day, we bonded in a way that I'll never forget. It was absolutely beautiful.

I remember telling him, "I wonder how you're going to feel when our child finally comes."

He looked at me and said, "It'll be different for us, because at first she and I weren't prepared for that child. It wasn't planned, but it happened. I have no regrets now of course, and I love my child more than anything. But I just know that this time will be special, because we have been doing all we can to have this baby."

He paused, slipped his fingers through mine, and continued, "I'm going to be ecstatic for you because I know how much you want this. I know what a great mother you are going to be."

We were never going to be perfect, and we had our problems in our marriage, but it felt amazing hearing him say this. We were going through all of these oppositions from the outside; despite that, we stood together, we fought for what we had, we fought for everything that meant the world to us. These were the moments where I loved this man with every fiber of my being, knowing that I had him to depend on.

I remember him teasing me by saying, "Are you ready for *that*?"

I was like, "Oh my God, the pain? No amount of painkillers will take it away."

You know it had to be supernatural; Allah had to be involved in every part of the creation, right up to the child's date of birth. Looking back now, it was my first experience of being that involved with a birth, and it's one of my most beautiful memories.

Before this uncertainty of a delay in having a baby, I was very naive to the problems that it would bring into the marriage. I was in my early twenties. Even though it was a journey I had embarked on with so much hope, the journey did take a big toll on my marriage.

As the need for a child grew, so did the problems, unfortunately. He had a beautiful heart. He had a beautiful countenance. People were attracted to him. His smile and his openness drew women in. The arguments were always based around a lack of hope, around wanting something that wasn't happening so much that it was overtaking our life. And the judgement I felt from his mother only added to the already fragile situation.

His mother was a hard working woman who went to any length to give the best to her child being a single mother. All her hopes and dreams were centered on her child and she experienced the love of a grandchild in his first marriage. The lack of the relationship she had with her daughter in law didn't fulfill the need to be the greatest grandma that she could. Because of this she felt like she hadn't really truly experienced the joy of being a grandmother as much as she wanted to. I think she had always dreamt of him marrying a beautiful young woman who was from a Jewish family, the same faith that they practiced. In the case of his first wife, she was Caucasian, Christian I think, and not everything that she wanted. He had not only had a child with a Caucasian woman at 19, but he had married another Caucasian woman whom he had his son with. By the time I came along her standards were even higher. I think the need grew even more after the two failed major relationships that produced children. To put it mildly, she was not accepting of me as a young black African woman and my relationship with her was far from perfect. I longed for a mother in law who would be a second mother to me. She was the mother of the man I loved. My love could encompass anybody that was in his family and accommodate anybody he loved and called his own. She didn't let me love her that way.

Her opinions were very hurtful, and they contributed to some of the problems in the marriage. I remember having conversations with her, it was one of the few ones we had about babies and one day she asked me, "do you even want to be a mother?" Before I could reply she went on to ask "Do you guys plan to have children?" We didn't tell her our plans or what we were going through in the privacy of our own home. The efforts we were making trying to have a child was personal. Most of the things that we were doing in our efforts to be parents were kept to us, we didn't share it.

When she saw me she saw a young woman who was full of life and enjoying life. I think all of that gave her the notion that I didn't want to have a child, or that I didn't want to disrupt my travels and partying lifestyle. I knew I was falling short of my expectations from her.

I remember this day very clearly in our home. Her son had walked away from the room and she piled on the questions one after another. "Do you want to be a mother? Are you planning to be one? Are you trying...what is going on?" It was a year or so after we had gotten married, and I looked her in the eye and said "Nothing in this world would give me more pleasure than having a baby with my husband. It is the biggest need of my heart; it is the cry of my heart. It is the pain I have to deal with every single day knowing that I can't." Tears filled my eyes but I knew I could not tell her any more information because she already thought less of me so I simply ended with "We're working on it just keep us in your prayers." I guess the answer was enough for her. When I finished she just whispered something under her breath and walked out of the room.

    I had to have a conversation about that with him and how it hurt my feelings, and the wrong perception she had of me. It was a tough conversation because nobody wants to hear certain things about their mother. At first I felt disrespected, overlooked, and like I was never going to be enough for her no matter what. She already did not care for me and the fact that I didn't have a child with her son made it worse. I know having a child would have bonded me with that woman in a way because I would have given her full rein into her grandkids life. I wanted a family of my own to love and nurture. That was one of the needs I've always had as a child. Regardless of how our relationship was, I would have let her experience in no small measure, the joy and completeness of being an amazing grandmother to a child that I had with a son. I was carrying a heavy burden, feeling like I failed not only him but everybody else that mattered to him. Being in a situation where you feel you're not good enough, it's as if every day of your life you're trying to prove not only to others, but to yourself that you are enough that you are worthy and valuable regardless of what you can't make happen.

    Even with all the issues it came as the biggest shock of my life when I found out that the husband I adored so much had stepped out of our marriage and was having an affair. I still remember the day I found out so clearly as if it was yesterday. I had a key in the door and I ran to him from across the hallway. I immediately started questioning him as I met him at the door. "Where have you been? Who have you been talking to? And why haven't you been picking up my calls, what's going on? I barraged at him as he opened the door and entered the house. I was so angry that I continued asking him questions as he entered without relenting. "Who were you talking to?" I demanded an answer and he casually responded.

    "Whoa, Whoa, Whoa. Stop with all the questions. What are you doing up anyway?" He said.

    I quickly shot a response back to him "Don't worry about that. Who were you on the phone with?" I asked.

"I wasn't on the phone. He answered right back, but without looking at me.

"If you were not on the phone, can you look me in the eye and say you were not on the phone with anyone this early morning?" I asked hoping he would confess but he couldn't meet my gaze. This wasn't normal for him. There was something very wrong somewhere. He was blatantly lying to me and quickly turned away from me to unleash the dog, using it as a distraction not to have to look me in the eye. This made me furious. My heart was palpitating. Every part of my body knew something was up. Some people call it intuition, some call it the woman's sixth sense, and on that day I was very much aware that something was wrong. As I looked at him squirm under my gaze, I didn't have the words to ask, but I knew I had to say something. "Bring out your phone, let's check if there is anything on your call log."

"'Why are you doing this? He shouted back "what is going on"
I looked at him knowing fully well that he was on that phone. Something in him couldn't let him tell me the truth. He quickly finished what he was doing and brushed right past me into the kitchen area. I followed him. I wasn't about to let him go. I need an answer. I followed him into the kitchen and asked again. "Bring out your phone."
" I don't have to bring out my phone"
"Yes you do. Yes. You do have to bring out your phone because you are lying to me. You know it. And I know it." As I finished my sentence I saw him make sure that he had his phone. He took the phone out of his pocket and he stood there with it in his hand. We had a joint account so the phone carrier would give him or me any info that we wanted regarding our account. I knew this so I yelled out to him saying "call T-Mobile right now." He stood there contemplating and murmuring, "why are you doing this? You're acting all crazy right now. I can't even recognize you"
He was trying to deflect and change the subject as he was there talking. I just launched for his phone, but I wasn't quick enough because he quickly pushed me out of the way and put the phone in his pocket. After the struggle, I stepped back to take a good look at this man I called my husband. As I took a step back to look at him, the first thing I realized was that he was changing every shade of red and sweating profusely. I didn't understand that because it was freezing in the kitchen. I screamed at him. "Why are you sweating right now?" It was at that moment that I knew something wasn't right and my hand covered my mouth in disbelief. "Are you cheating on me?" Before he could even say

anything, I ran into the hallway. I felt this bile rise from the pit of my stomach and I was just hoping I could make it to the toilet on time. I threw myself on the ground and wailed like never before. I didn't understand why I was actually throwing up. I felt sick to my stomach and one thing was lodged in my heart. One truth that no one could take away. I knew it like I knew I was Roza. I knew without a shadow of a doubt right there right then, laying on the fly mew.

I cried out laying on the cold floor, praying that this wasn't true. I hoped that my intuition was betraying me. I wanted this feeling to be a lie. I laid there feeling the cold floor on my skin, it was tingling and burning with fear, anticipation and worry. I wailed for the man that I loved with every part of me and for the marriage that was ending.

He took that opportunity to quickly flee the house after opening the bathroom door and looking at me on the floor. I remember him quickly closing the door and a few seconds later, I heard the front door slam. My life was never going to be the same again.

This was the start of dark times in my life and to cope, I threw myself into work. At this point, I had opened my first shop with his support, and I was on the way up. In the eyes of everybody out there, I was living the perfect life. His work was doing well. He was a self-employed business floor contractor and was making decent money. He had a business partner, and they literally were some of the hardest workers I had ever seen. At that time, I threw myself into things that I could control, and my work was one of them. At the age of twenty-two, going on twenty-three, I had the opportunity of owning my first beauty salon. I couldn't tell you how much that achievement meant to me, but even that achievement was marred by the fact that there was one area that I could do nothing about. My heart shattered into a million pieces. I had known pain in my childhood but nothing like this. Gone were the future plans, the dreams, the aspirations, and the knowledge that my need had a lot to do with this situation. We had fought. But eventually, there was nothing left to fight for. Everything that made the foundation of my life was now broken. Everything had changed.

4
LIES, HURT & BETRAYAL

After the separation, it was like death had come and snatched my love and my best friend away. It felt like my world crumbled; having to get up every day to face the day was much more than I thought I could handle. I sank into a low that was new to me. I wasn't devoid of pain, but I had never felt that helplessness of not being in control of my feelings and emotions. What people don't understand is the deeper the love, the deeper the hurt. I felt betrayed and used. I think I went through every emotion known to man. I sank into a depression that was so detrimental to my mental health, that my doctors were worried. I'm not proud to say this, but I contemplated very unhealthy thoughts in my head because I felt like my purpose had been taken away.

    I had made this man who was my world. I put him on a pedestal that no one could attend to. I'm the kind of person that when I love, I love fiercely. I don't know whether that's a good or a bad thing. It could be a blessing and a curse at the same time. I know people that are so much more in control of what they feel, and they give as much as they want to. I am not one of those people. I was at such a low place and there was no one there with spirituality to help me. It was so weird; it was as if my whole world had been split open. Not only did I lose a husband, but I had also lost mutual friends as well. I now had to deal with friends who took sides, who took it upon themselves to have an opinion, who thought I should concentrate on his good qualities and not the betrayal and hurt he'd caused.

    People had so many opinions and formed their respective boundaries. So many mutual friends that had been a huge part of our lives became not only strained but very uncomfortable. It was such a weird feeling, because one minute we were talking about dreams, hanging out together; or going out to eat; then all of a sudden these friends were strangers. I felt like I had lost out on those people. And then came the intimate personal friends that I had before meeting him. You see, he was a very charming person who could charm the birds out of a tree. He was friendly, he was nice, and communicative. People were drawn to him, and nearly everybody liked him. Even my friends thought they would benefit more out of a friendship with him than they would with me. They decided to cut me off.

Then there was our family. I mean, he didn't have much family; it was his mother and him. Even the extended family was taken away from me, and I was lost. I didn't have a clue what to do. So I did the only thing I knew and threw myself into work. I worked in the salon night and day, it was absolutely ridiculous. The hours I was working weren't normal. I was doing all of that just to fill his void and stop myself from having the free time to sit, think, and dwell on the life change that I was going through. People at work could tell I wasn't doing well. They knew I was trying to mask the pain. Just days after we separated, I learned that the girl that he had an affair with was pregnant.

Can you imagine how that hurt? I was there trying for a baby, and another woman thought she had the right to come have his baby when I couldn't. It was too much for me to take. I remember waking up one day, and I collapsed. I felt like I could no longer endure the pain of the breakup. I said a prayer to Allah, "Take me; it's time. I have nothing to live for. You know, this is over and I just don't want to live anymore."

That self-loathing came to helplessness, and the thoughts in my head were, *You're better off dead.* In my mind, that was the only way that would stop this pain. Those thoughts drove me to the point of no return. I woke up one day and gathered all the pills that I could find in the house.

I remember very clearly saying a prayer lying on the bed, "Just make it quick, Lord. Let's just make it quick."

I remember holding the pills and a glass of water. It was impossible to love someone for so long and undo it all. In fact, it's as if your heart wants to acknowledge the good and the bad. Your heart wants to keep beating for that person, and I had no control over it.

As much as I hated him, I still wanted to hear his voice one more time. I thought, *If I am going to leave this earth, the last person's voice that I want to hear is his.* It was crazy, I don't know why I felt the need to speak to him but I did. I grabbed my phone, and I dialed his number.

He picked up, and I said to him, "You have devastated my life. I see no point in going on, I can't go on with this pain. I see no way out, so I am done. I am not doing this anymore, I am done. I hope you have a good life. I hope you found what you were looking for."

I put the phone down and to me that was it. I was done. I had paid my dues. I had said everything I wanted to say, but in reality, I was a coward.

I couldn't call my mother or any of my siblings who lived about thirty or forty minutes away from me, because they would have turned up. I didn't know where he was, but I didn't have the guts to call my siblings. I couldn't put them through that much pain thinking they could stop it. I just couldn't do it. But I needed to hear his voice. I needed him to know that I couldn't do it anymore and that I was done with the hurt and the pain.

I put the phone down. I took the pills; I swallowed them all. I forced them down my throat, drank some water, and I laid back on the bed waiting for things to take effect.

I don't know how long I'd been lying in the bed, because I must have fallen asleep. The next thing I can recall was someone —who must have broken down my front door— rushing into the bedroom where I was lying. It all happened so quickly that it was like a dream. One minute I was taking the pills; the next minute, somebody was yanking, shaking, and slapping me. They were doing all they could just to wake me up. It all seemed like a dream, because I was in this fog, this haze; it was an out of body experience. I knew what they were doing, but I couldn't respond. I was so out of it. Eventually, they rushed me to the hospital, and they pumped my stomach to get rid of all the medication that I had swallowed.

I was very lucky because it hadn't even taken much effect.

The doctor said to me, "Another half hour or so and your story would have been different." As he stood there talking to me, he continued, "Why would you do this?"

I had never felt shame like that.

"Do you know how this will affect your loved ones? This isn't an act that is solely about you. You take with you everybody you love and whatever it is that they have done; whoever it is, they do not deserve this. Is it a problem with your husband? Apparently, he called the ambulance and told them to get to the house quickly."

I cried after the phone call I made to him, and in the ambulance. But on that hospital bed that day, I cried from the depths of my soul, from the depth of my pain. I cried not only for me; I cried for him. I cried for a family that I would have been affected for the rest of their lives. I cried for the mess of what things were; for what was to be; for the plans that were no more; for the future we would never have; for the baby I wanted so badly.

I felt like I was in a hole all by myself; it was just so dark, dreary and hopeless. That feeling was something very alien, and I prayed that not even my worst enemy would go through that.

The doctor stood there watching me as he said, "Yep, you've got to let it out. Crying is good. Those thoughts are exactly what drove you to this point. You were trying to be strong."

I started opening up. Why would he do this to me? Why did I deserve this? How could he? Didn't he know how I felt; didn't he know what this would do to me? I was rambling on. It was uncontrollably pouring out of me. It was like he had gone from being my doctor to a confidant that I could trust with my feelings. He stood there with tears in his eyes watching me and listening. Another nurse joined him in the room, and I didn't care who was listening or who was watching me sob on that bed. I was in such a bad place. I didn't care who needed to judge; let him judge. They weren't in my shoes. They didn't feel what I felt.

The nurse came into the room and stood beside the doctor. She just watched me. They didn't say a word. They just listened, and both of them tried not to cry with me. They saw a broken woman. That doctor patiently stood there with that nurse, listened to me, and gave me the time of day to ask the questions I wanted. Time to moan, to scream, and do everything I needed for relief.

When I finished, he said to me, "I am very sorry for what happened. If I could take it all away, I would. But I am going to help you. You're going through so much mental anguish right now. I'm going to have to make you rest with all of these things in your head. Being that you attempted what you did, we're going to have to keep you under watch, because we don't trust that you won't do it again."

He went on, "I'm going to have to chain you to the bed just to make sure that you don't harm yourself again."

I begged him not to, because I was already in a bad place. I didn't need to see myself in chains. I knew he was trying to do his job; he was trying to be professional. But after the words he said and how much they sank into my heart, I wasn't in a place to see them chain me up.

I willed up all the courage I had and I looked at him as I said, "Please don't chain me to the bed. I couldn't take it. I do want to rest. I do want to sleep."

He looked at the nurse. They had this unspoken message between them.

Pensively he opined, "Okay, in that case, I'm going to put you to sleep to give your mind the time to rest. You're mentally exhausted right now."

I said, "Yes, okay."

So he came over and touched me on the shoulder while he spoke, "You are going to get through this, but it will take every ounce of strength. This is going to either make or break you, so be ready. I know you can do it. I can tell you have a fighting spirit, because of the intensity of what you felt for him. Use that willpower to get yourself back to where you should be."

He walked out of the room, and the nurse came to prepare me for my sleep.

She assured me, "After giving you this medication, I'm going to let you rest. It'll take a few minutes, then you'll be off to sleep. I'll make sure I'll be here when you wake up, and then we can talk."

This was a female nurse, an older woman. I bet she'd seen a lot of people like me come and go in her line of work. Maybe she, in her personal life, had gone through similar circumstances. I could tell by the empathy with which she handled me. She went to the cupboard, got all the medication ready, and came to inject me on my arm. That was the last thing I remember, and soon after that, I fell asleep.

I must have slept for hours because when I woke up, I felt numb. I felt sedated. I felt like somebody had just stopped the thoughts in my head. The pain hadn't gone, but the thoughts in my head had calmed down. It didn't feel overwhelming anymore. I pressed the call button, and they came over. The first thing she asked was how I was feeling.

I told her, and she responded, "I've been waiting for you to wake up. You've been asleep for hours. At one point, I thought, 'Why is she sleeping so much?' You should have been woken up by then; the medication should have worn off."

Then she decided to drag a chair up to sit by my bedside. You see, this lady didn't just talk to me about the facts of life. She came to me to share some personal stuff about herself. She had felt glad to share these things, because she felt it would give me hope. She thought knowing that she had gone through similar stuff would give me hope and encouragement to move on. To say that it worked was an understatement.

She held my hand, and her eyes met mine as she encouraged me, "You are going to get through this. What is your faith?"

"I'm Muslim. I come from a very strong Muslim family."

She said, "Okay, well, I have a story to share with you. Regardless of your faith, I hope it will give you hope. I went through a really hard time when I divorced my husband. In fact, it wasn't just a divorce, he left me for another woman. We had three children together, so I was completely heartbroken.

He just sat me down and said, 'I am not in love with you anymore. I'm in love with another woman. She is a family friend whom you know, and we're in love. And there is no point in me staying in this marriage anymore because it's dead. There's nothing in it for us emotionally, we're just like roommates, we have nothing in common. We do nothing together. The children add a uniting factor in his marriage and it's not enough for me anymore. I'm done.'

I was broken. I was going to be a single mother of three kids and hardly made enough money to support myself, let alone them."

She paused for a moment, as if overwhelmed by emotion before continuing, "The first thing I felt was fear. It took over my whole being. I was devastated."

As I looked at her, my eyes filled with awe at her strength. I thought, *How did you go from there to here talking to me?*

She said, "Do you know how?"

It was as if she could read my mind. I could see this woman's pain in her eyes. It was one of the weirdest experiences I've ever had because this was a strange opening up to me about the most personal journey she had been through. She went on to say how she found God. When she said "God," she meant Jesus Christ, but this didn't matter to me because I knew she loved him in the same way that I loved Allah. I was able to empathize with her. My own faith has always helped me through.

She continued with her testimony, "I had no hope, no money. The house we lived in...he paid the rent. So it was questionable whether we were still going to be able to keep the home. He had bought the car; it was possible he could leave me penniless. And soon, that's what he did."

She was looking at me, eyes dewy with tears ready to make their descent down her smooth cheeks, "I found Jesus, or should I say Jesus found me. Let me tell you something about the Lord Jesus Christ and who he is."

She thought she was the first person to have preached Jesus to me. I ran a beauty salon; I met women from all walks of life. I met the single woman, the married woman, the lady of the night. I met the side chick. I met the one that lived her life as if there was no tomorrow. I had met them all through my line of work, and I was the kind of person that gave no judgment. As she sat there talking to me, it kind of took me back to some of my previous clients. Some were dedicated to their faith in Jesus Christ. And as I would be doing their hair,\ —even though they knew I was Muslim— they preached to me about how Jesus, the God of the Christians, is a *miracle worker*.

"You know, He's a way maker; He is the light of the world. He is the Savior. He is the one through whom all humanity will be saved. There is no other way to God except through him."

I'd heard it all. I had been invited to churches, for weddings, engagements, conferences, and sermons. I'd had the invitation but always declined respectfully. There'd been a few times that, because of my work, I had to go to the bride and the bridesmaids in a church setting. I would do their makeup, follow them through the church service, and get them all ready for the reception. So that was part of my work. I wasn't there to worship Jesus. I wasn't there to know Him. I wasn't there to visit, hear the sermons, and expect it to change me. I was there for my money, I came to do a service and I got paid for it. That was the extent of what I did with the Christians, since I had my own perceptions of them. I thought they were very forceful. They never took No for an answer.

All of this came to my mind as I listened to this woman at the hospital. I was thinking, *Here we go, I'm going to get another sermon right in my bed, in the hospital bed, like really?* I felt that. At the same time, I admired the genuineness of how she took her time to tell me these personal things that shaped her life. I didn't have a choice but to listen; there were no distractions. It was just her and I in the room.

She was holding my hand and talking to me while looking deeply into my eyes. As I listened to her, she told me stories of the things Jesus did. The hope He gave her. How He sent words of knowledge to her through random strangers to her. How He led her every step of the way. How she got up, enrolled in a college in her pain and hurt. While God was dealing with the healing, she was doing what she could do with herself. She went and got help from the government, got the children situated, moved into a new house, then she enrolled herself in college. She wanted to go and pursue her dream of being a nurse. She went on to tell me how God performed miracles financially. He emotionally gave her the peace of mind; the steadiness of heart for her to be able to go through college; to finish her degree to be a nurse.

She went on to say how people would bless her with money, when she needed her tuition fees to be paid. People would offer to look after her children; people would bless her with food; people would give a favor.

She told me her whole life story. As I listened to her I was so stunned that God had granted such miracles in her life. Her belief and faith seemed true, and it seemed genuine to her. I couldn't refute it, because this was a woman sitting there telling me and giving all the glory to God. As she spoke, I listened, I took it in, and I cried. She did as well. It was her words that captured me. She was so encouraging and so hopeful. I was looking at her, thinking she's so hopeful, not just for today, but for whatever the future holds. How could one live with so much hope? She had pulled herself right from the rubble, the pits of the darkness, and worked her way right through to find the light. She continued with her life with a driving force of her faith that was commendable.

All these thoughts were going into my head as she was saying them, and the woman jolted me out of my daydreaming and said, "Do you mind if I pray for you?"

The normal Roza would have declined and said, "No, I'm good, I'm fine. I don't need prayers."

But something in me, the genuineness of this woman, and the authenticity of what she had just told me changed my mind. I just couldn't say No, and I needed all of the prayers I could get. I mean, if nothing worked in my own ability, maybe prayers would. I thought, O*kay, why not?*

So, I said, "Yes, you may."

The woman took hold of my hands and started praying. She prayed from the depth of her heart. At one point, she went into a language I didn't understand. This must have been her native language, because she was black and African. She would pray in English for a while and then pray in this language that I didn't understand. It was weird, it was different, it literally jolted me from reality.

But I still let her carry on and when she finished she said, "Amen."

"Amen."

She looked at me and said, "You're going to get through this."

"I am," I said.

I actually believed it was true.

She said, "Yep, you are. You're going to get through this, because the God that I call upon is faithful. He will help you. He is faithful not just to the believer, but the unbeliever too."

"Thank you for calling me a non-believer. I'll take it, and thank you for the prayers."

She looked at me and said, "No man is worth this. You see, the same man that brought you into this hospital bed right now... I bet you he's on top of another woman."

That wasn't what I wanted to hear but it was the truth.

She implored me, "Why isn't he killing himself because he lost you? Why is he not hurting as much as you are? Clearly, he's got something to live for. How is it fair that you think you don't, and want to end it all? There are questions hidden in the depths of your soul, questions that set you free."

I felt like I needed to hear what the doctor said and what that nurse said at that point in time.

She rebuked me gently, "Don't do this. Get those thoughts out of your head. No man under the heavens is worth dying for. There's one that loves you more than you could ever understand; that's the one that gave up His life, because He loved you. That is Jesus. You're young, you're beautiful, and you're already on the right track. Get up. Go and run your business. Take care of yourself and live your life. You will heal; you will love again; you will make something of yourself."

This woman spoke with so much vigor, you would have thought she knew exactly how my future was going to pan out. When she finished, she told me she was going to be off the next day but would be back in a few days.

"Hopefully when I see you next, you will be feeling a whole lot better. I may be gone but you're going to be in my heart and in my prayers, you better believe that."

I thanked her profusely; she signed my patient file and told me, "We are arranging counseling and some other sessions for you to attend that will help."

You know, I've always heard of people being ashamed of seeing a shrink or a counselor to help their mental state of mind. I was among those people.

When she mentioned it, I didn't think I wanted counseling, but she said, "There is no shame in it. It actually empowers you to know you have issues you need to deal with. It can help you take control over your life. Don't listen to what people say, they don't even have to know if you don't tell anybody. I highly recommend it."

Eventually, I said, "Okay, I will see the counselor," and so she gave me the paperwork and I signed it.

She told me when my first appointment would be and made sure all my medication was in order. She also ordered my food; then she bid me farewell and left. I hoped I would see her again. Little did I know, I would never set eyes on that woman ever again.

A few days later, something had changed in me, and I didn't want to die anymore. I wanted to leave behind a legacy. Those few days in the hospital really put things into perspective for me.

One evening, they were so busy, I think there was some kind of accident or fire near the hospital. They were so busy rushing in new patients that I saw my opportunity to get the hell out of there. I watched the nurses running and trying to fulfill their duties. I heard people screaming, some crying, some bellowing. It was an absolute chaotic mess that day. As I looked at them, a thought crossed my mind. *They've come to trust you, that's why they didn't chain you to the bed. This is your opportunity to get out of here because they wouldn't let you leave on your own accord.*

They wanted to discharge me when they felt they were ready and yet, I was thinking, N*o, I need to go. I need to get back to my life*. I felt like my life was on a shelf at home waiting for me while I was stuck in this hospital. So, lying there, I made a solemn promise to myself that never again would I even entertain the idea of ending my life. With that thought in my mind I got up, packed all my stuff, and put it in a bin bag as if I had some rubbish to empty. I made my way through the chaos of all the nurses and doctors running to help new patients that were coming in from the fire.

I slipped down the corridor. A couple of them looked at me like "Where are you going?"

"I'm just going to put this in the rubbish bin."

They nodded to give their approval.

I turned around and looked at the hospital one more time and quietly slipped out through the hallway. When I reached the exit, I thanked God the door was unlocked. I yanked it open and started running down the streets, into the parking lot, and into the dark evening like my life depended on it. That's how I discharged myself from the hospital.

I never looked back. I hailed a cab, and I went home. I got all my stuff together. I was going to move to another side of town about fifteen to twenty minutes away, and that was it. My new life had started. There was hope inside me. I didn't know what it was called then, but I knew I'd found enough strength to go on. And that's what I did.

When I moved my stuff, I would have friends. I went over to the rental company and rented a nice little one bedroom flat, and I moved my stuff in a couple of days later. That was it. My life was starting again. I threw myself into work again, but this time something was different. I wasn't masking the pain; I was dealing with it. I started working ridiculous hours. I would open up at nine in the morning and finish at midnight or one o'clock. I was making a lot of money, because it was so busy. East London was so diverse and so busy that it never went to sleep. People were out clubbing at midnight. They would come to my shop to get their hair, makeup, or lash done, and go to the club.

On days that I felt like it, I would join my friends in the clubs. We loved to go to Trafalgar Square —which was in Oxford Street— the busiest part of the West End. That's exactly where I would go with my friends just to get away from the hurt and the pain which was still there. I was still going to counseling sessions. I didn't give up because I remembered what that nurse said to me. I reported to my counseling sessions week after week, and the more I threw myself into work, it was as if the heavens agreed with me, because it became so busy. I had about five girls and three barbers. The other part of the shop was rented by a guy offering money transfer services. Business was booming, and I took advantage of that. It was unbelievable. Then, I thought about opening another shop across the street on the other side. I couldn't control my personal life, but I could control my professional one. That was exactly what I did.

I wanted to start something fresh for myself. The first shop was called Real Friends, and this was the one I had started with my ex. It was very much tainted now. And so, I opened up another one and threw myself into work. The second one was called Roza's Styles Unisex Salon, and that was my baby that was birthed through my pain. It was time to work like I'd never worked before. I found a routine; the more successful I became, the more strength I had. I was going out partying frequently. I was traveling wherever I wanted to go. I was enjoying my life. I wasn't always ecstatic and joyful in my personal life because of the pain. It was still there. The counseling helped immensely. For once in my life, I was in control of my whole world, especially my financial world. That was amazing. To feel that level of financial security at a very early age from the work of my hands was very liberating, and I loved it.

When I wasn't working or partying, I would attend live musical festivals and gigs. There is one called Glastonbury Festival, which is one of the biggest live festivals in London. It was so much fun. That was my downtime; no matter how hard I worked, I was partying as well. That was part of my healing process. I was very content, but I was young. I was also beautiful. Men saw me and thought I could be another catch. The thing that made me want to decline was that most of the time, married men would approach me with propositions of what they wanted me to be. They wanted a concubine, a mistress. I would look at them thinking, *I bet this is the same proposal my ex made to the other single women.* In the same way, another woman had come with the morals of a stray cat and destroyed my marriage. I couldn't do that to another, and every time a married man would step up to me to ask me out on a date in this way, it brought out the wrong parts of me.

I remember my friends being very agitated about this because married men were very generous. They would buy you all the drinks you wanted in a club; they would pay for things for you and do whatever you wanted just to get into your pants. My friends were okay with it, but I was on the receiving end of what a married man had done to me. It was as if the tables had turned. I entertained them before, but now I don't. I had tasted the medicine that was just too bitter of a pill to swallow or entertain.

When we were together having fun in a club or festival or committee zone and a married man came at me, my friends would plead, "Please don't do it. She's having a great time; we don't want to ruin it."

They knew I was pissed at married men. I saw them as predators. I saw them as users and manipulators. They just had to get what they wanted from women. But when a single man approached me, that was something different. I would give them the time of day if I felt like going out with them. That was my choice. Life continued, but the hurt was still there. My ex lived on the other side of town, and rumors were flying around left and right. People felt the need to tell me everything he was doing. I don't know why people did that. When you break up with someone, the last thing you want to know is how they were faring. For me, I wanted him out of sight and out of mind.

I started having the confidence to say to people, "I do not want to hear what you have to say about him. I do not want to hear how he's doing. What we had is over, it's broken. It's finished, and I need you to respect that."

This was a boundary I had to set because people would go out of their way to call me to let me know how he was doing. That was hurtful because you can't just cure your heart. To say I didn't feel anything when they felt the need to fill me in on his life would be a lie. I did feel something. There were times when he would call, and I wouldn't pick up. He would come to the shop, and I wouldn't talk to him. I was just done. I had found a niche in this world as a single woman who was trying to hold it together, to find the strength and hope to carry on. There was no way I was going to retreat and go back to this man that had hurt me so much.

The days of wanting to work it out were over with. My business was doing well. I had my own place. I was driving a nice car. Life was looking up, and so the last thing I wanted was to get dragged back to think about this man that I had loved so much. I got to the point in my single life that whenever I went to a restaurant or a wedding and I saw mutual friends, I would just hide. And up until today, I don't understand why I hid. I think seeing those people was me confronting the past all over again, and that seeing those people reminded me of what wasn't there anymore, and it brought everything back.

And so, for a long time, no matter where the venue was, whenever I saw all these people that were in my past life, I would hide. I didn't have to be ashamed, but I was. Because truth be told, in every divorce you carry a sense of shame. It's as if you're damaged, because the experience has taken so much out of you that some things can never be replaced. It's almost as if your innocence is gone, as if one is losing her innocence. You're hurt; you're scarred with wounds to show your journey. You carry this sense of not being enough, because if you were that wouldn't happen. You carry this sense of failure that affects you and your family, because you were meant to have so much in the marriage. This burden can be carried for a very long time. I was broken, and in my brokenness, I had made my own world. I was very satisfied with it.

When I came to work, some of my male clients would hit on me, and I just wasn't interested. Some of my female clients took it upon themselves to hook me up with their brothers, their bosses at work, their friends, or even family members.

It was as if they all came together and said, "Roza is free. Let's do this kind of dating game."

But I wasn't ready to put my life into another man's hands and have him wreck it. I was very negative about relationships, and I was very cautious. I felt like none of them were worthy of my heart or my time. The salon was one of the most entertaining atmospheres to work in because you meet people from all walks of life. Everybody came with their own opinions, thinking they were right. So weekends in the salon were always my favorite. The male clients would be talking about how a woman had devastated them or how women are these days. Then you had the women on the other side who felt like they had to defend themselves. Before you knew it, the conversation was always centered around relationships. I could only speak about my own experience, and I was bitter. I was angry and it came out when I spoke about men.

I remember somebody saying, "Roza, you're too young to give up on men right now. You will heal; you will love again; you will have a family."

I always rebutted, "I am so good on my own. Even in the future, I am not going to want another man."

They would just look at me and laugh, because I guess some of them had been through similar journeys.

Some of them would go to the point of saying, "Roza, you are the type of woman that has so much to offer a man, yet you think you're better off on your own. You cannot do that to yourself, you know."

When they would start preaching to me about how there were good men out there, how men were different, how some of them were so good to the women, I wasn't interested at all. You could have put a camera in the shop to capture the conversations that went on, as it was so entertaining. It could have given today's reality shows a run for their money.

It was such a beautiful time. These were the people that had seen me at my worst. My employees had seen me at rock bottom. They'd seen me have a bad day; they'd seen me angry; they'd seen me sarcastic with an attitude. They'd seen every part of Roza. These people weren't just not employees; they were people that had walked my life journey with me. Some of them had been working for me ever since I was married, so for them to see me in this single situation was a big adjustment for all of us. But I loved my work. I loved what I did. I loved making people look and feel good about themselves. I could have a woman walk into the shop feeling so low, shoulders hunched down, beating herself up over words that were spoken over her. By the time she walked out of my shop, she was walking with her head held high with a different attitude than she had walked in with. It was as if my job wasn't only to beautify them but to give them that hope to see themselves in a different light, to love and appreciate themselves, to hold themselves to a better standard. My job was to not let the words of other people shape their lives.

These were all the things I did in my line of work to encourage my clients, but guess what? I needed those pep talks for myself. I needed to believe that more than they did. Actually, I was very good at giving the advice, but I had built walls around my heart that would take even Goliath centuries to scale. They were walls of pain, hurt, and betrayal that were solid and firm. They protected every parameter of my heart to the point that I wouldn't let anybody come that close to me again. I would never be that vulnerable with anyone again.

Sometimes I would catch myself dishing out advice to my clients and workers, and I'd think to myself, *I wish to God I could take my own advice and feel exactly how I'm wanting them to feel.* For a long time, I continued counseling and it helped. It made me see life from a different perspective. It gave me hope for the future. It started giving me the opportunity to make my own path, because I wasn't ready to just fold up and die. That wasn't an option anymore. I was ready to make my mark on the world.

There's something very beautiful in being alone, because when you're at rock bottom, there is no one else to look after but yourself. When it's time to get up, you have to work your way right up. And that's what I did. I did it with all the vigor I could muster. With all the strength and the hope I had in me. The marriage I had was beautiful until it was broken, and when it broke, there was no repair. My heart had an out of order sign, and I had no intention of removing it anytime soon.

This was my new life.

5
A STRANGER FROM AMERICA

About a year and a half into the journey of recovering from my broken marriage, I started to feel like life was taking a good turn. I thought I had settled into the life that I wanted. It wasn't perfect, but it was mine to live. I began to let go of the dreams of marriage, and the thought of having a child was so far away from the life I was living. It felt like it was a dream for another person in another life, because the life I lived didn't have any space whatsoever for a child. Those were the dreams of the past.

And now the dreams of the future were to work hard and make something of myself. To say it affected how I saw men would have been an understatement. The counselor had to work really hard to get me to change my perspective. Always reminding me that there were a lot of good men out there. There were men that would come into your life; men who could fit into your life like a glove and honor their promises to you. She even told me there was a man out there who would help put the pieces of my heart back together. I doubted all of this, but it was good to hear.

I dated but never really gave my heart very quickly to any man. I was in it just for fun. Casual dating, nothing serious. I didn't want to end up on my own but I wasn't ready to give my heart to anyone. For a while, it worked out okay. There was a long period of time where I could actually hear myself laughing from the pit of my belly. I wasn't a hundred percent, but I was on my way there. I had no idea that on one Saturday afternoon, an encounter was going to produce something that would last for the rest of my life.

On this Saturday afternoon, it was around six o'clock. We were winding down from the busiest day of the week, and I remember I was in the back in my office area relaxing.

One of the salon employees came into my office area and exclaimed, "There is someone here for you, you have to come and see him, Roza."

I had no idea who this could be or what was going on. Well, apparently there was a stranger that just walked into my shop and commanded the attention of not only the female workers, but even the males. Everybody knew he was different. Everybody knew he was a stranger and a foreigner. I guess it was the way he spoke, carried himself, and the presence with which he exuded without trying.

I walked in and standing in front of me was a tall, handsome, confident, stranger. He was very good-looking with a very nice body, ripped in all the right places, with really nice long dark hair. I think that was where the attractiveness came in, because he wasn't slouching. He wasn't walking in with an aura of *I don't know who I am or where I'm going.* He walked in with this air of sexy confidence. As I approached him, I was thinking, *Oh, God help me*, because the thing I felt for him was lust. I could feel his eyes on me taking me in with every step towards him. I could feel his gaze from the tip of my head, to the soles of my feet. He had his time to really check me out while I approached him.

"How can I help you?"

"I think he wants his hair done. Roza," one of the girls in the hair salon blurted.

I looked back at her thinking, *Well, obviously he's in a hair salon, not the doctor's office.* I guessed she just wanted him to notice her as well, or perhaps she hoped her words would make him laugh. For a minute, time stopped.

As we looked into each other's eyes, I directed my question back to him, "How can I help you?"

"I want to have my hair done," he said, and we all realized he was an American.

Immediately I thought, *What a beautiful accent.* But he also had the whole package. He was very pleasing to the eyes.

I looked him right in the eye and said, "We're kind of busy right now. But if you wait a little bit, one of the girls is about to finish."

He wanted a shampoo and to have his hair braided so I turned around and I said to one of the girls, "How long do you reckon you will be with that customer?"

And she said, "Oh, give me another twenty minutes or so, and I should be able to take him on."

But the stranger wasn't having any of it. Before I could even address him, he turned around and said, "No, I want you to do my hair."

My surprise must have shown on my face because he repeated himself. At that point in my day, I wasn't even busy.

But I lied to him, "You will have to come back because I'm busy right now. Give it about an hour and come back. And I may be able to do your hair. But if you come in, and it's busy, you will have to let someone else do it."

The moment he left, wearing the same confidence he came in with, the others turned to me with amusement.

"Did you see the sparks flying?" one of the guys teased.

I turned to him laughing, "You need help. You absolutely need help."

"No, Roza, everyone felt it."

One of the male clients was like, "Girl, for a moment, both of you forgot we were in the room, like it was just the two of you. And we all saw it."

"Roza just admitted it," another said.

"I've admitted what? "There is nothing to admit."

I was trying so hard to refute the fact that I found him attractive. I knew I did, but they weren't going to know that.

And so the teasing went on, "What? He's very nice. And by the way you were both checking each other out, there's clearly something there."

I had to leave the room just to allow myself not to blush in front of him. Thank God I was too dark to blush. But anyway, I knew exactly what they were talking about. It was called mutual attraction and chemistry. It was the same thing I'd experienced with my ex when we'd first met, which brought back some memories. I could only hope that things wouldn't end the same way here if I was to give him a shot.

And so they continued this conversation about our first meeting; I quickly ignored them and left the room. I returned to my own solitude, but I couldn't get him out of my mind.

It had been a long time since I allowed myself to openly admit that I found someone attractive. Even that was always too much. But you couldn't lie to the heart, and sometimes you found those people that you had an instant connection with. Somehow, I just knew he was one of those people for me. It's amazing how things happen, and we don't even know how much they will affect our lives. I went back to what I was doing. A client came in to have her makeup done so I threw myself back into work.

But in the back of my mind, I knew he was going to come back. He would have wanted to see where it ended, as I did. And so when I finished with my client, I stood in the mirror combing my fingers through my hair; checking my makeup; making sure I was ready. And I could see the anticipation on everybody's faces, as they all knew he would be here anytime. Everybody was anticipating him coming back.

I knew somebody had come to the point where they had to leave. Some of them had plans for the night. I turned around and asked, "Who's going to stay and work a bit late today?"

"Oh no, we have plans," said one of my employees.

"I have to go, but I wish I could stay just to see how things work out between you and this stranger," said another.

Then the doors swung open, and this stranger walked back in. This time he walked straight over to my station.

"Are you ready for me?"

"Have a seat and give me a couple of minutes. I will be with you."

So I went to the shampoo base to get everything ready, and I said to him, "You can come over this way."

Everybody was watching him as the girls reluctantly got ready to leave. He walked over to the sink and sat down, so I put the cape on him and I proceeded to detangle his hair before shampooing it.

"You are Roza?" he confirmed.

"Yes. How did you know that?"

"Oh, my dad comes here all the time. He was the one that actually recommended that I come here. He's a client of yours. He's been coming here for some time. And I bet you know him."

"Do I? What is his name?"

He told me the name of his dad.

"Yeah, I do know him. He comes to the barbers every few weeks to have his hair cut. I didn't know he had a grown son."

"Yeah, I live in the States. I live in New York and I visit him every so often. I have family in both countries, so it's a back and forth for me."

"Well, it's nice to know. I lived in the States for some time, too."

He continued, "Well, we saw you a couple of days ago. You were crossing the street to get into your shop. If you remember, I did a Wolf whistle, and you turned around to see where the sound was coming from. But you couldn't see me because I was in my car."

I thought, *Yeah, that did happen.* "So that was you."

He said, "Yeah, you looked very beautiful that day."

"Well, thank you."

Now I was so glad that he couldn't see me as I was combing his hair out. I was in the fashion industry and took pride in my appearance so I was used to compliments, but this stranger made me feel differently.

I think I knew there and then that I liked him.

"So how long have you been growing your hair?" I asked him.

"Oh, just a few years. I've been contemplating, you know, locking it up into dreadlocks or just letting it grow."

"Well, it's nice, thick and healthy."

"Thank you, I do spend a lot of money on maintaining it, which is why when I come to England. I have people that do it, but I didn't even know that there's somebody just around the corner from my dad's house that could take care of it for me."

He laid back a little more before sharing how long he was staying for. He was in town for a couple of weeks and he was very excited to find out about us.

"I've heard very good things about you. I hear you're very good at your job."

"From who?" I obviously asked.

"Well...my dad."

You see the thing about London is, everybody knows each other, but no one's got time to stand and chit chat. You kept it moving. It was that busy.

Every week everyone had a busy life. And so whatever little he knew about me, his dad really had passed onto him. And I was glad everything was good. My hard work had paid off. You know, it was a nice atmosphere here, very professional. So he was saying everything that a business owner loved to hear. I proceeded to shampoo his hair, because I was intent on giving him a good service. And so I started washing his hair and massaging his scalp.

My fingers delved into his scalp, and he closed his eyes, murmuring, "That's a really good hair wash. I needed one of those. You're very good at what you do."

"Well, that's the reason you're here, isn't it?" I teased him as I continued massaging his scalp, pushing my fingers in. I wanted it to be a good experience. And so when I was finished, I put the conditioner in, took the comb, and started working through his hair.

I had seen all types of hair, but I was just so happy to be working with hair that was just so well-maintained. The growth was beautiful. We started talking about mundane things, and I wanted to get to know him. I'm a very talkative person. It comes with my personality in my work. I like to get to know people. I loved people, maybe not men at that time, but I do love people. I loved meeting people, chatting with them, getting to know them, what they do, their families, their spouses, their children. People will talk about anything.

I always had this ability to make people comfortable with me, but *he* just wouldn't stop talking, and I loved it. He chatted right through the shampoo wash. I rinsed off the conditioner and I said to him, let's go over to my station. Now it was going to be interesting because he would sit in the chair with me right behind him, so he would see my face. He would be able to see my feelings and emotions on my face. I was one of those people who wore my heart on my sleeve. My emotions were always written all over my face. I knew that would be the toughest part of it and not the shampoo. And we went over to my chair.

I proceeded to oil his scalp and part the hair.

"So how do you want me to do your hair?" I asked him.

"Well, I am not sure," he said, "Why don't I leave it to your professional opinion? You can do whatever you want. As long as it's beautiful, I'm fine with it."

Okay. These strategies could just give me too much hope. You could tell he was trouble. But at the same time, it felt nice to have somebody appreciate what I was doing.

As I began working on his hair, the shop was winding down. There were two people in the shop, as well as the two barbers. All of them were listening, I could tell. They wanted to know exactly what we were talking about. But we were talking so quietly that they wouldn't just hear us properly unless we chose to speak more loudly.

I had just started doing his hair when he asked, "So, what are you doing tonight?"

"When I finish, I will be going home to relax. I am so tired. It's been a long day."

"Oh, okay. Well tonight is still young. You never know, you might want to do something later."

"I very much doubt it," was my reply.

I excused myself and went to the toilet. I needed to compose myself, to be professional and not let him know I was attracted to him. My past struggles with relationships had made me less trusting, which made me very weary of men. I didn't have time for anything that wasn't going to be within my control. But this American stranger had thrown me for a loop. As I walked back to him, I felt like I had composed myself. I was going to be in control of the conversation from now so they would not steer to personal territories. And so I went over to him and started parting his beautiful hair.

One by one, the people in the shop left, and the last bottle was tidied away. People were deliberately walking very closely to us to hear how the conversation was going. People were so nosy.

One of the guys said, "You guys have a wonderful evening."

The way he said it made me laugh.

"What is wrong with people?" I said, glancing and laughing again. He couldn't help himself either, and then we were both chuckling.

"Why are they teasing you like that?"

"Oh, they just do that. They love to watch me squirm and laugh"

He laughed, then said, "Well, I want to get to know who you are. I'm interested."

This stranger was saying all of the right things and I was intrigued to know more myself. I knew he was from New York. He was from a big city. He was very well-educated. I knew I was probably the thousandth woman in line that he had chatted to.

I said, "Well, I'm not sure I'm ready for all of that. All I know is that I can do your hair. When you come to visit, you will be looked after well. I'm not sure about everything else after that. And so well, we'll see how it goes then."

"Yeah, that's good enough for me."

There was some silence as I continued braiding his hair, and at one point he flinched as if I'd hurt him.

"Am I doing it too tightly?" I asked him.

"A little, but it's okay. I want it to last, so don't worry."

He laughed, and I found myself smiling. Even if I was a little nervous, I was enjoying his conversation.

"Well, I do braids tightly; my clients do say that. That's what actually stimulates hair growth. And you know, just take it as a man."

He burst out laughing, and was clearly unable to stop, "Huh?"

I feigned innocence, as if I didn't understand what he was talking about, "What? You want me to do a good job? Beauty comes with pain. I'm sorry."

"I haven't laughed that much in ages! You're a funny one, Roza."

He clearly knew I was teasing him and liked it.

I carried on with his hair and then the door swung open, and in came one of my really good friends. She was always told she was beautiful. She was a fashionista. She always looked good. She was one of those people that just made you laugh because of her great sense of humor.

She said, "You're working late again?"

"Well, everyone's left. I'm the only one here."

"Well, that's nothing new," we started laughing, "So what are you doing tonight?"

I was suddenly more conscious of the stranger from America sitting in my chair whose head was beneath my fingers and wondered if he was listening.

"I am going home after this. Why, what have you got planned?"

"Well," she said, taking a seat right next to my station, "Hi," she said, ignoring my question when she realized I was working on this guy and he turned to look at her.

"How are you?" They greeted each other, "I'm Jackie."

He responded, and she picked up on his accent then asked, "Are you from the States?"

"Yeah, I am of Jamaican descent but I was raised in the States."

So the conversation started about life in America. Jackie was talkative, curious, and educated. So we all got into this conversation about America: the good, the bad, the indifference. Everything that was so different from life in London. Jackie asked what he was doing in London, and he proceeded to answer that his dad lived in London. He had family in London, and he would go back and forth to visit. He was a very personable person. You could see that he was used to dominating the conversation, and he articulated himself very well. He was a charmer. He could charm the birds out of his trees. When he finished speaking, Jackie of course had something to say that caught me off guard.

"Well, I have an idea," her eyes lit up with excitement, "Why don't we show him exactly how we party in London and go out tonight?"

The American stranger in my chair quickly responded, "That's exactly what I was asking her, and she said that she is ready to go home".

"She works way too hard. So Roza, are you going to come out tonight?" Jackie replied while looking expectantly at me.

"I really am not feeling it. I'm tired and—" I did my best to decline but she interrupted me mid-sentence.

"Oh, you've got to come. This club is having a new DJ today. He's one of the well-known DJs in town, and it's going to be a full house. You're going to really miss out if you don't come."

So she turned to him and asked if he had ever been to the club she was thinking of.

"No, I haven't, but I'd definitely like to go, " he said with a tone that insinuated that he wanted me to come along.

"Well, I think this would be a great night to be introduced to this club. They have great music and it's not a young club with teenagers fighting; it's for grown folks with great music and great company. And there's a restaurant right next door that we could go to afterwards."

She was making it too hard to turn down. As much as I wanted to go home and rest, I was tempted. It was always a good night out with her. She was one of those people, even if you were wanting to be in your own feelings, she could literally snap you out of it. So eventually I agreed to go.

"Well, okay, why don't we exchange numbers and see where the night goes?" he asked after I conceded.

I was thinking that I really didn't want to give him my number, as I wasn't ready for that. So instead I said, "Well, I'm going to go home, get ready, and relax. Then we can talk later."

Jackie sensed my hesitance and said to the stranger, "Why don't you give me your number? We will call you and let you know what we're doing. We are going to make a night of it, I'll see you soon."

She walked out of the door. I heard it slam closed behind her, leaving me alone with the stranger.

"I need to shut this door before somebody else walks back in. Because if someone walks in to get their hair done, I'm taking them," I said aloud.

I walked over to the door, locked it, and returned to my station to the client smiling at me in the mirror.

"So she persuaded you to come out, then?" he said teasingly, "I thought you were too tired."

I shrugged, not knowing what else to say. After I finished doing his hair, I applied the olive oil spray on it.

He looked at it and said, "That looks really good, Roza."

"Well, thank you. I aim to please. I am very good at my job, as you were told by your father," I said, smiling a little.

I couldn't help myself, and I wanted to flirt with him.

He quickly matched my comment with his flirtatious tone, "I'm happy you like it." I really liked the style.

"Well, I was told that you would, but you really have delivered," he paid the bill, gave a generous tip and continued, "That's for doing a wonderful job."

I looked him in the eye and said, "Well, thank you."

"I really want to see you later on. And I hope you come out so we can have a good time."

He turned and flashed one last smile as I opened the door to let him out.

I closed the door behind him and sat down in one of the chairs and thought to myself, *What just happened?* It was so good to be there on my own, because now I could be honest with myself and process everything for myself. I had a habit of talking out loud. It was part of the therapy sessions, during which I read out positive affirmations to myself every morning or any part of my day, whenever I felt I needed it. I was doing it right there by asking myself questions I already knew the answers to like: *What are you doing? Are you going to go, are you going to chicken out? What are you going to do?*

I knew I was playing with fire. Something about this man smelled like trouble, but I couldn't help myself. When he left the salon, it was around nine o'clock, so I still had time to change my mind if I wanted to. This night felt different. It was a night that I'd had an invitation from a handsome stranger who —unbeknownst to me— was going to change my life in a very profound way.

Roza Perry

6
Unexpected Interruptions

My heart was beating a little bit faster than normal as I cleaned up the shop, thinking through my plans for the night. I was a little giddy with excitement as I locked up the shop, pulled the shutter down. and walked to my car. There, I picked up my phone and found several missed calls from Jackie and one of the girls in the shop. Everybody wanted to know exactly how it went with that stranger.

I thought to myself, *I'll call them right back once I get home*. Even though it was after ten at night, it was still active outside as if it was daytime. London was busy; people had places to be, and the nightlife was one of the most enjoyable things in London. There was never a dull moment. I looked out of the window and saw people all dressed up walking the streets to their destinations; groups of young girls all dressed up to the nines, laughing, joking; and people being very carefree about life. I looked at them and thought to myself, *That used to be me, but I am not that innocent anymore. I am wounded. I am scared with scars to prove it, and that makes me very cautious.*

I drove home with my thoughts all over the place. I was scared one moment and giddy the next, but I knew I had to make a final decision. I arrived home, threw my bag on one side of the bed, and went straight to the kitchen to make a cup of tea. I had to collect my thoughts before I decided what to do. As I made my tea, I remembered to call Jackie back. I picked up the phone and dialed her number.

She immediately picked up and said, "Hello, so what happened?" I knew she wanted every juicy detail about what happened when she left, "So who is he?"

"Like he mentioned, I do know him. I do know his dad, and his dad's young girlfriend as well."

I told her what little I knew about him and then said, "He is just absolutely gorgeous, isn't he?"

"You know, Roza, I could just tell that sparks were flying. It was like pheromones in the air and everything. It was just so nice to see. You can't fool me, girl. Anyway, I won't be able to attend."

"What? You basically arranged everything. I am not going if you're not."

"No, you've got to go and have a good time! What's the worst that can happen? He's going to be back on a flight to America next week. I can't make it, because one of my friends has called and said he's coming over. And I know for a fact, he's not going to want to go out. And I totally forgot that we had arranged to watch a movie and just chill."

"Well, why don't I come over to your house and be the third wheel?"

"No, that is not the plan you're having tonight. You go call him and arrange to meet him. I know you like him."

"I'm not sure," I said, a new anxiety creeping through me.

"Look, Roza, you're beautiful. No more shutting yourself away. It's time to live your life."

"Well, I'm not sure what I think about it. Are you sure you don't want to come out?"

"I can't. Another time, I probably will; just not tonight. I'm sorry."

"Well, okay girl. I'm not sure. I wish you were coming."

"Well, if you change your mind, give him a call. Go out and let me know how it goes tomorrow."

I thought to myself, one-on-one with this stranger was more than I could handle right now. I really couldn't do this. It was as if I had never dated before. There was something about this Jamaican American that was very different. I knew everything about him was different and exciting, and a part of me wanted to explore it. But the part of me that was so guarded just wouldn't let me; so I made my decision quickly after that that I wasn't going to go. I would have a nice shower and go to bed.

Only a few minutes later I fished in my bag for the phone number and held it in my hand thinking, *Oh God, what am I going to do? What am I going to do?* I found myself dialing the number to tell him that I wasn't going to make it as the phone rang endlessly. Then he picked up and seemed to know it was me.

"So, is it good news? Where are we going? What are we doing?"

I said, "Listen, I'm sorry, Jackie couldn't make it tonight. And unfortunately, I don't feel up to it, either. It's been a long day and I'm exhausted."

"Well, that's a shame. I can understand Jackie not making it, but why can't you? I'd like to spend more time with you. We can still go out and have some fun."

"I know, but I'm just not feeling it right now. I'm tired, but I'll speak to you some other time as usual."

"So, I can't make you change your mind?"

He proceeded to try to tell me what a night I would be missing out on and that he wanted to really spend some time with me and get to know me. His tactic didn't work, because I still stuck to my guns. I couldn't muster up the courage to go one-on-one with him.

He finally gave in and said, "Well, okay then. I guess I'd love to invite you some other time."

I said, "Have a good night, and enjoy yourself if you do go out."

"All right, then. Thank you. I'll speak to you soon."

I put the phone down and stared at it for a moment. I had actually chickened out. The night was mine to do exactly what I wanted. As I was holding the phone, a text came through: *It's such a shame that you can't come out tonight. I was really looking forward to spending some time with you, but I guess it will have to wait for some other time. Have a wonderful night and I'll see you soon.*

After reading it I thought to myself, *Here we go, now he's got my number.* I didn't even bother replying to the text, because I was so scared. He was going to start a conversation that I wouldn't be able to control. I put the phone down and got ready to have a shower, watch TV, and go to bed. As I lay on my bed that night, thoughts ran through my head: the events of the day, leading right back to this stranger. I fell asleep with a smile on my face, because for the first time in such a long time, I had met somebody that I actually wanted. But I had to fight myself on every emotion.

This morning, I slept in a bit later than normal because it was my day off. It was a Sunday and there was no need to wake up early. I would just have to do some food shopping, probably run some bits and bobs, and come back home. And as I checked my messages, I saw messages asking me to call back. They weren't a priority. There were messages inviting me out at night. They were messages from clients wanting to know one thing or another, and then there was a message from him, wishing me a good morning and asking what plans I had for the day. I just knew he wasn't going to leave me alone.

I texted back right there on my bed and said, *I've just woken up. And I have a lot to do today.* Again, he texted and asked if I could meet him somewhere for lunch or for an early evening dinner. I gave him one excuse or the other. Then I proceeded to go through my day, cleaning my house, and making a shopping list of the things I wanted to get.

The supermarket was just down the street from me, so it wasn't time-consuming. I moved through my day and he texted again, asking if I was going to go out with him.

I said, "No, I'm getting ready for Monday, which is a working day for me."

I spoke to my friend and relayed everything that had happened to one of the girls. They were shocked to find out that I hadn't gone out with him, but I guess people didn't just realize how hurt I was. I mean, I was laughing and joking so it might have seemed like I was healed. But my heart had barriers around it. I texted with him right through the evening and went to bed Monday.

I got another phone call asking for us to go out. He just wouldn't relent. He wasn't going to let go until I said I was going to have dinner with him.

By Wednesday he had worn me down. My defenses were low, and I found myself agreeing to meet him at a restaurant for dinner.

"You choose where you want to go," he promised, "And I'll meet you there."

"Okay."

It was all agreed. We were going to meet around seven thirty at the restaurant. I picked a place with excellent food and excellent service, which was actually one of my favorites.

I took extra care of my appearance on that day and went all out to make sure I looked stunning. I'll never forget it. I was wearing a little mini dress, my long jet-black hair all the way down to my back, and my makeup was meticulously done for the evening. I finished the outfit with some high-heeled pumps and a nice little clutch bag. I knew I looked good.

As I looked at myself in the mirror to take one good look before walking out the door, my phone beeped. It was him.

The message said, *"I'll see you soon, beautiful."*

He knew exactly what to say to make my heart flutter.

I put the phone down after I told him I was going to meet him soon then picked it up again to call Jackie. I wanted to let her know where I was going and what I was up to with this stranger.

She answered instantly with, "So, what's going on young lady?"

"Well, I'm going out for dinner with him."

"That's amazing, Roza. I'm so happy for you! Now, go and have a good time. Get to know him." She was clearly excited to see me getting ready to take the plunge, and I felt good. I was excited and happy that she was glad to see me taking that leap for the first time in so long.,

I promised to call her afterwards, and that was it. I put the phone down, locked the house, and proceeded to drive to the restaurant to meet this stranger.

I walked into the restaurant confidently, thinking I had arrived early. But as I walked in through the reception area, there he was. I told the waitress I was meeting up with him, and she led me to the table and gave us the menu before she left. As I sat down, I felt his eyes all over me. Truth be told, I felt them the moment I walked into the room. Other diners were looking my way, and I felt very confident taking my seat opposite to him.

The moment I sat down he said, "You look absolutely stunning tonight."

I looked at him and blushed, "You don't look too bad yourself."

We started with small talk about the restaurant. I told him a few recommendations on the menu and did my best to hurry things along to get the food ordered. I wanted to get things going; chit chat was going to lead to personal conversations in territories I wasn't ready to discuss. As we checked the menu out, he started telling me about himself. He had a son who was under a year old and he seemed like a good father. His son was the pride of his life. He also told me about his mother and his siblings; he was very forthcoming with this information. It was nice getting to know him better.

I felt the need to reciprocate. I told him a bit about myself, not as much as he had told me. I was pretty sure he already knew a lot about me from his father. I knew he knew things that I didn't want him to know. I knew my ex-husband and the breakup was a part of a story that he already knew.

As we started to talk more, his phone started ringing, but he ignored it. We continued; the phone started ringing again. As the waitress came over to take our menu, his phone was still ringing.

I thought to myself, *He is busy.* This was a red flag for me! I thought to myself, *I'm not stupid. I've met men like him. A thousand times. I've seen them with my girlfriends. I've seen them with my clients, the men that get so much attention from females in private and in public. Something isn't right."*

As he tried to ignore his phone, I noticed there were people turning around and looking at us, because we made a good pair. We looked very good together. He commanded his own attention from females, just like I did with the men. Together we made one of those really good-looking couples that people would take time to look at and admire. We knew we were getting a lot of attention in the restaurant; he even mentioned it.

When he stated his observation, I was thinking to myself, *Well, your phone's been ringing so much I am surprised you noticed.* I knew how busy one could be with my own business. My phone was always ringing at all hours of the day with clients inquiring, booking appointments, or whatever else. I was used to that. It was part of my job. I had two phones, one for personal things and one for business. The business phone was never off the hook. It was always ringing.

As we sat there, a text came through on his phone and another call.

The interruptions were so undeniable that it came to a point when I said to him, "You can answer your phone. I do not mind, it looks like whoever is calling really needs to speak to you."

"You don't mind me taking phone calls?"

"No, I really don't mind."

"I do have to take a phone call."

I said, "No problem."

As we spoke his phone rang. He picked it up and he said to me, "Excuse me, I'll be right back."

"Okay."

As he got up to walk away from my table, I took a good look at him. I wasn't stupid. I wasn't naive anymore. I wasn't a teenager who believed that he was all innocent. No, I knew there were demands on his life from women. I knew maybe he even had someone else waiting.

Attractive as he was, there was something about him that wouldn't allow me to relax. This man was going to have to walk the whole earth in a day and a half to get to my heart.

For me, to be vulnerable and let him fully in would be very hard. I knew that he wasn't being a hundred percent honest with me. Sitting there lost in thought, waiting for the food to arrive, the waitress approached to make sure we were okay and didn't need anything. When she walked away, I saw him reenter the room; whatever conversation he had with the person on the other line he made it very brisk.

He took his seat, and we resumed chatting. And right in the middle of the conversation, his phone rang *again*. This time it wasn't ringing aloud, rather it was the vibration that I could hear. He hadn't switched his phone off completely, and now the vibration was maddening. He ignored it twice before he actually powered it off. I knew it was a lady on the other end, but it wasn't my place to ask. I didn't want to be interested. It was only dinner. So I just took it for what it was the rest of the evening.

The food came, we laughed, joked, and got along well. We even had some things in common. We shared hobbies and interests in common, and he wanted to get to know me deeply. He was not shy or bashful about asking questions. I did my best to answer honestly, but I was still very much guarded.

It was almost time to leave. We had dessert and didn't run out of conversation, but the night was getting late. I had a working day the next day.

Eventually I said, "I think it's time to go home."

"Why don't we just stay a bit more?" he asked politely.

"I have a full day tomorrow, and I really think it's time to get going."

Reluctantly, we ended the night.

He paid the bill, and I thanked him for a nice evening. As we walked to my car, he bid me good night, thanked me for coming out to meet him, and asked if he could see me again.

"I'll let you know, I have work."

"You work all the time. Don't you?"

"Yeah, it's the priority of my life."

"I admire that. You're a woman that has a purpose and is following through."

"Yes I am."

I looked into his eyes and was able to put enough space between us so we didn't have to touch. I thanked him again for dinner, got into my car, and quickly left. As I left, I looked back into my rear view mirror, and there he was standing for a minute. He looked at my retreating car and eventually walked over to the other side of the road to where he parked. I had a good time. The food was lovely. Service was efficient. All in all, it was a very good night. But there was still that part of me —that little notch in the side of my heart— that was saying, *Don't fall for him*. By the time I got home, he had texted me to see if

I had gotten home safely. I thought was very thoughtful of him. This guy was saying all the right things, doing all the right things, pulling only a few punches, and really going for what he wanted.

I texted him back when I got home, told him good night, and that I would speak to him the next day.

The next day unfolded, and I received text messages from him. As I got to work, everybody wanted to know how the date went. I told them that it was nice, and he was quite a gentleman.

Right on cue, as if he knew we were talking about him, a message came through on my phone. He was asking me out again. This time he was asking me out during the weekend so we could go out to a club, dance, and have fun.

I said to him again, "I will let you know."

The week flew by, and I was still trying to avoid getting into deep conversations or phone calls when talking to him.

The weekend came; he called me and declared, "We're going out tonight, and I'm not taking no for an answer. You told me you loved music. There's this nice club not too far away from where you are. Tonight is one of the best nights."

I thought, *What's the worst that could happen? I mean, everybody's encouraging me to go out with a stranger. I am encouraging myself to go out with the strangers, guarded as I am."*

Reluctantly, I said, "Yes, let's go dancing."

That was exactly what happened.

I called Jackie and invited her, but she had other plans. I called another friend of mine, but nobody wanted to be the third wheel. Everybody just wanted me to just go out and enjoy it on my own without anyone in tow. So for the second time, I stood in my apartment getting dolled up for this stranger. I knew I commanded a whole lot of attention, especially in those moments. I capitalized on it and I wanted to look absolutely ravishing that night. That was exactly what I did! As I got ready it was exciting. This time, it wasn't going to be a dinner date where you sat there and chatted politely. My mind was excited at the thought of dancing with this stranger. I was so nervous, being that close to him. It was frightening. All kinds of thoughts were going through my head as I was getting ready. I took one final look at myself in the mirror and knew without a shadow of a doubt tonight was not going to go exactly as I planned. I kind of knew dancing with him was just going to open up a can of worms. I knew it. I mean, you wouldn't go to a club and let me dance on my own. So I was kind of getting myself all psyched up and ready for what was to come.

You wouldn't have known how nervous I was just by looking at me. When I arrived at the club, I could hear all the whistles as I made it from my car to the entrance.

The moment I went into the bar area to get a drink, I heard, "Hey, beautiful."

I turned around and there he was, looking as scrumptious as ever. He knew how to dress. He had an eye for coordinating his clothes to suit his frame. Everything just fit his body in all the right places. Nice shirt, nice shoes, hair looking all nice. I couldn't deny that he wasn't only an attractive man, but he was a very good dresser. He went on to compliment me.

I complimented him right back, and he asked what I was going to drink. I think I had ordered something light, like a glass of wine. I wasn't going to get hammered with this stranger. I didn't trust myself to let my guard down. So I slowly sipped a glass of wine as we stood there, chatting and talking about everything. People were dancing in the middle of a dance floor, and I was there nodding to a song.

He noticed that I was feeling the music and said, "Why don't we go and dance?"

We put our drinks down at the nearest table. He grabbed my hand, and led me to the dance floor. All of this time, my heart was beating so fast in my chest because we had never been that close together. The moment we got to the dance floor, he pulled me closer to him, and we started moving. It was as if the DJ knew it was time to slow dance because the song became a slow one that required close proximity. He put his hand on my waist, drew me closer to him, and I breathed in his cologne and he smelled so good. We started swaying to the rhythm of the music. As we danced, I found myself relaxing in his arms. He was a good dancer. He did everything well. I had a love of music and had taken dancing classes. I had been to enough clubs to know what the latest trends and dance techniques were, and I was a good dancer myself.

Very soon people took notice of us, and started moving away to give us enough space. We took over that dance floor. We danced seductively and even though we couldn't see each other's faces, I felt every movement. When this song came to an end, I quickly said I needed to get back to my drink. He led me out of the dance floor. Everyone was looking, and I was very aware of that.

We went back to our drinks. We chatted, and other men he knew approached him and said hello. Before I knew it, we were standing in the midst of some other friends whom he introduced to me. The night was going well. Then he grabbed my hand when another song that he liked came on, and we went back to the dance floor. This time I was a bit more relaxed and we started dancing, and it was wonderful. By the end of the night, we had had a few more drinks, and it was late.

I said to him, "I think I have had enough to drink, and I am all danced out. I've had a great time, I think it's time to start heading home."

I think he wanted to stay a bit longer, but I was ready to go.

Reluctantly, he agreed. We bid goodnight to the other clubbers and made our way out the door. When we went outside the door, he asked if I was able to drive home safely. Even though I told him that I could absolutely drive home without a problem, he insisted he would take a cab from my house over to his own. I wasn't hammered, but I'd had enough to make me feel relaxed. The chemistry was high and we obviously liked each other. My guard was down; I was happy and carefree. Almost against my will I heard myself agree to let him drive to my house. I could have driven, but I let him; he took the car keys from me. I got into the front seat. As he drove I was thinking, *When we get to my house, I'm going to get my keys from him so he can go to the nearest cab station and take a cab home. That's what we agreed on.*

On the ride to my house we talked about unimportant things. When we got to my house, he looked me right in the eye and asked if he could come up for a minute.

Followed by, "I would just like to spend a bit more time with you, and then I will head home."

As a grown woman, I should have known exactly what was going to happen. But because of my undeniable attraction to him mixed with a bit of alcohol in my system, I found myself looking at him and thinking *You can't just send him home like this. At least let him come upstairs and have a nightcap before he goes home.* I still think back on that decision and wonder had I said No, what would have happened? But there is no changing it now.

He came up, made himself comfortable, and I asked him if he wanted a drink. He said yes, and I proceeded to bring him some water. As I handed the drink to him, he took it, and then reached out for me. He pulled me closer. Prior to this, he had been quite a gentleman and didn't try to do anything funny. I guess he knew I was very guarded, but there in the privacy of the room, it was just him and I. My defenses were so low. Even through my feelings of fear and nervousness, I was ready for what he wanted. He pulled me in and took a good, hard look at me and proceeded.

As I saw his face coming closer to me, I thought, *Oh my God, it's happening.* When his lips touched mine, I knew I was done for. Attraction took over, and he just crashed his lips into mine with a fierce hunger. I wasn't only shocked, but elated. Everything outside of this moment was forgotten.

Lust is something that takes a lot of self-control to push away. It took over us, and before I knew what happened, we were tearing at each other's clothes. He led me to the bed and began doing some beautiful things. Right in the middle of it, I stopped him and asked about protection. I wasn't that lost in lust to let this happen this way. As it turned out, he came very prepared. He reached for his wallet and brought out a condom.

We proceeded from where we left off. Right in the middle of it, the condom broke. I felt instantly that something was different.

"Oh shoot," I said.

"What?"

"The condom broke."

He looked down and confirmed before saying, "Well, if it makes you feel any better, I'm clean."

"Well, everybody says that."

" No, I actually am clean."

"I hope so. I don't make a habit of doing this, and I'm going to have to take your word for it."

The conversation ended as quickly as it began and we went right back to business. The second time around, we didn't even bother with the condom. What was the point now? Having gone through fertility treatment for all those years with nothing happening, I knew I wasn't going to get pregnant. The worst that could happen was a sexually transmitted disease. I threw caution to the wind and had a wonderfully memorable night with this man. He made me feel wanted, and he made me feel very good about myself. Every touch of his hand was welcomed by the fact that I craved it. I hadn't had a man in my bed for quite some time so all the feelings that came with him that night nurtured my loneliness.

After he finished, I guess he wanted to spend the night, but that wasn't an option. It was one thing sharing my body and a totally different thing to share my space. This was my privacy, and it had been so long since I woke up with a man in my bed. I wasn't ready to share that with him.

I said to him, "I think you have to go."

" I don't mind spending the night if you want me to."

"Let's take it slow. I just want to be on my own now."

He didn't push it. I watched him get up and put his clothes on. I laid there watching him from under the sheets thinking to myself, *What are you doing sending him home?* A part of me wanted him to stay, cuddle me to sleep, and let the night go on forever. But the other part of me wasn't ready to let this man into my heart willingly. It wasn't going to happen. As I watched him dress, I was happy that he was actually doing what I wanted him to do and not pushing it too far to get his way. He got ready, and gave me another kiss. I scrambled out of the bed to put my robe on and walked him to the door.

He gave me another kiss and said, "I'm going to call you tomorrow morning. Is that okay?"

I looked into his eyes and said, "Yes."

He gave me another kiss and walked out of the door. I closed it behind him and leaned into the door thinking, *Oh my God, what just happened?* All kinds of emotions and thoughts were running through me. I took my robe off in my bedroom to climb into bed with a huge smile on my face. I drifted off to sleep as moments with this stranger replayed in my mind.

The next morning I woke up to a text from him telling me what an amazing night he had. He said he could not get me out of his mind and wanted to see me again. A smile broke onto my face. I just couldn't help it. As I drove down the street that led to my shop, my eyes drew to the pharmacy that was literally two doors away from my shop. This was the pharmacy that I'd gone into to buy my female essentials. I knew I could go in there and get the morning after pill just to be safe. The thought left my mind just as quickly as it came into my head. I even laughed and reminded myself that I couldn't get pregnant. It was even co-signed by the voice in my head! I decided to just forget about it. I wasn't ready to share this with anybody so I told myself sternly, *Don't say anything.* Then I quickly reverted my eyes and mind to the main road as I drove to work.

Everybody could tell I was in an extra good mood that day. There was a spring in my step. They picked up on it quickly. These people knew me. They had been with me through the hardest days of my life. They knew something had happened, even though I didn't say it. They said there was a glow about me. There was a difference. I didn't fully divulge what happened, but I didn't deny when they asked if I was seeing him. According to them it was instantly obvious that we were going to date.

I listened and offered no extra information because everybody was just running ahead on speculation. All through the day, he was sending me messages. I remember Valentine's Day was coming up, and he sent flowers and chocolates. It was obvious that he was trying to court me. I was enjoying it, but he still didn't have my heart. I still didn't trust him. There was something about him that just wasn't going to be very easy to place my heart into. Something kept stumping me.

Even in my resistance to officially dating, he declared how he felt for me before he had to go home to America for a week or two. I saw him right through the time he left and took him to the airport. I came back home wondering what was going on and where this was going to lead. He'd made promises to call, but I wasn't expecting anything. We were not boyfriend and girlfriend; we weren't even exclusive. While he was in America, he called me and said, "I think I'm in love with you."

I didn't reply and he proceeded to say, "I know this is happening quickly for you. I know your past and things that happened to you, but you're going to have to take a chance on me."

I cared about him, but I did not love him in the way he confessed love for me. To be honest with you, I did miss him a bit when he left, because he was always calling and texting while it was in America. We were in different time zones, but he still called and texted. Sometimes I found myself wondering what he was doing and who is with as days went by.

The second week came.

We were talking on the phone, and he said, "I'm coming back. I just have to see you. I miss you so much."

He was trying to break my defenses and climb those walls that were built around my heart. The out of order sign was still on my heart, but I would be a liar if I said I wasn't happy that he was coming back so soon.

"Why do you want to come back so soon?"

"Because I want to be with you. When I come back, we'll talk about it. Think about being exclusive with me?""

He was saying all the right things, the appropriate things. As scared as I was, there was a part of me that was just so elated that I had found a man that I was attracted to, a man who actually had feelings for me. And as much as I liked him, I knew that he was not to be trusted. I just knew that he had other women. I didn't know how I knew it, but I just knew it. I mean, what woman wouldn't be interested in a fine specimen of a man like that?

He told me he was going to book his flight, call me back, and let me know exactly when he was coming back. I was living in anticipation and hope of his return. We talked about almost everything, but I hadn't told him that something in me had changed. My body was changing. I was feeling more lethargic and I thought it was just me overworking myself. I had started feeling very nauseated at certain times of the day, especially in the mornings. And when someone walked into the shop, the smell of perfume that I used to love was starting to become irritating to me. It was little things like that, but I never mentioned it to him. I never acknowledged it. I just brushed it off and kept on going. Some people had noticed in the shop; it had been going on for about four to six weeks. I'd never been through that and I'd never known the symptoms really of a pregnant woman. I've had pregnant clients, and they said it differs from one woman to another. I really didn't know my body well enough and it didn't even occur to me that I hadn't seen my period. Pregnancy was the last thing on my mind so I went about my business.

He called one evening and told me he was coming back and had booked his flight. I was really looking forward to it. That day, I was doing a client's hair, and I was feeling really rotten. I was just so tired, weak, nauseated, and very run down. This wasn't like me. I normally partied, worked hard, and still had energy left over for anything else. So it was a very weird feeling which I wasn't really used to. I found myself telling the client in my chair all these things that I was feeling. The more I told her, the more her eyes widened.

Eventually she said, "Roza, you do know I am a nurse, right?"

"Yeah, I do. What does that have to do with this conversation?"

She said, "Everything you just told me fits the symptoms of a pregnant woman."

I was like, "Nah, hell no. I can't have a child. I've tried before."

She interrupted me, saying, "Roza, I promise you. Everything you've told me is the symptoms of a pregnant woman. When was the last time you had your period? What was the last time you had unprotected sex?"

I was thinking, *Lady, stay in your zone. These questions are a bit too personal for me to share.*

She swung the chair around and got up while asking me to open my eyes. I complied and opened my eyes.

She peered deeply into them and conjectured, "You seem to be very low on blood."

I was still not a believer, and she clearly knew it. It didn't stop her though.

She proceeded with her examination saying, "I'm going to feel your breasts."

She literally grabbed at my nipples through my clothes. It was sensitive and nearly painful. I shrank back from her. This was a client that I had been working with for some time. So we had assumed some kind of a relationship, but I wasn't ready for this. We were whispering as we carried on this conversation that I was not at all ready to have.

"You are pregnant. After you finish my hair, go do a pregnancy test. Call me when you're done."

I tried to brush it off and make light of it, but something about her words and the fact that she was a nurse made it stick.

I managed to finish her hair.

She bid me goodbye and said, "Do it today. Don't let it wait. You need to know for your own sake and your sanity."

I called one of the girls over quickly. I told her to get the money, go to the pharmacy a couple of doors away, and get me some pregnancy tests. I asked her to get me three different brands. I needed to be sure.

"Who's it for?" she whispered.

I knew I couldn't lie. So I told her it was for me.

"What? You think you're pregnant?"

"I don't know. I really don't know. I hope not, because I'm not ready for this. I didn't ask for this."

I was nervous. I was scared, and I think she could tell from my voice.

"Well, if it happens, it happens. It's a good thing. You've always wanted a child. I know you fought against it. I know you've given up on it, but what if this is it? Just preparing yourself for it?"

She grabbed the money from me and made it out the door. The moment she returned I went straight to the toilet. I mustered up all the courage that I had. I will never forget how my heart just dropped as I lifted the first pregnancy test, turned it over and looked at it.

"Oh my God. Oh my God. Oh my God," was all I could say.

I was sweating profusely as my eyes just went straight to the window that showed two pink lines. I could've dropped it. All I could think was this can't be true. There has to be a mistake. I picked up the second one and again, two pink lines.

I was like, "Oh my God, no, this isn't happening. It's not right. It can't be."

I'm talking to myself. I picked up the third, with all three of them staring back at me saying that I was pregnant. I cannot tell you how I felt every emotion known to man, fear at the root of it all. How did I let this happen? How did I let this happen? Oh my God, I am dead. My mother's going to kill me. I was so scared. I was shaking, literally shaking profusely. I heard a knock on the door a second time, banging on the door.

I could hear her calling out, "Roza, what's going on?"

She could hear my denial through the door, "No, this can't be happening," I opened the door and continued, "Nope. I think they're wrong."

I was in absolute denial. My thoughts had not even gone to him. My thoughts were all about what would happen to me being an unmarried mother from a religious Muslim family. I knew my mom was going to kill me. I was just so scared of the repercussions and the consequences that were going to come my way. Oh my God. I couldn't tell you how scared I was.

And I said to her, "Go back and grab me another three. Choose different ones from these ones. I do not trust these ones."

She looked at me and asked "They're all positive."

"Yes, but," I irrationally added, "they are wrong. It can't be, I need more proof. Go get me three more. Please get me three more."

"Roza—"

I abruptly cut her off mid-sentence, "Will you just go get me three more?"

She saw the look in my eyes and thought she better not to argue. She ran back out and I closed the door. I couldn't believe it, and I started reciting all of the things I had learned in the Muslim faith from the Quran. I pleaded with Allah not to let this be true, to let this be a hoax, a false alarm. I started promising how I would never sleep with another man again; I was making all kinds of promises pleading with Allah to take this away.

Then I turned to myself and asked how could I let this happen? How could I let a total stranger come into my personal space? What was I thinking? How stupid was I? Why didn't I stop? I had all kinds of regrets. Why didn't I stop in the pharmacy and get the morning after pill? I wasn't stupid. I was a smart young woman. I knew what happened when you had unprotected sex.

It felt like hours before I heard another knock on the door. When she handed me the bag I started tearing the packets open, and repeated the same process. I turned them over so I wouldn't see them change and waited for the appropriate time. One by one again: positive, positive, positive. I was done for, and I just sat on the floor.

I started wailing from the pit of my heart. I howled. I wailed. I cried. I was impregnated by somebody I barely knew. This guy could be a murderer, a killer. He could be whatever the worst thing could be, because I didn't know him enough. And here I was, pregnant by him. And to make it worse, he wasn't even in the country yet. He was in America. What was I going to do? How would I tell people? Oh my God, it was terrible.

I heard a knock on the door and someone saying, "Let me in, let me in," I reluctantly opened the door and she entered saying, "You're pregnant aren't you?"

"Yep, it's happening. I'm done. I'm just dead."

I started crying and she said, "Roza, this is a good thing! You will see."

"How can this be a good thing? How can you even say that to me? I don't even know him that well. Do you know what happens to unmarried mothers in the Muslim faith? You bring so much shame to your family. You're a stigma. You're a loser, and no one's ever going to marry you."

I just started lamenting.

Ruby told me, "You cannot work like this. Go out the back door, and just go home."

And that was exactly what I did. She brought my bag over with all my essentials. I slipped right out of the back trying to make it to my car before anybody saw me. Looking at me, you couldn't tell yet that I was pregnant. But I was so paranoid that anybody who looked at me would know the truth. I was pregnant. That was the longest walk from the shop to my car. I quickly took off from the place I normally parked my car, took a right, and my eyes went straight to the pharmacy.

This cannot be true. I found myself parking right in front of the pharmacy. I went inside and headed straight to the section with the pregnancy tests, finding three more. I didn't care. I just needed to know for certain. I knew the owner of the pharmacy very well.

And he inquired, "What's happening? I mean pregnancy tests have just been flying off the shelves today. I just sold some."

I wasn't in the mood for any chit chat. I quickly shoved the packages for him to scan. I paid for it, grabbed it, ran out of the shop, and went back into my car. I couldn't wait to get home. As I was driving home, I was in such a state. I still couldn't believe I'd let this happen. I thought, *Okay, I got another three that could say it's a negative. Hold onto that thought.*

I quickly got home, and went straight for the toilet. And for the third time, all three of them were positive. I was devastated. I cried over and over. I heard my phone ringing and saw that it was him calling from America. I wasn't ready to have that conversation.

Usually whenever he called, I would pick up. Even if I was busy with a client, I would pick up and tell him I would call him back. Now I didn't pick up. I was pacing the floor, going out of my mind.

He kept calling and texting and calling. I was in such a state. I didn't know how much time had passed before his texts started showing his concern.

"What's going on? Are you okay? You're not picking up my calls or returning my texts. It's not like you; what's going on?" his voicemails opined.

I wasn't ready to deal with it. I wasn't. I didn't pick up the phone that night. I didn't return his texts and calls. I went to shower and looked at my belly thinking, *There is a child inside me.* How? I mean, this was something I had always wanted, but not in these circumstances. And so I didn't even see it for the blessing that it was. All I could think was that my life was over. My family was going to be totally ashamed of me. I was going to be a cast off; no one was going to want an unmarried mother. And I sat down in the shower as the water poured right from my head onto my toes. I was devastated. I dragged myself from the shower, dried myself, and got into bed in the fetal position. That was a position I had come to know due to the heartache of the past. Whenever I felt alone or sad, it was a position that brought me some kind of comfort. And as I lay in bed in the fetal position, I couldn't sleep that night. I was tossing and turning throughout the night.

His messages were getting more frantic. He had called the shop and knew I wasn't at work. Where was I? Oh my God, I couldn't believe it. When morning came, I couldn't wait to get out of bed and go literally face my day as if nothing had happened. And the realization of what I was going to do. I called my client back and told her I took about nine pregnancy tests; she was right. They're all positive. But I'm thinking of going to get more.

She said, "Don't waste your money. Don't waste your time. You are pregnant. It's time to accept it. And then think about the next course of action."

I cried with her on the phone; she understood my fears, my predicament. But she also wanted to try to make me understand that it was a blessing in disguise, knowing my past and what I had gone through.

She said, "I hope you come to the right decision before you make a choice."

I told her, I couldn't have this child. There was no way I was going to have the baby. I was going to arrange for an abortion. I asked for advice on what clinics to go to, where I could get it done quickly. By the time we put the phone down, I'd made up my mind that I was going to call and find out exactly how long an appointment was and everything else.

I called around; I had an appointment in the afternoon. I said to myself, *I need to make that appointment. I need to go find out exactly what was going on with my body, how far along I was and to make the preparation to actually have the abortion done.*

I couldn't wait to find a clinic very close to my home. I called my work, and told them I was going to be late. I dashed over to the clinic and pretended as if I had not done any tests at home, because I wanted them to do another one that was going to confirm I was negative this time. They took my urine.

I sat down to wait and they called me into the office.

The nurse exclaimed, "Congratulations! You're going to have a baby. You're pregnant."

Her smile dropped when she noticed my blank expression, "What? You're not happy?"

"No, I'm not. I do not think I want this pregnancy."

And I started crying, and she told me to give myself time to think about it. What she didn't know was that I already knew that I was pregnant. And so again, I began explaining to her why I couldn't have it.

She looked at me and said, "I know a lot of people trying for a baby. And they can't; so to me, babies are always a blessing."

And I thought to myself, *If only you knew. It would have been a blessing at one point in time in my life, I wanted it more than anything else. And it didn't happen. And I'm not ready for it. I'm not prepared for it.*

You know, what we had doesn't even constitute a relationship to begin with. And here I am, pregnant. I felt like heaven was playing a big joke on me. I was so upset. She came back with the paperwork, gave me some info about clinics that would actually perform the abortion. I was just under twelve weeks.

"When did you last have sex? When did you realize the changes in your body?"

I wasn't ready to share anything. And then she went back on my dates and told me exactly when she thought I got pregnant. And it was the first time that the condom broke. I wailed on the way home; I beat myself up. Why didn't I go and get the morning after pill? Why did I just let it slide? I beat myself up the whole way home. I got home and proceeded to call the clinics to make an appointment.

Meanwhile, he was going crazy in America, calling and calling. And I wasn't picking up, not ready to share this news with him. I needed to know what I was going to do. This wasn't something I had wanted to happen. I was going to deal with it on my own before I even got him involved.

Fear had taken over my body. I couldn't sleep. I couldn't eat. I managed to get hold of a hospital that was willing to see me, because they just didn't book abortions. They needed to give you a counseling session first to make sure you knew the repercussions of what you were doing and that you knew the consequences that followed. I just wanted to go right past that and straight into the abortion, but they wouldn't let me. And so they booked me in for a consultation, first for us to go through whole process of the abortion. I booked it. I think it was a few days later and I hadn't been to work because I was waiting for this. It was like I was hiding away. It felt like anyone who looked at me would know I was pregnant. So hiding away gave me comfort. I woke up that morning, and I was so ready to get it over and done with. I wanted to see if I could get rid of it before he even came back. That would have been the best for me.

I went to the hospital, dreading every step that I took, as if everyone was going to know. Everybody knew what the hospital did, especially that part of the clinic. It was just uncomfortable. I just had this sinking feeling of, *Oh my God, I'm about to do this.* I'm about to actually embark on doing this. So I went in, registered with my name, and sat down to wait for my name to be called. As I sat down there, I grabbed a magazine and I started opening it.

The magazine was about pregnant people, new mothers, giving birth and the baby; there was so much information that I didn't even want to know. All I wanted to do was get rid of it. If they could even bypass this consultation period and take me straight into theater, that would've been perfect for me. But every page I turned, there was a child smiling back at me or a delivery moment where they put the child on the mom's chest. It seemed like I waited forever before I heard my name called. A lady came and ushered me into a room. We went into a room; the moment I sat down, I started crying.

She said, "Tell me what's going on."

I burst into tears. You see, there's something about knowing that you can offload to a total stranger who doesn't know you and won't judge you. This was a job she had done day in and day out for years. I wasn't the first upset mother that she had seen. And so she listened to me until I finished. I wailed, I lamented. I said it all.

When I finished, she responded, "I don't think you're ready for this."

"What?"

That wasn't what I was expecting from her.

"I don't think mentally you're ready for this, you're too emotional right now to make a decision. But I'll tell you the other side of what you're not seeing. First of all in my faith, just like in yours, abortion is a sin. Secondly, every child is a blessing, regardless of the circumstances they come in. And from what you have told me, you have a good financial basis to raise this child if worse comes to the worst. Also, you'll think about it for the rest of your life. You've got to live with the fact that you took a life. It is a life. It might not be showing right now, but there's a life inside of you right now."

As this lady was speaking to me, time stood still. She was putting into my head thoughts that I didn't even dare let myself think. It was the most surreal experience of my life, as she told me how some women would give their right arm to have a baby. And here I had the opportunity of having one. And I couldn't see the blessings that came with it. And she went on to tell me how she was a single mother, and her children were the best things that ever happened in her life. And she felt exactly like I did, but once she had a kid; she knew that she had made the right choice to keep them. As she spoke to me, every word found a place in my heart.

And just like that, I felt ashamed like I had never felt before, not because of another person or what their opinions were going to be. I had shame at the thought of taking a life, a life I had prayed so long for, one that I had wanted, a blessing I had knocked on heaven's door for many-a-year. Now it had happened, and here I was thinking about getting rid of it. And something clicked in me, *Wait a minute, you are about to have a child that's going to love you like you've never been loved before. A child that is going to be yours forever to love and nurture. Yes, the circumstances aren't right, but this is what you've always wanted.*

That part of my heart that was dormant for so long, because I let go of the dream, came alive. I felt this nurturing need and love for this child that I had always wanted, but never even dreamt of. For so long I thought it was over and done with, because in my head I wanted a child with my ex-husband. I hadn't even thought of a child with this one. That was the funny thing about it. In my heart, the dream was with him; the dream couldn't come alive without him. Something switched in my head, and I cried.

"Well, I think you're right. I really don't think I want to make this decision now, because now I'm thinking about how much I would have."

It was the consultation which put me on the right track. I cried some more, but my mind had been renewed. And then in that office, in that short period of time, this woman had managed to lay my fears aside and tell me the reality of what I was about to do. And it changed my heart and my decision like that. She printed out the paperwork, which was mandatory for her to do.

And she said, "The choice is yours, but I really hope you do make the right one. And from what I have seen, I think you are going to make the right choice."

She handed over the paperwork.

"Thank you."

Slowly, I walked to my car and drove home where I threw myself on the bed and cried. I apologized to Allah for even thinking of taking this life. I thought, *I will get through the pain. I will go through the shame. I would go through the rejection.* I would go through everything I needed to for my child. Because I knew how much I would love and nurture him or her, how much I wanted them, and what I had been through for them.

As I sat on my bed, stroking my belly, I found myself telling my little one, "I am sorry, this is not going to be a conducive normal setup, because me and your dad aren't married. In fact, we barely even know each other. But I think I'm going to keep you. I'm going to love you. I'm going to nurture you. I'm going to lay my life down for you, because I'm going to be that one person you can depend on. The whole world will walk away, but you will always have your mommy."

I had always wanted a girl. I started right there addressing her as a girl, it was as if a knowing came over me. I was thinking, *You are my everything.* I had gone —in less than twenty-four hours— from aborting this child to looking forward to being a mother. I felt a sense of elation come over me that I had never known. And as I cuddled myself again in the fetal position to go to sleep, I knew there was no way I would get rid of my child. It wasn't going to happen at all. I had made my choice right there and now; it was time to tell the whole world.

That was another step that was going to take every ounce of bravery in me. I went to sleep that night with my hand protectively on my belly.

6
UNFAMILIAR TERRITORY

I woke up in the middle of the night, and my first thought was my child. Words failed me when I tried to describe it. That was when I first started to accept what was happening. I remember going back to work and constantly having all these missed calls and messages. Everybody was worried about me because it wasn't like me to not pick up my phone. People knew I was reliable, that I would get back to them in a certain timeframe. I walked into work, and people were relieved to see that I was okay. I didn't realize that Ruby had blabbed a little bit to everybody. So everybody was just more caring than normal. I wasn't used to them treating me that fragile. They knew I was strong enough to look after myself. They knew I was the ice queen.

But seeing how they were treating me, I looked at Ruby and said, "What's going on? Did you tell everyone?"

"No, I didn't tell anyone, but they're not stupid. They know something's going on."

I just thought, you know what? Might as well start now, since these are the people that I'm closest to. I spend more time with these people than family or any other person in my life, at least ten to twelve hours of my day. I could trust them with that information. I turned around, not caring who was there and who wasn't.

I just said, "We're having a baby, everybody."

I had never felt so loved and supported.

The moment it left my mouth, they congratulated me. These people knew my past. These people wanted this for me. They'd waited with me for a day like this.

Everybody dropped what they were doing, and they came to hug me saying, "We kind of knew. We suspected when you started running to the toilet and throwing up. We kind of knew, but we were just scared to say anything. Oh my God, you're pregnant. You know, we can't wait. I hope you have a girl. We would do her hair!"

It was beautiful. It was absolutely beautiful. The clients even joined in. Those people even knew I was pregnant, while the father of my child didn't even have a clue. I knew it was time to talk to him. They were not going to say anything. It was nice to work with a set of people that you could trust with the most intimate stuff. I knew word was going to go around quickly, and I needed to tell him. So I made up my mind.

That evening after everyone had gone, I was going to call him back and speak to him on my own time in private. And that was exactly what I did. I prayed again.

I picked up the phone, and the first thing that came out of his mouth was, "Are you okay? What's going on?"

I was quiet for a while, not sure what to say.

He continued, "I have been calling and texting; how can you do this? Just not pick up the phone. You know, everybody's been worried about you. I've even called the shop, and they were very dismissive. They didn't know what to say to me. What is going on? It's not like you to do this."

I let him finish then said "Listen, I have something to say to you. I need you to listen to me very carefully and not interrupt until I finish. I don't think I'll have the courage to continue if you keep interrupting."

But he ignored me and said, "You're pregnant, aren't you?"

Oh my God. I couldn't believe it. I asked him, "Who told you?"

"No one did. I just knew."

"Well how did you know?"

"I kind of suspected it right before I left."

"Oh my God."

"I knew. I suspected very strongly that you were pregnant. Now, what have you decided to do?"

"Listen, I thought about having an abortion. But I decided against it because I don't think I could live with myself if I did it. And I wanted this child for so long. And it hasn't happened. Now it's happened with you. I do not want you to feel pressured into having a relationship or raising her with me."

"Whoa, wait. Who said you're having a girl? You don't know what it is."

"No, but I have a very strong feeling it's a girl. You are allowed to freely leave right now. You don't even have to come back. You can stay in America if you choose to. I will understand because this is as much a shock for me as I know it will be for you. So don't feel pressured to do the right thing if you don't want to. You can go. I can take care of her. I can look after her financially, and I'm in a position to give her a good life."

"Stop. Nope, I'm not going anywhere. We are having a baby, and I'm going to be there every step of the way."

Now that was shocking. I was used to hearing stories where men bolted out of the door the moment they knew they'd gotten a woman pregnant. I thought he was going to run faster than Linford Christie himself. But here he was telling me he wanted to have the baby. I tried to reassure him that I would understand if he didn't want to stay and raise this child. I just needed him to have a clean break where he would just go ahead with his life and forget I was even pregnant. And that was it.

He continued saying, "I'm not going anywhere, so you might as well get used to it. I am in love with you. I'm going to stay by your side. We're going to do this."

He was reassuring me, telling me from now on that I have to eat carefully, not work so hard, and that he was going to be there very soon.

"I'll be there next week to help you take care of yourself, feed you, and nurture you."

I was shocked. That was not the conversation I was expecting from him, but he said it.

"Are you at home?"

"No, I'm in the shop. Everyone's just left. I'm about to close up."

"Okay go home, and I'll call you. We'll talk some more."

I cleaned up the shop while thinking, *Did this conversation just happen?* I couldn't believe it. I cried my eyes out on the way home as relief washed over me. It felt like a heavy burden had been lifted.

But I still had my family to tell. Now that was going to be one challenging thing. But for now I was just so happy that the person I was having the baby with was so open to the idea of co-parenting with me. I didn't want to expect anything from him. I just wanted him to know he had a choice to make, and I wouldn't blame him for choosing another and not wanting to be a part of her life. I was ready for that.

I drove home. I had to shower again. I had started being so protective of my body. I spent a lot of time in the shower, just stroking my belly, and talking to her. My life was about to change in a very profound way. And even though it was unexpected, the need that I'd had that laid dormant in me for so long came alive with such a ferocity. I wasn't ready for that. I climbed into bed with my phone in hand. He called me, and we spoke through the night. By the time we ended the conversation, we were talking about how he wanted a son and I wanted a girl. We talked about names and made guesses about who she was going to look like. We joked about African genes being so much stronger than Jamaican genes and that he or she's going to come out with Bob Marley locks in his or her hair. We just laughed right through the conversation. I couldn't believe it had happened, but I was grateful for what he had said to me.

That night, as I put the phone down, the realization set in that now I had just one more person to tackle. And she was the matriarch of all. She was my mother.

I woke up the next morning, and went about my business. Everybody in the shop was treating me like I was a fragile China doll. It was so sweet to see them making sure I'd eaten, had enough water, and was eating vegetables. Everything had changed in a matter of twenty four hours. The way they treated me was just so beautiful. Even if I coughed, they made sure I was okay. The way they nurtured me was just so beautiful. I thought, *I'm going to enjoy this for a while. My mother can wait for a little bit.* Then a thought came into my head that wouldn't go away: *Tell her before somebody gets to her. She wouldn't like to hear it from other people and you know how word travels fast.* I got home that day and looked at the phone number. I couldn't bring myself to do it. I chickened out.

So another day went by and another one. It was just so troubling until one day I said to myself, *You know what? I need to tell her.* I don't have the confidence to call her myself, but I knew someone else who did. I called my auntie, who was really my mother's cousin. The fact that they were family gave me comfort.

I told her, "I'm going to come over to your house, and you're going to help me tell my mother."

When I told her, she said, "Oh God Roza, how can I?"

I told her, "You'll find a way of helping me. I just can't do it on my own."

"I'm happy for you because I know you wanted it for so long, but also I know the situation. You know, I have been there."

That was why I had the confidence to go to her somehow. I knew she would understand. I drove over to her house.

I walked in, she looked at me and she said, "Oh God, are we going to do it?"

"Yep, let's do it before I chicken out. I have dialed the number and hung up so many times. Let's do it."

"What do you want me to say?"

I told her to say the right things like: sometimes things happen outside of our control. Doesn't mean it's the end of the world; it's just another challenge and a trial to get through. I told her to also speak with her faith because my mother was dedicated to hers.

My auntie knew how much her religion meant to her, along with keeping up appearances and doing right.

"Okay, let's do it," she said.

My heart was pounding so fast in my chest. I thought I was going to collapse any minute. I sat there, literally shivering, as my mom picked up the phone. My auntie engaged her in a short greeting before she went straight into her speech. It flowed like a well-rehearsed poem. She just wasn't into telling her how God has all power and allows things for his purposes to be established.

Right in the middle of this my mom said, "What's going on? Why are you telling me all of these things?"

My aunt went on to say, "I just need you to be at peace with what I'm about to tell you. It's not the end of the world."

Out of the blue, my mum just cut us short and said, "What is it? It's Roza, isn't it? What's going on? Is she pregnant?"

When I overheard this, I nearly collapsed. It was one thing for the father of my baby to suspect I was pregnant even before I knew, but this lady? She was all the way in Africa.

"How did you know?" my aunt uttered, flabbergasted.

I was thinking, *Someone's beat me to it and told her that I'm pregnant. Like how can people be so careless? That was my news to tell her.*

I snapped out of my thoughts when I heard my mom say, "I had a dream about her, so this isn't a shock at all.," she took a brief pause before saying, "I'm surprised because she's always been very responsible. How did she let this happen? She knows it's wrong to have a baby out of wedlock, and that our faith doesn't tolerate it."

Before she could even go any further, my aunt just picked up from where she left off in her sentence, "Yes. We all know that, but you don't cast away your children because they've done wrong. She hasn't done wrong. She's pregnant with a child."

My mother clearly wasn't going to let this go easily and made it known by saying, "She should have known better. She's always had a good head on her shoulders. How did this happen? Who's the father?"

My aunt ignored her barrage of questions and firmly stated, "Listen, she's right here. It's time for you guys to have this conversation."

And she passed the phone over to me.

Oh my God. The amount of pressure.

I picked up the phone, but before I could speak to her, my mum asked with concern in her voice, "How are you doing?"

I said, "I'm doing good. Not as good as I want to be but good enough."

"How did this happen? How did this happen to us?"

"I'm sorry. I didn't mean for it to happen. It's quite a shock to me."

She said, "I understand you went through so much in your marriage to have a child. I understand that. But it still doesn't give you the right to do this. When something like this happens, it affects the whole family. You could have been smarter than this."

"Yeah, I know, Mommy. I'm sorry."

It was all I could say, with tears running down my face.

I think she knew I was crying, and she said, "Well, it happened. There's nothing you can do about it. I guess it's time to really get up and tighten your belt. It's not going to be an easy road. Motherhood isn't easy, especially when you're not married."

"I know, but the father is supportive so I have that, at least," I said once I finally calmed down enough to speak.

I knew I wasn't going to get, *"Hooray, let's open a bottle of champagne and celebrate because I'm having a grandchild,"* but her response was a good enough blessing for me. I quickly apologized once more before letting her know that I needed to go and would call her later. When I hung up the phone, I felt relieved. It felt like somebody had just reached down and taken all my burdens away. Everyone that was important to me was informed.

I was free to tell the world and to enjoy my pregnancy. I was free to go about my business. I didn't care very much about what people thought about me, to be honest. I looked after myself and had a roof over my head. I had a beautiful car. I was in the process of buying a home. I was in the right place, and I didn't really care what anybody else thought because my life was my own creation. I had respect, love and admiration for my mother, which was why I felt terrible. I hadn't taken help from her since the age of sixteen or seventeen, so nobody could really stand in front of me and tell me what to do or have an opinion that was going to affect my life. I didn't care. I was free, and I couldn't express that enough.

    I thanked my auntie profusely, picked up my bag, and I ran out of the door. I got into my car, and then I realized I was low on petrol. I stopped at the next gas station. As I got out of my car, I heard a man whistle so I turned around. There was a guy there trying to chat me up; he came over to me and started laying on the compliments.

    I listened for a few seconds before interrupting, "Dude, you wouldn't want to hook up with me."

    "Oh yeah, I do. Why would you say that?"

    "Because I'm pregnant."

    "You're not pregnant. You're just saying that."

    I stroked my belly and assured him, "I very much am. I just found out, and I'm elated."

    The last thing I needed right now was another man. As I said this, he was backing up slowly.

    I laughed and said, "Yep, you better back off. You don't want to be responsible for milk nappies, late nights, and all of that."

    I laughed all the way to the main kiosk where I paid for my gas, because I knew I was free now to tell the whole world. That was the first person I had told after the people who were close to me.

    After that, I went home and called people. I called Jackie and I called everybody. I was like, I'm pregnant. People couldn't believe it, some were shocked, some were elated. It just depended on how long they had known me. That constituted their reaction to the news. But it was amazing.

    I couldn't wait to go and buy the baby books. I made a list of all the things that I wanted, went to the shops, and bought myself some baby books. I needed to learn all over. Prior to this, I didn't have many friends who had babies. I didn't know much about them. I didn't even know much about pregnancy.

    I had to buy a pregnancy book to tell me what to expect every month, like how big my child was growing in gestation. It was just such a surreal experience narrating how my day went to the man that I was having a baby with. It was just lovely. He was just really supportive and always there to hear what was going on inside my body. Soon it was time for him to come back to London from America. When he came, I picked him up from the airport, and he hugged me. The first thing he did was put his hand on my belly and ask how I was feeling. I assured him that I was good and had been eating well. He had to take it upon himself to tell his family, and I didn't want to be the one to deliver the news. I asked him to tell his family before people got to them. He went home to his dad, put his suitcases down, and spent some time with them.

Then he was right over at my house. He came to my house that night and we got into it straight away. This time, there were no condoms. It was a new experience to be free to know it was already happening. It was time to make the best of it. It was different. That night, as we had sexual relations, it was in the back of both of our minds that we were going to be parents very soon. I think that was the first night that I actually let him stay over. As I laid down, I started seeing him in a different light. He was no longer just the man I had sexual relations or a good night partying with. This time I looked at him, thinking, *You're going to be the father of my child. We are having a baby together.*

As he drifted off to sleep, I stayed awake looking at the features of his face. I wondered if the baby's nose was going to be like his, or if she was going to have his long lashes. I wondered if she was going to be hairy like him. I couldn't sleep and, for a long time, I just stared at him. I watched him, knowing that my life was never, ever going to be the same, knowing that I was going to be tied to this man for the rest of my life.

The next morning, he woke up early and had errands to run. He was going to his dad's house, and I laid in bed for a bit because I wasn't going to work for a while. He was just so attentive and concerned about what I ate, how many hours I worked, and so much more. After I assured him that I was okay, he left to go to his family and I got up and went about my day. I went to Costco and I started buying Pampers, and I went shopping at Gap. I went to baby shops. I was so excited. I couldn't stop once I started shopping. The retail therapy was great for me; it kind of hit home when I saw myself bringing home baby clothes.

The days went by, and I was so into myself that I just didn't realize that things were slowly changing in my daily routine and in my work. And to be honest, even with him. There were times where he would go out on his own. He would invite me, but I didn't feel like going. I was still going through the morning sickness, and I had appointments to make with different doctors. On top of that, I was still working, even though I wasn't feeling a hundred percent. I still didn't want to alter my routine, which still involved so much work. So he would do a whole lot of what he had to do during the day. He would go to work with his dad and sometimes help out there. Then he had his own time. Even though we were dating, I didn't want to claim all this time or make demands. I allowed him to come over when and if he wanted to. He would come over. The days turn into weeks. Sometimes he would spend the night at my house. We would go out to eat or listen to some music. We were just getting on with it. My belly was slowly getting bigger. Everybody knew about it. People would stop me on the road to congratulate me.

By this time, my ex had gotten the word that I was expecting. I think he didn't believe that I was actually pregnant. He had to come and find out for himself, since it was something that I couldn't achieve and had wanted so badly with him. And now that I was embarking on the journey to motherhood without him, it kind of hurt a little bit sometimes.

I continued working because I wanted to provide a good place for my child. My house came through; the government helped me secure it, because I was a single mother. It was an incentive program to help people like me. I was so happy as things were coming together nicely. We were going to get a place; it wasn't huge, but it would be ours. I remember the day that I signed the papers, and they were getting the house ready for me. I went back to the shop to tell them I was moving into my own home and that I'd finally secured a place. It was going to be a permanent home unless we decided to move. My life started to take a new shape while I prepared for the baby.

I noticed he was going out more and more on his own. The calls were coming through, but they were now fewer and further apart. It didn't crush me, because he still didn't have my heart. I wasn't as guarded as I was in the beginning, but I was still very much in control of what I felt for him. Honestly, I think the experience of being a mother had taken hold of me, and nothing was going to spoil it.

Sometimes women know things without even knowing how. Some call it a sixth sense. Some call it a woman's intuition. Everyone has a name for it, but I knew I never trusted him completely. I kind of always felt like there was something more going, but I didn't have time to dwell on all those things. When I found out I was pregnant, the more I accepted it, the more I was making a plan for just me and my baby. It didn't matter whether he came along on the journey or not.

One day, I was in the shop working. My belly had grown a bit to the point that it was now obvious. I was about four and a half months pregnant. I think I proceeded into my office at the back to relax and chill when there was a knock on the door. One of the salon workers told me that there was someone looking for me, apparently she was causing a scene in the shop about my baby's father. I came out of my office, and standing right in front of me was this tall, dark Jamaican woman. She didn't look good at all. It seemed like life had given her a whole lot of hurdles to cross. She was irate.

I took a deep breath and asked her, "What is going on?"

"I have been trying to call you, but clearly I had the wrong number. Are you Rose?"

Back then people called me Rose because Roza meant Rose in English.

I responded, "Yes, I am. People do call me Rose now, what is going on?"

I saw her anger building; that apparently was the wrong question to ask in the open, because she immediately started with her rant right then and there.

I interrupted her, "We are not going to do this right here; let's go to the back."

So we did, and I sat down, knowing I was about to hear something that I didn't want to. I just knew it. I felt it. She was just huffing and puffing and in such a state.

"What is going on?"

She looked me right in the eye and said, "I'm pregnant."

"Well, what's that got to do with me?" I asked.

"I'm pregnant by *your* baby's father."

I sat in disbelief for a moment, trying to gather myself before responding, "Okay. And how long have you guys been seeing each other?"

"It started years ago, way before you came into the picture. We have been seeing each other all the time, even when he goes back and forth to America."

I was angry, not so much that it happened, but because I was lied to. Up until this point, I had a feeling but no proof; now the proof was right there in front of my face. I had questions, and it turned out that she had three or four kids. She was a single mother. I was shocked to think that he would go and have relations with a mother that he knew was vulnerable and already struggling with kids. It was shocking. She proceeded to tell me what car he drove, which was actually my car that he would use to pick her up or run errands.

It was just so laughable; compared to the devastation I had to come from, this was minor. But I think my pride was injured looking at the woman with thoughts running through my head like: how many times she had slept with him, and now we were both pregnant by the same man.

I picked up the phone. I called his father and told him I was coming over to meet someone. He asked who it was. I told him not to worry about it, and that he would see soon enough.

I put the phone down, got up out of my chair and said, "Let's go and meet his dad, because I don't want no denials. I don't want lies. I just need people to know the truth."

His dad was the primary person in his life in London. He lived down the road from my shop. We got in my car and drove to his house. We knocked on the door and there was another person there to open the door, just as he was walking into the room.

He saw me and immediately asked, "What's going on?"

"Meet your future daughter-in-law; she's pregnant by your son."

He had a look of disbelief on his face, followed by a befuddled, "What?"

"Yeah, he got both of us pregnant, and now the truth is out. She's your future daughter-in-law. I'm done with him."

And that was it. I turned around, opened the door, got into my car, and drove off.

In the car on the way over, she had started talking about how she wanted an abortion, because she couldn't have another child. He also hadn't been returning her calls. It reminded me of how I had wanted to get rid of my own baby when I found out. If I wasn't going to have my hands soiled in blood for my own child, why would I get involved in someone else's? I was done.

It upset me, because now I knew I was definitely going to be a single mother. My pride was injured. My ego was injured. The uncertainty of the future was stronger now than ever, because I knew this child was going to depend on me so much more than him. I didn't care whether he was going to stay or go bac. And all this time, I hadn't even told him what was happening. People had come to me in the past and told me they had seen him in a club dancing with this person or that person. Sometimes I would even catch him in a lie where he told me he'd been at his father's house, and I found out he was out at a party;

it would just be trivial to me. When your heart isn't involved in a situation, you handle it differently. I started thinking about all the reports I had got about him. I went to work, picked up my bag, and went home.

I sat on my bed, called him, and fired away, "How dare you? Why did you lie to me? What made you think you were going to get away with this? You knew you had other women you were dealing with way before I came onto the scene. Not only that, you were dealing with mothers that have already had many kids, like…"

My voice trailed off, as I didn't know what else to say or how to control my rage. The emotion was festering inside me.

"Oh, I wasn't sure what you and I had. I didn't know if you wanted me. You acted cold one minute and hot the next—"

The excuses just kept coming, but I interrupted, "I always told you I was afraid of love. You knew I was reluctant to give my heart away; you knew it would take time. I told you that from the beginning, so you can't say I didn't make that clear before. Do what you like, I'm done!"

I paid it no mind. If I could go through a breakup with someone I completely adored and gave my life to through vows in the presence of God and man, I could walk away from anything else. It was trivial.

I told him that whatever we had —whether it was a relationship or not— and whatever I was to him —a side chick, a concubine, a mistress— was over. I was going to raise my child on my own.

He started defending his rights as a parent, saying that I wasn't going to push him to the side. He wanted me to just separate my feelings of hurt in doing what he classified as "the right thing" for my child.

I couldn't take it. I told him to stay away from me, my shop, and everything else that had to do with me. I was done. After I ended the call I remember sitting on the bed crying, because I couldn't believe that I had been such a fool. I was a fool to ignore the feeling that he wasn't being one hundred percent honest with me when it came to others. It still hurt to be lied to and blindly taken for a ride with another deceptive man. I cried on the bed; I cried more for what was to come. I laid in my bed stroking my belly, talking to her, telling her how much I loved her, how much she was going to have me, all of me. And even if she never had a dad, it would have been okay. I'd be the mother and the dad she needed. I made so many promises to my child. I was far enough along to feel her moving slowly within my womb. It was as if she was reassuring me that she heard me, and it was one of the most beautiful things that night.

My child was very active within my womb. It was as if she was feeling the heaviness of my heart, the uncertainty of the unknown future.

I woke up the next day with so many texts and calls from people in the shop, as they knew something had happened. I got up, showered, put my makeup on, and dressed really well. And I turned up at work. They were shocked because I think they thought I was going to be home wailing and licking my wounds. No, that wasn't going to happen. I was concentrating on my child. I packed up all of his stuff and brought it to work.

I sent him a text that said, "I'll be dropping your stuff over to your dad's house, so you don't have to come anywhere near me or my salon."

After that I blocked his number, because I didn't want to talk to him anymore. I was done. It was time to face my future.

There was a baby growing inside me. A baby that wasn't going to stop growing because the dad had proven himself to be a liar. I needed to be prepared for her mentally, physically, and emotionally. That was my priority. People were shocked at the way I handled it. Some even said I was careless, but it wasn't that at all. I was about to have the one thing in the world I wanted, and nothing was going to stand in the way of that. That was more important than anything else. I had started a journey that I couldn't change, and I was going to make the best of it, regardless. I carried on preparing for the birth of my child, going shopping. I went out with my friends if I wanted to, ate well, and continued to work hard at the same time. Life had to go on, and it did.

My hospital visits made it hit home, because he had been with me at the previous appointments. Now I was doing it all on my own. As I laid there hearing the machine and the galloping of the heartbeat, it was just so beautiful. But he wasn't there to see it. I wasn't going to let him stand in the way of that. The nurses would ask where the father of the baby was, and I would tell them he was no longer in my life. I didn't even need to give an explanation. This was my experience, and I would make the best of it. I turned up at my appointments alone. I went shopping on my own. I worked and went home on my own. All this time, he got on with his life, and I got on with mine.

People would come and tell me what they felt like I needed to know. He was out doing his thing at this club or that party with another woman. My life was about to change, but his was going on as if nothing had happened. He picked up from where he left off, and that was what women didn't understand. We get to pay the price of having a child and being there for the child, while the man can go free if he chooses. He did his thing; I ignored him for a while, until one day I will never forget.

I had a really hard day at work. I finished early, came home, and laid down. I could tell I was kind of tired, but nothing out of the normal happened. My baby was very active, moving around a lot so I laid in bed, and I talked to her. I put some music on and I was following all of the guidelines I had learned from reading the pregnancy books. I had changed my whole diet and was eating vegetables, which I hated initially. I was eating the appropriate foods to boost up my energy levels. I had everything I needed to take care of myself. It really wasn't that hard, because I had built a life around me. I remember going to bed at night thinking, *Well, my baby is very active tonight*, and I tried to calm her down so I could sleep. I remember curling up in bed, watching TV, and just talking to her. I picked up the book to read ways that I could calm her down when she's overactive in my belly at night. I saw that a nice hot bath helped, so I dragged myself out of bed, had a nice bath, and came back to bed. I rubbed my belly, because I didn't want to have stretch marks. My belly was growing. My mound was easy to see. I wasn't huge, but you could tell I was pregnant. I was twenty four weeks pregnant. During the night she had moved a couple of times. They were very strong movements that kind of jolted me out of my sleep, but it didn't seem like anything out of the ordinary.

Then, I woke up, used the toilet, and felt a lot of pressure down in my abdomen. But I just came back and went back to sleep.

It was the morning of the fifteenth of September, 2009. I got out of bed, feeling very heavy and weighted. I could feel this heavy pressure down below, and I'm thinking, *Wow, your body changes from day to day, during pregnancy. You never know what to expect every day.*

I woke up thinking, *Oh God, I'm not feeling too great today, maybe I should take the day off and just stay home and relax.* I dragged myself out of bed and went to make a cup of tea. The moment I laid the cup on the nightstand, I felt this tight grip down below. It felt like my bladder was being ripped open.

All I felt and heard after that was this gush of water. It didn't smell like pee. It was just gushing down.

I looked down and thought, *Oh my God, my water broke.*

According to the baby books, that only happened when the baby was about to come. Panic shot right through my body from the depths of my soul. I was only twenty four weeks pregnant. How could my waters break right now? I knew that wasn't right. I stood there screaming and literally scrambling for my phone to call someone. The first person I called was the ambulance, and soon after, my neighbor next door said she could hear howling and screaming.

I didn't even know what to do. I didn't want to move so I sat with the water dripping on the bed. I didn't want the baby to come. She wasn't ready. I wasn't ready. I sat on the bed making frantic phone calls and soon enough, I heard the siren of the ambulance. I could hear it getting nearer and nearer. My neighbor frantically ran into the house to open the door. To this day, I have no idea how she got into the house. Nonetheless, she started helping me wrap the towel around me and told me to just lay still.

She consoled me saying, "The ambulance is here."

There was so much commotion going on in my fear that I didn't register everything that was happening. I was just lying on the bed, praying to Allah. I was so deep in my thoughts about the child I had come to love so badly. My prayers were all about her. I wanted Allah to save her and let her be okay. This wasn't meant to happen, I knew from the baby books that she was not viable to live this long, because she was so little in the books. This panic and fear was multiplied times one hundred; it compared to nothing that I have ever felt in my life.

I snapped out of my thoughts for a moment when two people rolled me up onto a stretcher, shouting out commands of how to move me gently down the stairs to avoid any motion. As they put me on the stretcher, I felt pain like I've never, ever felt before. It tore right through me, and I screamed.

One of the emergency workers said, "I think she is contracting."

When he said that my eyes flew wide open and I asked, "You mean I'm having the baby?"

Before I could even finish the sentence another one came. I was in labor. I knew that contractions came during labor. I started screaming.

"You've got to calm down because when you're agitated, it's going to stress out the baby. You don't want them coming right now."

I had found out a couple of weeks before that the baby was going to be a girl.

So I said, "It's a girl. It's a girl.," that was all I could scream, "it's a girl. It's a girl…."

I must've come across very crazy to them, because it was as if I was rambling nonsense. But, I was rambling about things that were in my heart. I felt the fear, even as they tried to reassure me. They took my vitals. I realized I was very low in blood, and I was anemic. They had already told me that in the hospital, and I was dehydrated as well.

And so they were just doing their job, trying to stabilize my child, and me in the process. Very soon, we were at the nearest hospital. It felt like it was forever, but it was about fifteen or twenty minutes away. We were at the Royal London hospital in White Chapel. This was a hospital that was best known for groundbreaking technology for babies, mothers, and everything concerning pregnancies. Knowing that they had brought me to the hospital calmed a few of the fears of my heart. It made me feel like we were in the right hands. We arrive, and there was so much commotion and shouting orders. By this time, the pain was getting stronger. They wheeled me into the hospital and straight onto a bed.

I could hear someone saying, "We can't let her come right now. We have to do all we can to make her stay in."

So they lifted my legs up just to keep her inside. They were telling me not to push, even though I felt this urge bearing down below. And soon enough, a client and a family friend of mine came. More and more people were just turning up at the hospital, because they were all concerned. They all knew it was in time. One of my good friends showed up and wouldn't leave my side. They needed one person to be in the room, and she volunteered to be there, which I was grateful for.

As I laid in the bed, the doctors were wiring me up to one machine and checking the baby. There were nurses checking my vitals, taking my blood levels, everything else. It felt like it was all a dream. I couldn't believe it was happening to me. I handed my phone to my friend and asked her to let her father know. It was all happening so fast, and it was so weird. When she had my phone, my ex-husband called. She told him I was in the hospital, and it looked like the baby was about to be born. She told everybody that called to pray because I was going to need support. I will never forget what she did. She brought her Bible with her even though I was a Muslim, because she was going to call out to her God on my behalf. I was lying in bed reciting all the Muslim prayers I knew in my head. I was pleading with Allah to save my baby's life, to give me another chance, and not to take this baby away from me after all I'd been through. I was pleading with heaven to give my baby a chance to live.

As I was doing that in my head and screaming at the contractions that weren't stopping, my friend was pacing the floor with the Bible open in her hand praying and calling out to her Christian God to help. I didn't pay much attention to her because I was in my own space where I had to call upon the God I served and knew from childhood. I was calling out to Allah more than I've ever done. It felt like the doctors were doing all they could, but whenever the pain was too severe, I would scream out for a nurse.

At one point, I remember saying to the nurse, "I feel like my private parts are going to explode."

The pain was so severe that I thought I was going to pass out. I was drifting away, and they slapped me just to keep me awake. Hours later, they had done everything they could to stop my baby from coming, but that was not going to happen.

Eventually, one of the doctors looked at the nurse and said, "She's dilating way too fast. I'm going to have to check her to see what's happening."

When the nurse and the female doctor started coming at me wearing their gloves to do a physical, I panicked. It was just too much going on already, and it was too painful.

I started speaking quickly, saying, "Get away from me. I can't take this pain. Leave her alone, leave her alone. Just don't disturb it. If you touch it, she's going to want to come out."

I was just going on and on in a state of hysteria that no one could stop.

The doctors tried to calm me by saying, "Roza, we just want to make sure that if she's going to come, she won't be breached. If you don't let us help you, we can't do our job."

Reluctantly, I said, yes and instantly felt the doctor touching me down there.

Shortly after I felt the touch, the doctor spoke out to the nurse saying, "She's coming. She's about six centimeters dilated. It's going to be sometime soon."

They started running around; they brought in this little incubator and positioned it right beside my bed. Then they started putting towels under my bottom. They were getting ready for delivery, and it was so shocking to me. As they were getting ready, I laid in the bed weeping and begging with them to help me so she would not come. I knew it wasn't time yet. I was shaking my head with tears running down my face. All the while, my friend was still in the room praying profusely, ferociously and fervently, for her God to intervene. I thought to myself, as I watched her, *Why would your God intervene when I'm calling out to the one that I believe in?*

In the middle of my thoughts, I had this urge.

I called out to the doctor pleading, "I can't hold on anymore. I need to push."

He urgently told me not to push and to wait as they were fixing this little incubator. It was going to be home to my child. If she was alive after this, there was no way she was going to be able to breathe on her own.

The doctor was explaining all of this as they were setting it up for her and wiring things on me.

Eventually, I moaned, "Doctor, I can't anymore. I'm going to push. Please come and help me pick my baby up."

"You're going to have to push."

The doctor ran over while screaming orders for the nurses to stand by. The machine was on. Everything was ready, and he finally told me to push. I pushed once and felt a bit overleaf, but nothing happened. Soon after, another contraction came, so I pushed again.

The doctor yelled out, "I can see her head. Just one or two more, and she'll be out. You can do this."

I had about eight medical professionals in my room, and it was one of the scariest moments of my entire life. The look on their faces didn't give me much hope either. It was as if I could read their thoughts. They all scrambled to do whatever they could. I held my breath and mustered all the strength I had left in me, even though I was so tired and depleted. I howled from the depths of my soul as I bore down and pushed.

All I heard was, "She's coming"

I continued pushing and screaming. Then at my final push, I felt relief. It felt like something was leaving my body.

The doctor shouted out, "She's here! She's here!"

My baby girl was born, but there were no cries. There were no screams. There was nothing. It was just total silence in the room. I started panicking.

"Why isn't she crying? What's wrong? Somebody, tell me what's happening."

I was screaming and crying out for answers.

To this day I've never seen the doctors move so quickly in my life. They grabbed her and wiped off all of the fluids then quickly stuck her into the incubator. They were gone in less than a second. I was only able to get a glance of her, and I noticed she looked extremely tiny. She was covered with soft, fluffy looking hair on her body. I strained to take a better look, but their movements were swift. The nurses gathered around putting all kinds of wires on her before she was pushed out of the room. She was gone, and I couldn't contain myself. Grief and confusion filled me because I hadn't even had the chance to hold my child. I didn't get to experience what I had read in the books. I was supposed to have her laid on my bosom to have a little snuggle and get her first milk. It felt like I was watching it happen to someone else. All I saw was them wheeling my dream away in a flash.

On that day, the fifteenth of September 2009, my baby girl came into the world. She weighed nothing more than a measly six hundred and thirty grams. As they wheeled her out of the room and the door shut behind them, I knew my life would never be the same. At five and a half months pregnant, twenty-four weeks and a few days, my baby had decided it was time. Or should I say, heaven decided it was time for my baby to be born into this world. Born into a world without being able to cry or even breathe on her own. I laid my head back in exhaustion, and knew I was about to step into a different territory. One that I had never walked through before. One that I never imagined even in the worst of times. I was a mother. I had gotten what I always wanted, but the uncertainty of not knowing what was happening to my child broke my heart. I laid in the hospital bed and sobbed until my body began to shake from exhaustion. Another chapter of my life was about to start.

8
BROKEN AT A CROSSROAD

After giving birth, I was drained of emotions. I was absolutely exhausted. In the midst of my outcry, I heard the nurses coming towards me. They were trying to get me ready to pass the afterbirth. By then, I was so exhausted and don't even think I was fully conscious. They pushed and tugged on my belly Finally, I felt it come out. The moment it did, I knew I didn't have any more strength to hold on. I laid myself back down on the pillow, and the last thing I remembered was praying that Allah would save my child. I wanted her to live, and the fear that gripped my heart at the thought of my child not making it was unbearable. My heart had just leaped out of my chest when I caught a glimpse of this little baby that I had created. It was terrifying having no control over what happened to her while she was in the doctors' hands.

As I closed my eyes and surrendered to sleep, the last thing I remember was the prayer on my lips, "Allah, please save my child."

I slept for hours, because when I woke back up the room was dimly lit with the afternoon sunlight. My friend was still sitting at my bedside when I quickly tried to get up to bed.

"Lay back down," she said.

"How is she doing? Have you heard anything?" I asked, not worrying about myself.

I wasn't going to lay there and not be with my child, knowing just how much she needed her mother right now.

I tried to lift myself from the bed again only to hear my friend sternly say, "Lay back down on the bed. I'll get a nurse."

She ran out of the room and came back shortly after.

"How is my child doing?" I urgently interrogated the nurse.

"They are still working on her," she said softly, "Remember, she was born very small and very early. She will be staying in the hospital for a while. They've taken her to the intensive care unit, after which they will transfer her down to the NICU."

The nurse tried to reassure me that they had a specialist in the NICU department whose specialty was working on these little babies. They would help and nurture them until they were full term and could go home.

As I looked at her, questions swirled in my mind. I wanted to know if my baby had cried. I wanted to know if she was moving. I had so many questions, and I asked her a few of them.

"I don't know," she said, rubbing hand, "all I know is that they're working on her; that's all they've told us. In the meantime, let's help you get cleaned up and hopefully you will be able to see her later."

She left the room for a moment, and I burst out crying. I couldn't believe that I wasn't even allowed to hold my child. Every part of me was yearning to be with her. It felt like it was a separation worse than divorce. It felt like somebody had taken a huge part of me away. As I started to cry, my friend got up and started pacing the room praying, calling into the God of the Christians whom she served. She was fervently praying. I didn't care as I needed prayers now more than ever. Anybody could pray for me.

When she finished, she turned around and said to me, "Let's get you to the toilet. Let's get you all ready, because you are going to need all your strength for your child. She's going to need you like no one's ever needed you before."

Just as I was about to leave the room, my baby's father walked in. He had missed the birth. He said he was stuck in traffic and couldn't get there in time. It was okay, because I had stopped depending on him emotionally or physically. It really didn't bother me that he was not there for the birth. All I wanted was to be with my child. It didn't matter what anybody else was doing, who was there, or who was not; all I wanted was my daughter. Both of them helped me off the bed. I was so weak and lethargic. It felt like I was run over by a semi-truck. There was no pain anymore; it was just this deep hollow emptiness. As I looked down at my belly walking into the shower, it dawned on me again. My baby had arrived. I stood under the shower as the water rushed down my face, and I couldn't help but go back to the picture in my mind's eye where my child looked so fragile. I burst out crying again, and sat on the floor in the hospital shower room. Right there on the floor, I prayed to Allah on this day. I prayed more than I ever prayed before, because I knew a child born at twenty four weeks had a long way to go. I had heard stories of babies being born early who didn't make it. My fate and that of my child was in God's hands. I didn't know how anything was going to be. It's as if you're being led into a dark room —a place you've never been before— embarking on a journey that is alien to you. I can't remember how long I sat in that shower. Finally, I got up, washed myself, and went back to my room.

I picked up my phone and made phone calls telling people that my baby was born. Everybody was shocked; most couldn't believe it. They thought I was playing a sick joke on them. Just like me, everybody wanted to know what was happening. They wanted answers, and I had none to give. I couldn't explain to them what she looked like. It was as if I was scared to tell people before they jumped to the wrong conclusion. I asked everyone to pray, as everything in me knew she was going to need them. When you come to a situation where you know everything is out of your control, suddenly you start looking at the power that is beyond you. You start looking for that sovereignty that is way above your capability. You start reaching out for something you never had use for in the past. I was never a spiritual person, but I found myself calling everybody and asking them to remember her in their prayers.

I sat in the room for hours anxiously waiting for the doctors to come in.

Eventually, a doctor came in and said somberly, "We need to talk," his demeanor was gentle but his facial expression was serious, "I don't have many answers."

"What do you mean you don't have many answers?" I screamed, "No one wants to tell me what is going on with my child."

By now it had been some time after the initial report from the nurse, so I knew nothing else. I was a sitting duck, just waiting in limbo for anybody to come and tell me what was going on.

"It is not looking good. She's very tiny right now. She's unresponsive. Her heart rate is very faint. You can see she's been through so much, so we're not getting much out of it right now, but we're not going to give up yet. We're still going to continue working on her.

You will not be able to see her for a few hours because they will not let her out of their sight for the time being. So all we can do right now is pray."

As he spoke, all kinds of emotions were running through me, fear being the most prominent one.

With my face in my hands, I cried helplessly, "I just want to see my child. All I want is to see and hold her."

The doctor was clearly moved by my tears and crouched down next to me saying, "You will see her in due time. We just need you to be strong. We need you to take care of yourself so you can be there for her. Go and get something to eat and to drink, and regain your strength. You've been through a lot these past few hours."

I looked at him and said, " Do not worry about me. I need you to just do whatever you can do for her, whatever it takes, just help her."

The thought of my child being on our own with all these doctors working on her broke my heart.

"Has she cried yet?" I asked.

"No, she hasn't. Like I said, we're getting very little out of her right now, and it is possible that she will be on a ventilator for a very long time. At this moment, her lungs are very small and severely underdeveloped. She won't be able to breathe on her own for some time."

"You mean she's going to be hooked up to a machine that's going to be breathing for her?"

I didn't understand. I had never been subjected to anything like this, and I hadn't read about premature babies. It was never part of my plan. In my hopes and dreams, I was going to go to full term and give birth to a beautiful, bouncing baby girl. That was my dream. This was not part of the plan, and so it was out of my control.

As the doctor looked into my eyes he said, "I promise you, we are doing everything we can to save your child."

I locked eyes with him, "I appreciate all that you're doing. Thank you," I said through my tears, "As soon as they are done working on her, may I see her? Being here without her hurts."

He cast me a warm smile and said, "Okay, let's make a deal. If you don't fancy any of the food up here, go down to the canteen, and get yourself something substantial to eat and drink. Get your energy levels up. Take care of yourself for now. And when the time is right, I will come and personally get you to come and see your daughter. This is where we all pray and hope that a miracle happens.

I've seen babies leave this hospital after being born early, she is the youngest we've had this week. I'll tell you more when I know more."

I thanked him as he walked away; I was so emotional knowing that my child's whole life was in his hands. What a pressure he and the other doctors and nurses must have been feeling, looking after all these tiny babies on a daily basis.

I had become used to being in control of my life and had built a life for myself. I had the perfect master plan, and —until this situation— I was the driver. In one day, all of a sudden, I found myself at the mercy of somebody else. I felt utterly hopeless and powerless. As badly as I wanted to, I couldn't help my child at this point. As I sat in the wheelchair sobbing, the doctor's words triggered in my mind, *Let's pray for a miracle*. The Muslim way to do to the prayer was standing up and kneeling down. But as I sat in that wheelchair, I looked up to heaven, and I prayed to Allah. I prayed earnestly, and I asked him to save this child of mine. I asked him to save the love of my life, because I had come to love my child, regardless of the circumstances of her conception. I had come to love this little person that I spoke to; that I sang to; that I whispered to in the middle of the night; that I caressed; that I had felt moving within me. A love had literally erupted in me for her that I couldn't contain. As I sat in the chair praying to Allah, my friend came back into the room.

"What did he say?" she asked.

I did my best to relay the message that the doctor told me.

"Well, I think he's right. I think, right now, what we need to do is pray. That's all we can do right now."

I looked at her and thought, *That's all I've been doing ever since I got here, but would Allah even want to hear from me when I haven't really been spiritual or sought to involve him in my life?* I guess she must have seen the look on my face. She said that from today, we are going to be praying for her every single day. When she said "we," I assumed that she meant that I could pray in my own faith while she did the same in hers. This woman had a very strong faith in the God that she served.

"In the meantime, we have to take care of you. I will go to your house for you in a bit and gather some things you may need. For now, I'm going to take you over to the canteen and get you something to eat so that you can be strong for your child. That is the only way I am going to leave you and go get things you need, okay?"

I reluctantly agreed.

As she wheeled me out it, felt like all the nurses were looking at me as if they knew something that I didn't. I bet they had seen thousands of women coming there to give birth to premature babies that stayed in the NICU and another thousand gave birth to a bouncing baby who would go home with the parents soon after. In my mind, everybody was looking at me with an empathetic smile. Some of them even looked at me as if they were sorry. It was as if I could read their thoughts on their faces.

I asked her to stop by the reception, and as she stopped, I said, "Did you notice any news on my child?"

"Has anyone been to see you?"

I said, "Yes, the doctor has, but I just want to find out if there's been any developments."

"Let me find out," she said before picking up the phone to call the intensive care unit.

She spoke on the phone and asked.

She put the phone down and looked at me and said, "No, no developments at all. They're still working on her. They have no news other than what the doctor told you. But they said the moment they're done, they will come and get you. Where are you going?" she asked me,

"I'm going to go get something to eat."

"Come right back so you do not miss it if they come for you ."

As we left the Maternity ward, in the outskirts of the corridor to the elevators, my friend looked down and said, "You've got to stop crying Roza, you've got to have faith. You got to look after yourself and trust that God will look after your baby."

Whenever she mentioned God, I wondered which God she was referring to. But I guess it was hers. This woman loved and trusted her God in a way that was very refreshing to me. I had known her for a few years, and I knew her well. God was a huge part of her life. Not that it had ever interested me anyway.

And so she wheeled me into the canteen, ordered my food, found a chair at a spare table, and got me seated before saying, "I need you to eat whatever they give you right now, whether it's good or not, because I know you don't feel like eating. I know you don't want to be here, but this is where we are now. So eat, drink, and I'll take you back to your room then go to your house and get everything that you need for you and your child."

They brought the food and put it in front of me, but my stomach was in knots. I couldn't eat. The last thing on my mind was taking care of myself. How could I do this when I couldn't even take care of my own child? I forced the food down my throat. Everything was just so tasteless and devoid of any flavor. It just didn't feel right for me to be sitting there eating. But I knew my friend wasn't going to take no for an answer, and our deal was already made. I had to uphold my end of the deal and take care of me for her to fulfill her end of the bargain. She sat and watched me eat. I quickly pushed it down my throat. I just wanted it to end. A few minutes after starting, I was done. I took a sip of drink, then she was taking me right back to my room.

We passed the corridor again, and I asked the same reception lady if they had any news.

"No, not yet."

My frustration began to build again, and I told her, "I'm going back to my room, but please let me know when they're ready."

"Of course."

When we got back to the room, I got into the bed, because as much as I was trying to muster up the courage to be physically awake for when they needed me, I was exhausted.

As I arranged myself into bed, my friend said to me, "I have to go get your stuff. I will be back in a little while."

Before walking out of the door she came over and she looked at me and said, "Roza, you are going to get through this. Whatever the outcome is, you are going to be fine. You've already been through so much yet you are still here."

She was speaking hope that I didn't feel. When you feel like the very existence of your life and your child's is in the hands of another, you begin to feel like you're not enough or you did something wrong. .

After she left, my thoughts moved on. What could I have done to stop this? What did I do? Why did I work too hard? Did I overexert myself? What did I do to result in her being born early? What could I have done to prevent this? All these thoughts were in my head. I must've done something. I laid there going back over my actions from the previous day, trying to piece together the reason why she had come early.

In the middle of my thoughts, a nurse came into my room.

"How are you doing?" she asked.

"I'm hanging in there."

"That's what you need to do now, and just pray."

As she was walking out the room I called out to her, "Nurse. Can I ask you a question?"

"Yeah, sure."

"What causes a woman to go into premature labor?"

She looked at me and said, "Don't do it."

"Do what?"

"Blame yourself. I see a lot of women do that. You don't need to add that to your plate right now. It's going to be a long journey for you whatever the outcome, and you don't need to be beating yourself up with this. I'm going to tell you the God's honest truth: these things happen, and no one knows why. There's no reason for it. Some babies just come earlier than others, and that's just how it is."

"You want to tell me this happens all the time?" I asked.

"Yes. Well, not all the time, but it does happen quite often. When you get to the NICU department where all these babies are being watched over, you will understand exactly what I mean. But I can tell you right now, it is not your fault. There is no way you could have stopped this. Your child was ready to come. You were already dilating quite fast when you got here. So please stop blaming or looking for answers where there are none. The best you can do for her right now is take care of yourself emotionally, physically, and mentally so you'll be strong enough for her. The worst that can happen is for you to fall apart while she needs you.

You are a mother now. It ceases to be about you. It's about that little girl upstairs being worked on, whose whole life depends on you and what you make of it. It's a huge responsibility, but it's also the most beautiful journey because you're going to have this person who's going to love you like no other. There is nothing like the love of a child. Trust me, I know."

Then she went on to tell me how a cousin of hers had a baby quite early at thirty weeks.

I interrupted her saying, "But mine is only here after twenty four weeks."

"I know. But her baby made it, and yours can, too. They were in hospital for months, but now he's a bright little boy. He is the joy of his mother's life, you will get through this. Right now, just get some rest. Hopefully, in a little while they will have some news concerning your child."

She walked back over to me and helped me get settled in the bed, and she looked me in the eye and said, "I will be praying for you and your child. I will be remembering you in our prayers."

Then she turned and walked out of the room.

The moment she left the room, my thoughts of guilt returned. Even though she said not to blame myself, I couldn't help it. I was still trying to think of any possible reason why this would happen to me after everything I had been through in the pursuit of a child. The journey seemed surreal that I had fallen pregnant by a total stranger on our first night together. Now fate had decided that I would have to go through this journey with her, if she made it.

I tried not to let myself go to the territory of thinking that I could lose her. I couldn't think of that, so I held on to what little tiny fragment of positivity I could. The last thing I remember doing was calling out to Allah again before falling into a deep sleep. I slept for hours. According to my friend who had returned with my things when I was sleeping, not only did I sleep, but I was talking in my dreams. It was incoherent, but I was speaking earnestly and fervently to someone. I truly believe I was praying in my dream, because I didn't dream of anything I could remember. It was restless but very deep sleep.

When I woke up, she was sitting right next to me.

She said, "I didn't want to wake you; you were sleeping so deeply."

"What's the time?" I asked.

"It's about eight o'clock in the evening."

My child was born around two in the afternoon.

I looked around the room for a moment before asking her, "Did they come in while I was asleep?"

"Nope. I haven't seen anyone. The nurse did come to check up on you a few minutes ago, but you were still asleep. I asked her, but she had no news."

I started scrambling out of the bed.

"Do you need me to get the wheelchair?"

"No, I can walk."

As I took the first step, I felt my body responding. I needed to know what was happening. This waiting game was over. It was just too much. It had been five —almost six— hours, and nobody was going to tell me anything unless I pushed for it. I walked slowly with my friend at my side helping me down to the reception.

"Lady? It has been nearly six hours since I gave birth to my child and I still haven't seen her. I still have not held her. They keep telling me they're working on her. What is going on? I need to know; I can't take this anymore. I need to know what's going on with my child."

I was becoming hysterical.

"Give me a moment," she said before picking up the phone again.

This was now the second time that day she had done this for me.

A few minutes later she turned to me and said, "They are still working on her, but they're nearly done. They're quite confident that they'll be done in the next half an hour. So why don't you just go back to your room and wait patiently. They're coming."

"That's easy for you to say," I retorted back, "How do you think it feels not even knowing how my child is doing? They're not saying anything except that they're working on her. What is going on? I need answers."

"Calm down," she said, "you don't need to get yourself into this situation. I promise you when they're ready, they will come for you. I am sorry. I totally understand your frustration."

"No, you don't," I threw back at her, "How could you even understand how I'm feeling right now? I need my child."

I started sobbing again, tears running down my face.

My friend came and gathered me in her arms, comforting me, "Let's just go back to the room and wait."

We got back to the room and she sat me down on the bed. I could see in her face that she was concerned about the way I was unraveling.

"I think we need to pray."

She held my hands and looked deep into my eyes.

Then she said, "Just agree with me in prayer."

I had no idea what that meant. I guess she wanted me to say, "Amen." I think she could tell in my face that I didn't understand, because she confirmed my thoughts.

"Okay."

She held my hands and prayed almost endlessly.

All she kept praying was, "We need a miracle, Lord. We need a breakthrough. We need you now more than ever."

As she was praying, the tears were just streaming down my face. This lady was consulting her God on my behalf, throwing her faith out there in collaboration with mine. Even though I was of another faith, she had faith enough in the God that she served that he could do something. As she prayed, my thoughts wandered away from the prayer into the possibilities of what could happen.

Her words jolted me back out of my daydream.

"Whatever happens you are in control."

She ended it and I thought to myself, *Oh my God. So she is literally dabbling with the idea that my child couldn't survive.* We cried together.

She held me and prayed again before saying, "Now we just wait and see."

We were sitting silently in that room, looking at each other. Sometimes silence is the solitude you need in a situation that you can't comprehend. I didn't want to say a word. I was done talking. I started to think of the possibility of what she said about her God being in control. That really hit home and brought with it so many other thoughts.

The same doctor that saw me earlier entered the room and was ready to give me more information. I had to get up.

He saw my efforts and told me to be careful, "I have news for you."

I looked at him with hope in my eyes, trying to gauge from his face exactly what kind of news he had for me.

"How is she doing?" I asked.

"She's still unresponsive, but we are not done doing all that we can. She is on a ventilator that's breathing for her right now. It's like a life support machine. She also has some aids to help her heart beat stay normal."

I could see him searching for the right words to say.

"I need to just prepare you for what you're about to see. This could be very traumatic for you. This is your first time as a mother in this situation. So I need you to just understand that everything you see is helping her. She's not in pain right now. Right now, we're just trying to get her heartbeat going and her breathing right with the machine. Her heartbeat slows down to the point that we are concerned, and that's what took so long. That's why we couldn't come and tell you anything, because her heartbeat was very irregular. At one point, we thought it was going to stop, but it didn't. You have a fighter on your hands," he looked at me with a hopeful smile and continued, "If she is fighting to stay alive, the least you could do is fight to be strong for her."

"Yes, I will. May we go and see her now?"

"Yes, let's go."

Then he grabbed the wheelchair and helped me to get settled into it. He must have seen the resistance in my eyes, because I wanted to walk to see my child.

"You're going to need this because it's a long way away. You need all your strength." I reluctantly sat back. They were treating me like I was so fragile, like I was about to break. It was as if they knew what I was about to face, and I needed to muster up all the strength I had in me as he wheeled me out.

I asked, "Has she cried?"

"No, she hasn't. She hasn't done anything because of how tiny she is. The only thing she did was sneeze. That was her getting out all the gunk in her nasal passage and that actually helped."

I had something to hold onto. She sneezed; my child actually sneezed. That was good enough for me, for now.

As he wheeled me over, he started telling me exactly what to expect. He said I wasn't going to go through this alone; there were other mothers there as well. There were about eight to ten babies in the room with different ailments born at different gestation periods. He said it would help me to find strength in those people. It would help to socialize with these mothers in the mother and baby room.

He said, "You will have to feed her at some point."

My body was in so much shock that I had even forgotten that I was meant to feed my child. I knew she wasn't going to be able to latch onto my breasts for sustenance. I looked down at my breasts, as he said this.

"I have no milk."

"You don't have any milk because your baby wasn't meant to be born now. Your body is in shock. We have medication that will help the production of milk, because we will need you to physically extract the milk with the machine. That way, we can feed it to her because that milk is very important. I hope you don't mind."

"No, I don't. I'm going to do everything that I can to help her."

This was my child, and the least I could do was produce enough milk to feed her. I couldn't wait to get to the room. It felt like it took forever on the journey to the other side of the hospital, where the babies were.

As we entered the NICU department, we crossed the room and went to the receptionist.

"This is the mother of the baby we were working on," he told the nurse.

She turned around and said, "Congratulations."

I thought to myself, *Why would you congratulate me in this situation?* But I supposed congratulations were in order because I had given birth.

"We're going to take very good care of her."

It was a very busy ward. There were nurses and doctors in their white coats going up and down inside the rooms, and I saw nurses monitoring. I saw people who were crying. We came to a little room.

"I am going to need you to go into that room and change into this."

It was like a bodysuit, which I presumed was for the protection of the babies so I wouldn't spread germs. I put on this bodysuit that was covering me from the neck down, and then I put on a pair of gloves. It looked like I was getting ready to go to space. When he finished dressing in the protective wear, he took me to a sliding door, punched in a number, and the door slid open.

In that moment, it felt like I had left my world and entered one that only a few people got to see. There were about ten tiny cubicles with a baby in each one.

As I scanned the room, fear returned in full force and I asked, "What is this room?"

"Welcome to the NICU department. This is where we work on our precious little ones."

He stared at my face, where my fear was probably on full display and said, "You'll be fine."

He wheeled me across the room to the other side where my child was. I couldn't help but look at these cubicles with these lifeless babies hooked on all kinds of wires; none of them were moving or making a sound. It was as if they weren't even alive. The only thing showing that there was vital life and breath in their body were the machines that were flashing and beeping. I had never seen anything like this in my life. I was so scared, and lost in my thoughts.

As we moved from one cubicle to another, he finally came to one.

He stopped and said, "There is your baby."

That was the first time I had seen her properly since I'd given birth. She was the tiniest, most fragile thing I had ever seen. She had wires on her chest and head. There was a small pad covering her eyes. Her skin looked so light and transparent like it would just split open if you touched her; and she looked so dark.

"Why does she look like this?" I asked.

The doctor went on to explain that she had come out of the womb with all of her body hair intact. She didn't have time to shed it. I looked at her, and from the depth of my heart, overwhelming nurturing and protective feelings came over me. I just wanted to grab her and breathe into her lungs. Tears started running down my face.

The doctor said, "Get to know your child, familiarize yourself and you will get better. This initial shock will pass. I'm going to give you some time to spend with your child. I'll be back in a few minutes."

When the doctor left, I inched closer. I needed to have some form of physical contact with my child but that was impossible because these little cubicle pods were so secure. The only thing in and through them was the wiring that ran from the child into the machines. I laid my hand on the cubicle. I looked at her, taking in every length from the tip of her head right to the little tiny toes. I had never seen any babies so tiny or fragile. *Are they sure she's even alive? The* thought crossed my mind, because there was no life in her. There was nothing about her that showed signs of life or even movement of any kind. The machines were the only indication that she was still with us.

As I looked at her, I started sobbing.

Through my tears I began to speak to her saying, "I am sorry. I love you so much. I need you to be strong. I need you to fight because I'm going to be out here fighting for you, willing you to live, willing you to get through this."

I don't even know what came over me. I just started speaking to my child as if she could hear me. We had already bonded whenever I used to sing to her in my belly. On the nights when she was moving so much in my belly, I would speak to her. I would tell her to calm down, because Mommy needed to sleep. I felt like the connection was already there. Now, all she needed to know was that her mom was here. I laid my hands on the cubicle for a moment; then I went around to the other side to count her ten tiny fingers and toes.

Her little chest was going up and down in fluid movements that were very slow and faint. I looked at this machine that went into her mouth and down her throat. I took in the sight of the wires that literally started from her forehead down her throat to her chest, to her belly then her legs, even her toes were wired up. It looked like she had about thirty wires going in and through her. The image of my child being in this position was devastating. Something deep inside willed me to keep talking to her, to give her the strength that she needed. Whether she heard me or not, I was going to tell her I was there even through my tears. I told her how much I loved her, how much she meant to me, and how much I had wanted her for so long. How I am sorry that she had to come early. How her first fight in life was the fight of survival. How she was going to make it. I told her that we were going to have a beautiful life together, and she was my world. I loved her so much, even before I hadn't seen her. Seeing her being so helpless, I was going to do all I can to make life easy. I started promising her that she wouldn't want for anything. She wouldn't lack anything. Not as long as I had breath in my lungs. I spoke to my child from the depth of my heart and from my soul, I felt an outpouring of love for this tiny little human being, who was my world.

I don't know how long I was there. I supposed the doctor and nurses saw me bonding with her and gave me time with my child. I studied her facial features and concluded that she looked more like her father. I looked at her tiny little nose. I looked at the space where her eyes were meant to be and wondered how big or small they were. Everything about my child was perfect to me because she was mine. This was a child that I had created with another human being. This was a child I was going to be connected to for the rest of my life. The weight of that responsibility hit me. She was everything I wanted. I wanted a little girl who would be the mini me. I would dress her up in pink every single day. We would go and do girly things. We'd go to the nail salon, go to fun places, and explore the world. I had plans for us.

As I looked at her, I didn't want to leave. I just wanted to sit there and look at her, but I heard footsteps coming towards me. I turned around and a female doctor came over and introduced herself.

She informed me, "Your baby is under my care. I know it is hard to see your child in this situation, but I wanted to tell you that this is what we do. We see these babies grow and overcome every obstacle and hindrance in their path. We see them healed and fully grown to the point that they're ready to go home with their parents."

She wanted to know whether I was married or single, if I was going to have any help with her.

I told her it was just me, since her father and I weren't even in a relationship. I wasn't holding him to any responsibility at all.

She looked at me and said, "Well, this situation is hard enough on its own. You will need to rely on family, friends, and loved ones to help you through this. We do allow only parents to come see the children for their own safety. Since it's only you, we will have to put you in the books as the only visitor."

"Put him on as well. I don't want to stop him from coming in just because we're not together. He's her father, after all."

"Okay, I will do that for you. I'm going to give you time with your child. When you finish, I need you to come to the office and sign the paperwork concerning some things. I will explain to you exactly what needs to be done. We're getting it all ready, and we will let you know. If the paperwork isn't ready when you leave here today, we can get onto it tomorrow morning.".

"Yes," I replied.

"And another thing. You will have to extract some milk. I can see you, haven't got any, so we are going to put you on some medications that will kick in within twenty four to forty eight hours. It would help the production of milk, because we'll need that first one. It's loaded with so many good nutrients that she will need. Every few hours we will need you to extract some more. You can take the machine home and do it in your leisure time there as well as when you're here. The nurse will come in and bring those medications that you need."

"Do you think I will produce any milk?" I asked.

"I bet in the next few hours, once you've relaxed that part of the body that tells the brain that you've had a child, it will kick in. The production of the milk will start."

I looked at my breasts, and I thought it didn't look likely. But I decided to take her word for it. At least my child was relying on me for something. It felt like they were doing everything for her, and I was just left on the back burner. Being able to extract some milk for her gave me the motherly duty I was craving.

Before the doctor left the area I looked at her and said, "Is she going to make it?"

I could tell she was uncomfortable answering. She clearly didn't want to build my hopes up too high, but also didn't want to leave me heartbroken and hopeless either. I watched her choose her words very carefully.

She said, "Right now, it's a bit too early to make a prediction. She is not alone. Each and every one of these babies is fighting for their lives. Try to keep your thoughts positive. I don't know if they told you this, but there are a good number of them that do make it. Hold onto that thought, and do everything in your own power to help her in this journey."

"How long do you think it will take?"

"That all depends on how well she does and how quickly her body recovers and grows. The main concern for us is her lungs —which are very tiny— and her eyes —which aren't very well-developed. And she has a murmur that won't allow air to circulate properly into other parts of her body. Her female genitalia hasn't fully developed, so we have put in a tube to collect all the fluid that is meant to be in her bladder to help ease the pressure down there."

She went on to say that there would be another doctor coming in, to explain the ailments, treatments and surgeries she would need.

I immediately interrupted, " What do you mean by surgeries?"

"It is very likely that she will need surgery to help rectify some of the deficiencies she has."

I looked at this tiny little baby on the life support machine and thought, *She can't do anything right now, and the doctors are already thinking about surgery.*

The doctor interrupted my thoughts saying, "We will explain everything another time. Right now I just came to give you the preliminary of what to expect and to get you all informed on what we know, as we're running a lot of tests right now. By tomorrow, some of the results will be back. We'll be able to tell you more, but I just needed you to know that the process has started. We are going to do everything that we physically can. This is one of the best hospitals in London when it comes to premier care. The Royal London Hospital is recognized for groundbreaking care and technology when it comes to these babies."

We were in the right place with the right people that could help her. What if I had given birth at the community hospital that was near my house? It was a smaller hospital and less equipped. That thought gave me a tiny bit of hope. The conversation ended, and I still had a lot of questions. But I knew she didn't have the answers yet, and I needed to be patient. I had to wait at the right time to ask the questions that needed to be asked. The doctor left my side. I watched her go from one baby's cubicle to another, checking them all out. You could see this lady cared so much about these babies that were in her care. She moved from one cubicle to another, looking at them and untangling some wires in some of them before she eventually left the room. When I first came into the room, there were no parents in there. By the time she left, there were about three mothers in the room sitting by their baby's pod. One was reading a magazine. The other one looked like she was lost in prayer in her own world. The other one just literally was just staring at her child.

As I looked at them I thought, *Oh my God, they understand how I feel. We are going through the same experience and the same emotions.*

I looked at these mothers holding on to every shred of hope. All of them were sitting there, not knowing what tomorrow would bring. It kind of made it feel real. Nobody else understood how I felt but these ladies in the room.

On my way out, one of them looked up from the magazine that she was reading, and she nodded to me. That nod said a thousand words.

Without any words at all she said, "I feel your pain and I know how you feel. I know, because I feel exactly the same. We're all in this together. This is going to be our home for however long our babies are here."

I nodded back, acknowledging her tenderness. I knew that this woman, without words, knew and understood me more than any person ever would that day. We were in the same predicament. I made a mental note to speak to her some other time. My gaze landed back on my child one last time before leaving the room. I took in what the doctors were telling me. I watched her little chest willing for her lungs to grow and for her heart to just start beating right. I was lost in thoughts of my child and her needs.

"How is she doing?" someone asked from behind me.

I knew that voice. It was her father.

"As you can see, she can't breathe. She's on life support. They've run some tests, and they won't get them back until tomorrow."

As I was speaking to him, my voice broke. We went over to her pod, and he stood as close as he could. I was trying to read his face to gauge from his reaction what he was feeling, but he had this poker face. It was hard to tell what was going on in his heart and his mind.

He went around the crib, looking at her.

"She's so little," he whispered.

"I know. She doesn't even look like she's ready for all that is happening to her right now," I replied.

He went around the little pod, taking in every sight of this little person we had both created. He again apologized for not being there at the delivery.

"It's fine. I understand."

Honestly, in my mind at that moment, that was quite irrelevant in the scope of things. What mattered most was what was right in front of us. I watched him look at his child. I looked at her, and I looked back at him trying to just make sense of the whole thing.

"How do you think we're going to get through this? Just look at her."

"You have to be positive. You have to be strong for her," he assured me tenderly.

Emotionally, he was much stronger than I was, and I was glad that he wasn't breaking down or losing hope. Even though we weren't in a relationship, I needed his strength at a time like this.

He interrupted my thoughts by saying, "I'm going to be here for her. I'm going to visit. I want to be here for you as well. We will go through this together."

Whether I believed it or not was irrelevant; just hearing those words gave me a small measure of comfort. He knew I was going to need all the help and the support in the coming days, weeks, and months.

"They want to see us tomorrow. The moment I know, I will update you. I need you to be there so we can hear about everything together."

I didn't trust myself to go through that on my own but I was kind of bracing myself for what was to come.

I continued, "But at the same time, you have a choice. Only if you want to."

"I will be there," he said while standing alongside the cubicle pod, looking at her.

We stayed like that for quite some time, just taking in the sight that was in front of us. We watched every one of her movements in silence. This was the child that we had made, and she was fighting for every breath that she was taking.

The nurse came over to check up on her.

"This is her father," I told her.

They exchanged greetings. Then, the nurse then told him that she was responding to treatment. She wasn't out of the woods yet, but at least she was responding to the breathing machine. It all looked good. It was as if they were professionally taught to not say too much. They could speak to you for ten or fifteen minutes and still not be any closer to giving you a definite yes or no. I listened to her go on with the same stories as before about how they were fighters. As we both listened to her, we looked at each other, passing knowing glances. We were praying and hoping that that would be our case in our minds.

So she went on to tell us how to clean our hands, and she ran us through all the health precautions.

"Do you want to touch her?" the nurse inquired.

"Am I allowed to?"

"Yeah, you can touch her, but you have to wear a new pair of gloves."

As I began pulling the old gloves from my hand, she brought me another.

She did the same for her father and said, "Be careful. Touch her as gently as you possibly can."

She opened this little tiny hole in the cubicle, and I put my hand through. I touched her little fingers. The moment I came into contact with her body, it felt like I couldn't hold it in. I just cried and started talking to her. Feeling her skin for the very first time inspired new emotions that I hadn't yet felt. I watched as her father did the same on the other side. It was one of those sights that would have been amazing to capture; the emotions we were feeling clear on our faces were priceless.

With tears running down my face, I stroked my baby's fingers. She didn't respond. It was as if no one was touching her. Part of me thought the moment I came in contact with her skin, she would somehow know that Mommy was there. That Mommy was touching, that Mommy was having her first skin to skin contact. Even though it was really gloves, it didn't matter. But she didn't realize. The nurse stood there and looked at us. She gave us all the time we needed, after which she came and closed both of the openings.

She looked at us and she said, "Now the journey begins. She's going to need both of you to be strong for her."

And then she walked away.

We stood there for another few minutes, not talking, just looking at our tiny daughter.

A few moments later, he turned to me and said, "I'm leaving now. Call me if you need me. Call me if anything changes, whatever time, night or day. Just call me."

"I will," I whispered.

He took a final look at her and then turned towards the door. I watched him retreat through the sliding door, out into the corridor. My gaze reverted back to my child.

"That was your dad. That was your daddy."

I felt like I was introducing her to the one other person who was going to love her as much as I did. I didn't know how he truly felt about her since the pregnancy was unplanned and thrown into both our lives. I knew what I felt for her, but I didn't know what he felt at that moment in time. But from what he said and the concern he showed, it felt right to tell my child that that was her father.

I rambled on about who he was and that he didn't live in London, that he lived in another country on another continent. But I really didn't know what was going to happen between the two of them. All I knew was that as the heavens looked down on me and my child, I made one solemn promise right there. I promised my child that I was going to love her and be there as long as I had breath in my body.

I didn't want to leave her. My mother's heart had awakened. I didn't want to leave her, and I sat there for some time until the nurse came.

It was nearly 2:00 a.m. when the nurse approached me.

"You need to get some sleep. You can't sit up all night and not rest. Then, you won't be able to face your day tomorrow. Then you won't be able to produce milk, because your body will be so tired. And she won't be able to benefit. When you take care of you, you are taking care of her. You're going to have to eat, sleep, be hydrated and take care of yourself. So I'm going to need you to go back to your room in the maternity ward. They haven't discharged you yet. They will be doing so soon but for now you are going to go. I'm going to have to ask you to go get some rest by tomorrow. We will find you a place in the mother and baby resting area where you can have a bed. So when you want to rest, you can actually go in that room and extract milk for her."

"Can I come back in the morning?"

" Yes, you can. But for now, just like she's resting, you need to rest as well."

Truth be told, I was so tired. I took one final look at her.

"Okay," I said, as I sat back into my wheelchair.

As she was trying to get me out of there, it felt like it happened too quickly. She was briskly wheeling me from one side of the room. As I left, she pressed the button to open the door, and I turned back to take one final look at my baby's incubator. It felt like I was leaving a part of me behind. It took all of me not to just jump out of that chair and run back to my child. This feeling of separation, this feeling of being taken away from my baby was just so painful. I didn't think leaving her the first time would affect me like that or hurt so bad.

As soon as the door was open and she reeled me out of the room, I burst into tears. I cried as this other male nurse came to take over for her to wheel me back to the other side of the hospital, where my room was. I think shame was gone. Composure was gone. Everything was gone. I put my head in my hands, and I cried. I was being taken away from my child into this other place where they were going to take care of me with all the medications that I needed. My heart felt like they were forcing this separation that I wasn't ready for. Even though I knew it was the best thing to happen, because they were right. I had to look after myself. I still couldn't control what my heart felt. Every beat of my heart yearned to be with my child.

I got to my room and climbed into bed. I didn't want to eat or drink. I just wanted to be left alone to take in everything I had seen. But the nurse came into the room to get me settled in and to wish me good night.

"How is she doing?" she asked.

"She's got so many wires going through her and she's on life support. I got to touch her, but I don't think she knows I'm there."

"That's day one. It gets better after today. I promise," she said, "Now you get some sleep. Are you hungry?"

"No, I am not. I just want to get some rest; I am so tired."

As I was talking to her, more tears filled my eyes. It felt like I had cried more in that twenty four hours than I had ever cried in all of my life. I settled into my bed in the fetal position that I had come to know whenever I was hurt or dealing with a situation that was beyond my control.

In my head, I was pleading with Allah. I was praying earnestly, asking him to save this one person that meant everything to me. If there was any exchange to be made —my life for hers— I would have gladly done it. As I laid there lost in the bargaining stage of grief, that was more powerful than anything I could ever muster to do for my child.

Then, sleep overtook me. The last thing on my mind was the picture of my child in her incubator. The love of my life was born. The most important person in my life was here. And, for that, I was grateful.

One thing I knew beyond a shadow of a doubt was that my life was never going to be the same again. Life as I knew it was gone because no matter the outcome, good or bad, I was never going to be the old me.

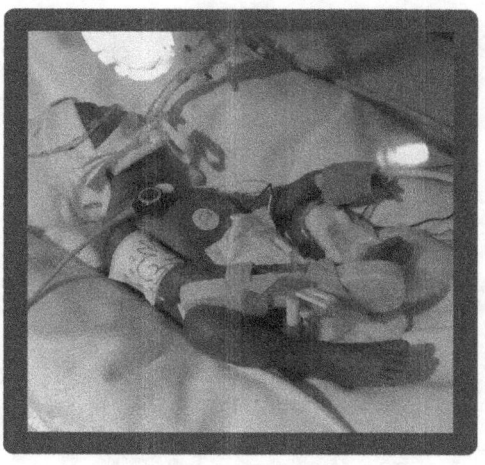

9
24 Hours to Live

The next day, my friend came back to get me from the hospital. I was allowed to go and get all my essentials. I was ready to come back for a long stay with my child. Before leaving, I was put on a steady dose of domperidone to help with my milk production as I scrambled to get things in order. The milk produced for the first days after birth was called Colostrum. It contained antibodies that would protect her fragile body from disease and infection and activate her underdeveloped immune system. In my case, it was like liquid gold. On my ride home, I passed the pharmacy. I bought a manual breast pump, in preparation for my body to be able to produce milk that my child would feed on. In the meantime, they were going to give her other milk that was donated by other women who were in my situation but were producing way more milk than me.

Before returning to the hospital, I stopped by the salon. When I walked into the shop, they didn't know how to treat me. They could tell I was heartbroken, and I must have looked so fragile. I was scared. I was nervous and everybody just wanted answers that I couldn't give. They all knew I had given birth after only twenty four weeks; nobody was expecting the baby to come this early. I tried as much as I could to be positive and relax as the doctors told me. I quickly delegated everything to my shop manager, because I knew I wasn't going to be back for a while. My priorities had changed overnight. I had a sick baby in the hospital who needed her mother. She needed me. Nothing else was going to come before her.

While there, I was delegating the duties of the shop, trying to get things in order so they could efficiently run the business in my absence. In the midst of that, my phone rang, and it was my baby's consultant from the hospital. She called to tell me that they were ready to have that meeting with me. They had done some tests and the results were back. That afternoon they wanted to see me and possibly her father along with the doctors that were going to be caring for the baby. I listened to her on the phone telling me to brace myself and come with an open mind. I wanted to know exactly what was going on. It felt like something had happened, and they didn't want me to know.

I broke down in the middle of the shop over the phone, and she tried to comfort me saying that nothing had happened.

She assured me that it was just something that they needed to do, and they would prefer to have both parents attending. We scheduled a time, and I told her I would be there. As I put the phone down one of my workers saw the fear on my face. I had never had a problem answering my phone as a business woman, especially when I had two shops. My phone was constantly ringing off the hook. But after that phone call, I did not want to pick up. My mind ran wild with scenarios of what could happen. I dreaded the moment they told me to get to the hospital immediately, because she was no longer alive. The fear of losing her swallowed me whole as I looked at my phone.

Even with this fear, I had an important call to make. I dialed his number, doing my best to follow the doctor's request to have both parents present. He picked up on the second ring, and I relayed the message that the doctors wanted to see us that day at around three thirty in the afternoon.

I remember saying to him, "You're welcome to be there if you want to. If not, it's still not a problem. I'm still going to attend and find out exactly what was going on with my child."

"I will be there. Like I said, Roza, she's my child, too. I'm going to be there for the both of you."

We ended the conversation, and I hung up. On my way out the door, I gathered some of the things I needed from the shop. I made sure the register was all accounted for; I was happy that I had a good team of hard-working professionals who could run the shop without me.

I got back into the car, and my friend was patiently waiting for me. She still wouldn't leave my side. I believed she was praying to her God the whole time I was inside, because she never lost her positivity. I sat there as we rode to the hospital, and I couldn't stop crying. It felt like I was bracing myself for the worst that was to come. I was crying for the news that I was about to receive.

She did all she could to calm me; again, she started speaking faith, positivity, promise, hope, and mentioning her God in every sentence. She told me how he could do miracles, and she was confident that her God could do anything. I realized for the first time ever that I didn't mind her sharing those comforting words. Before, when clients and friends tried to share their faith with me or tell me the miracles and wonders they had experienced with their own eyes, I wasn't in a place to receive it. But now, knowing that everything was out of my control, I welcomed it. In the flow of our conversation she reminded me that I had to tell my family so they too could be in prayer for my baby. It hadn't even occurred to me to call them. I didn't have the words to tell my family and those closest to me, because everyone had questions. I had many questions myself; most had no answers.

I thought to myself, *I will wait until I feel ready to tell my family, because right now I'm just a nervous wreck.*

Finally, we reached the hospital, and I couldn't wait to see my child. I went in through the front door, to the front desk. My heart was beating and pounding out of my chest.

The first question I asked the nurse when I reached the desk was, "How is she doing?"

She looked at me and said, "Who?"

"My child."

In my head, everybody knew she was mine. But this nurse clearly wasn't there on the day I gave birth to her.

"Remind me of her number and I'll find out for you."

By this point, I hadn't given my child a name yet. They gave her a number, and that was how they referred to her. After everything was confirmed, she gave me the okay to go back to see her. Before going back, I looked over at my friend one last time, as she couldn't come back with me. I could tell from her facial expression of comfort that she would be waiting when I came out. I went into the special changing area and followed all of the precautions. I put the protective overalls on top of my clothes, disinfected my hands, got my hair out of the way, and made my way to the sliding doors to where my baby was.

The room was so serene, almost like everybody was scared to make any noise. As I scanned the room, I saw some mothers sitting by their children; some were faintly humming, and some were talking quietly to their babies. Others were sitting there looking nervous and fearful. You could read all kinds of emotions in their eyes.

When I reached my child's incubator, the first thing I realized was that her tiny body had these jerking movements. She would move her leg but in a very awkward way that made me realize that maybe she didn't even know she was doing it. The coordination was all wrong. I called the nurse and asked her to come over.

She came over and I said, "I just got here, but I realized she's moving. She just flexed her leg."

The nurse listened and responded with a reassuring tone, saying, "Oh yeah, that's normal. It's nothing to worry about. These newborn babies have spasms and uncoordinated movements. It's the brain working; don't worry about it. It's all going to be fine."

When she finished speaking, I looked over her shoulder to the clock and asked her to let the consultants know that I was there and ready for our meeting. She noted that down as I took a seat and focused on my child. I just sat there watching her. This was the second time I was seeing her. And if the first time didn't register, this really dawned on me. I can't remember how long I was sitting there praying in my head, talking to her, watching every move. I was watching her little heart beat through her chest slowly in a rhythmic kind of way.

For the second day, I was lost in thought looking at my child when I heard, "How is she doing?"

I turned around and her dad was there.

"Have you seen any of the doctors?"

"The nurse knows we're here. We will speak to them soon. I wonder what they're going to be telling us today. I am so scared."

"Don't be scared. At least today, we will know exactly what is going on. Just be strong, and be positive."

The conversation ended, and we stood there in silence. Somehow the silence was comforting. At that moment, I wished I had telepathic powers to speak to my child like only a mother could.

A few moments later, the same nurse that I had spoken to earlier came over and notified us, "The doctors and the consultants are ready to see you now."

I knew we were waiting for that but the moment she said it, there was no going back. It seemed like the longest walk following the nurse out to the room to the conference area that led to the doctor's office. There were three doctors present: a female one that was in charge of my baby's case and two other doctors that were there to help her with the test. They specialized in interpreting the various scan results. As we entered the room, all three of them got up and introduced themselves. The main consultant was a neonatologist, who was usually the most knowledgeable member of the team. She came over and shook my hand to introduce herself as the others introduced themselves to my baby's father. Once we were done with introductions, she gestured for us to have a seat.

I was anxious, so I got right down to business, "How is she doing?" I asked.

"She's doing as expected," when she said that, I wasn't comforted, because I didn't know what to expect.

She continued, "We will keep you informed of what's going on at all times. We will not give either of you any false hope, but at the same time we will be tender enough not to eradicate all hope and positivity."

When she finished the speech, she glanced over to the other doctors and they handed her this paper that she looked over. She reached for a file, the one that contained everything concerning my child.

"As I go on," she said, "if there's any questions you have, please feel free to stop me. Ask me right away, because I do understand it's a lot to take in. We do understand that most of the medical terms you will not understand," she paused for a moment before continuing, "First of all, as you or know, your baby was born at twenty four weeks and two days. She is severely premature weighing only six hundred and thirty grams, which is just over one and a half pounds."

She went over more of the basic information that we already knew like the ventilator and the irregular heartbeat before telling us that my baby suffered from something called apnea.

"Apnea is an episode where the baby forgets or stops breathing. The baby's breath will shallowly drop for about five to ten seconds and then pick up again. This is very serious, because this can affect brain function and possibly cause some neurological and developmental problems."

As she was talking, my heart was beating so fast. None of this sounded good so far. I felt my palms sweating profusely. I had never had anxiety like that. I'd been nervous in situations, but this was far worse. I couldn't bear sitting there, hearing what she was saying, and trying to connect what I had seen in the NICU. I wanted to know how long she was going to have tubes in her throat, nose, and every other part of her body.

"We're not really sure, because unfortunately, there were a few situations in the night where her heart rate and oxygen level dropped dangerously low. We will keep watching over her recovery."

Her dad took over asking, "So taking all of that into consideration, what do you think will happen regarding her breathing and her overall health?"

The consultant looked us straight in the eye and said, "The next twenty four hours are critical in helping us determine where we're headed with her. If she makes it past these next twenty four hours, there will be a little more hope. But if she keeps deteriorating like she did last night, we're in for something else."

As she said that, my tears started flowing uncontrollably. I didn't think I could even sit through a whole meeting. Just hearing her say that my child had twenty four hours tied to her existence in this world broke my heart. Again, I put my head in my hands, and I started sobbing. How could this happen? Why was this happening? I didn't realize I was speaking out loud.

Her father tried to reach over and comfort me while the consultant was there profusely apologizing for everything. They were all trying to reassure me that these things happen, and they really didn't know the cause of it.

The lead doctor told me, "Your baby was really fighting to stay alive, and she pulled through every time we were about to lose hope. I do have to continue and tell you everything that you need to know about your baby. Do you need time to collect yourself?"

"No, I don't need a break, just tell us what's going on," I replied, and did my best to regain my composure.

"Okay," she said, "after we reviewed the test results we found that your child suffers from chronic lung disease of premature babies, the medical term is Bronchopulmonary dysplasia (BPD). This is when a baby's lungs are not fully developed, and it causes a small opening in the heart. It is very common in low-weight infants born more than two months early. Your baby also has a murmur and a condition called Patent Ductus Arteriosus (PDA). It's a congenital heart defect in premature babies."

We listened with the same look of bewilderment on our faces; she clearly sensed it, because she began to draw out a picture to explain it to us better.

As she drew out the diagram she spoke, saying, "Ductus arteriosus, which is the vessel connecting the pulmonary artery to the descending aorta, fails too close. So it's like a hole in her chest, and because it hasn't closed properly, it allows some of the baby's blood to bypass the lungs. If untreated, it can lead to pulmonary hypertension, cardiac arrhythmia, or congestive heart failure."

Hearing this, I thought to myself, *Oh my God, this is unbearable.* The doctor went on to explain that ninety percent of babies born prematurely had heart murmurs with this problem. Finally, we had arrived at the point that was most interesting to me: options.

"We can do an echocardiogram, which uses sound waves to capture motions in the heart. This will help us find out exactly what's going on, because the conditions she has can cause an enlargement of the heart. In some cases, it's severe and will require a surgical procedure called a PDA ligation. This will help us insert a catheter into the femoral artery or vein to close the opening. If she had gone to full term it would have closed up on its own but that was not the case, so it will need a little help."

I couldn't make sense of any of her words. My heart dropped into my stomach.

"Your baby's heart is larger than usual and if we can't repair it with the ligation procedure, the worst case scenario will be an open heart surgery."

Again, I burst out crying, because in my head all I could picture was my poor fragile baby going through open heart surgery.

Almost against my will, I blurted out, "I don't think she can go through that."

The doctor tried to reassure me by saying, "That is the worst case scenario, but I do have to tell you so you can prepare yourself, because according to the x-rays, the hole is quite big."

"When would she have to have this open heart surgery if we're going to do it?" I asked her.

"Well, as soon as possible. We'll give her some time to gather her strength back, because she had a really rough night. But as soon as the doctors get together and see how her levels are, we will set a date to have the surgery done."

I sat there wondering how my baby was going to survive this because she was already having a blood transfusion, because she didn't have enough blood in her body. I couldn't fathom the thought so I sobbed. I looked over, and for the first time, I saw worry on the face of my baby's father. Nobody wanted to hear that surgery would happen for a little baby that was barely moving or breathing on her own.

The doctor gave us a moment.

When she felt like we were ready to continue, she asked, "Do you have any questions?"

"How many babies have survived this procedure?"

"Well, it all depends on the baby. It varies from one child to another, but we have had a good rate of babies recovering from this surgery. I am fully confident that if we do it quickly, it will definitely help the breathing and respiratory problems. Because your child has respiratory distress syndrome, RDS, the chances of her getting better without treating the heart murmur are very slim."

I looked at her, fear coursing through every part of me and said, "In your professional opinion, what do you think we should do? Are there any other less invasive procedures that you could do before thinking of surgery?"

I knew I was clutching at straws, but I needed to know.

And again, she looked at me and repeated, "The hole is severe. We recommend a surgery that could give us the end result we want, and to not go through so many avenues that may fail."

I said, "Okay."

"With this kind of situation, the child may grow out of it years down the line, but she will also have respiratory problems. Like when they have colds or flus or any kind of respiratory problems, it will be more severe than a normal child that was born at full term."

I watched her telling us these things with so much ease and poise. I supposed it was a part of that profession to be very much in charge of the situation and remove emotional feelings and attachment. No matter how hard it was, she had a job to do. And part of it was telling us the most devastating things about our child. You could see she could feel our pain, but she had done this a thousand times during her career. I had to commend her. She was so professional and empathetic at the same time. It was written all over her face.

"My second concern—"

My baby's father stopped her, "Can we talk more about the heart condition later on? You can go on now. But later on, once I read about it, would you be able to, you know, give me more in depth insight into what we're actually looking at?"

"Of course. By all means, I'm just giving you a synopsis of what we're dealing with, but feel free to call after you research and find out more about everything I'm telling you. Anytime you're ready to have another sit down, I'll be here. We have a meeting every few weeks to sit you down, and tell you what changes have happened, good or bad.

The second concern is that the tests have shown that she has something called retinopathy of prematurity. This is a blinding disease that is caused by abnormal development of retinal blood vessels in premature infants, especially those born before thirty one weeks, weighing less than three pounds."

When I heard blindness, I was thinking that this conversation had no silver linings. It was one bad report after the other; would she have any good news for us at this point? First, it was the heart; now, it was the eyes.

Again I blurted out without fully realizing I was talking aloud, "Is she blind?"

"Well, it's too early to say, but I'm going to be very honest with you. It can cause impairment to her vision or even blindness. We've seen certain situations where the babies have never recovered their vision."

I do not remember exactly what I said or did, but I know I was on the verge of going frantic.

I recall the doctor trying her best to calm me saying, "I cannot tell you right now if she's going to be blind or not, but I can tell you, it causes abnormal eye movements called nystagmus. It causes cross eyes called strabismus and a severe nearsightedness called myopia."

I sat there listening to these "best case scenarios"; if she wasn't blind, she was going to have these conditions. Another condition she mentioned was leukocoria, which was curable but would add another procedure to the growing list. The worst case was blindness but the best case didn't sound much better either. The treatment would be a laser therapy that burns away the area around the edge of the retina, which has no normal blood vessels. That procedure could save the sight in the main part of the visual field, but at the cost of peripheral vision. The thought of her eyes being invaded brought me to tears. This was becoming ridiculous. Everything they were saying was leading to the fact that I was going to have a severely special needs child who would need help every single day of her life. There were five different stages of this retinopathy of prematurity. This fragile newborn was between stage four and five.

From our earlier introductions, I knew the team of doctors specialized in neonatal care. They brainstormed to come up with the best solutions to fit the child, according to their gestation period and condition.

"Do babies ever fully recover from this after the operation?" her father asked with a voice heavy-laden with overwhelm.

"Again, it varies from one child to another. Sometimes they do, but then the infants can be of a higher risk later on in life. Even if they don't go totally blind, they can be at a higher risk of developing certain eye problems. In many cases, they can be treated or controlled."

As much as I wanted to know everything that was happening to my child, a part of me wanted to just leave the room and not hear anymore. I could tell there was more to come.

I braced myself in the seat and asked, "Is this the worst of her conditions right now?"

"I wish it was, but there's another concern that we have as well. She has something called PVL, periventricular leukomalacia. This is an injury that affects the brains of premature babies. The condition involves small areas of the brain tissue around the fluid-filled areas called ventricles. The damage puts holes in the brain. It's as if it's poking holes in the brain and leaving gaps; it causes a nervous system dysfunction that affects brain development and mobility."

"Can you explain that better?" I said, between my tears.

"It's a neurological problem that can affect the vision and eye movement and cause trouble with movement and tighten muscles. In addition, it can lead to developmental delays, which means the child's brain function may be slower than that of a full-term child. And she will likely have mobility problems. She may have impaired coordination. Babies that suffer from PVL sometimes have problems like speech impediment. Some of them are even non-verbal, because the part of their brain that deals with speech and facial movement is not fully developed due to those holes in the brain."

I had to stop.

My head was spinning as she spoke and I probed, "What are you trying to tell me? That she's going to be disabled? Is that what you're saying? That she's going to need help getting from one place to another. That she won't speak, walk, or talk? Give it to me in layman terms. Help me to understand."

She looked at me and said, "That is a possibility, but we don't like to get to the end before we even start. But yes, these conditions can lead to a situation where the baby later on in life will need around the clock care."

"So is there any treatment for PVL?" I asked.

She clarified, "There is no treatment to cure PVL. Babies that suffer from PVL may need special care after discharge from the hospital, or for the rest of their lives. Some of them do get better with physical therapy, occupational therapy, and speech therapy."

I felt like I was finally getting a scope of everything, and it was starting to make sense why they thought she wouldn't make it past the twenty four hours. If my baby made it, there was a chance that she would be disabled and paralyzed with breathing tubes, respirators, and oxygen tanks.

The image filled my heart and mind with horror, and I cried out for help, "Oh, doctors, you guys have got to help me. Please, do whatever you can to help her. Please do it."

The situation sounded hopeless, and I sat there crying, absolutely devastated.

Again, I had to gather myself, because she had a little more left to share.

She said, "Those were the major concerns; some of the lighter ones are a urine blockage that she has had since birth. She hasn't emptied her bowels.

She hasn't urinated because the opening of a private part where the urine should pass was also underdeveloped. The urine blockage condition is caused by Spina Bifida, which can affect the spinal cord."

I can't recall her exact wording but she continued, "Urine blockages in newborns can be serious. In a case where it threatens the life of the baby, they will have a fetal surgeon do a surgery to insert a shunt —that's a small tube— to correct the problem causing the blockage. In other words, because she couldn't naturally push the urine out of her system, especially with her private parts not being properly developed. It was very important and not invasive, so we already had it in the works. At some point they will have to find other measures, but that was one of the less invasive treatments that they could use at the moment."

I sat there thinking that it was unfair that my baby couldn't even do the most basic things that we take so much for granted. I had to force myself to return to the conversation.

When I brought my attention back to the doctor, I could hear her saying, "During the night, she has developed a fever. This indicated that there was obstruction in the urinary system, and they had to do something quickly to relieve her of the buildup of urine in her bladder. The urinary problem is called Hydronephrosis; it is the enlargement of the renal pelvis. This is the basin in the central part of the kidney where the urine collects and hydronephrosis can occur in one or both kidneys. Both kidneys were affected in your baby."

As I listened to her, I thought to myself, *How can a urine blockage have anything to do with Spina Bifida?* I had heard of it before, but didn't know much about it.

So I asked, "How will this affect her spinal cord?" Before she finished I added, "I know the spinal cord is very important for mobility. And I've heard of situations where people have literally been paralyzed for life."

Her reply was brief but enough to put it all together for me, "It's like a domino effect. One affects the other.

The last time I saw her, it looked like she was developing a skin condition called Jaundice, which causes a yellow discoloration of a newborn baby's skin and eyes. Often, it develops because the baby's blood contains an excess of Bilirubin. This is known as Hyperbilirubinemia."

It was a never- ending circle. I didn't have a clue exactly what I was to expect regarding her skin and the coloration, but it was apparent that she didn't look like a normal baby. I thought her coloring would change on its own.

When she mentioned that, I raised my hand and asked, "Will this affect her skin? Because it looked like you could literally rip it up if you touched her."

"Her skin is thin because the outer layer and the middle layer are much thinner and less developed in premature babies. Your baby has fewer layers of skin because she was born early and never developed those extra layers that a full-term baby does. This is also why the chances of them contracting a disease through their skin is very high compared to a full-term child."

I nodded as she spoke and became crystal clear on why they took all the precautions and made us wear a covering to see the babies. As a stylist, I knew how important the hair was, but I didn't realize the severity of this skin issue until now. There are over thirty two layers of skin on a baby born full term and less than five in newborn babies. Her toes and the tips of her fingers were so red, and I worried it was hurting her. I knew every inch of my baby; I had taken a mental picture of her and was revisiting it often as the doctor spoke.

I forced myself to stay present at the table as the doctor moved from the skin issues and told us, "There is a high chance of cognitive or hearing impairment, because she was sixteen weeks premature. She could be partially or fully deaf, but this is something that we will find out later on. We haven't quite done the test yet."

At this point, all I wanted the doctor to do was keep quiet. I wanted this meeting to end. I felt like I couldn't take any more. Every word that came out of her mouth was a blow to my heart and mind.

I looked at her and said, "I cannot wait to see my child again. I just can't believe this is happening. This is just devastating. Why is this happening? Why me?"

"Babies of African descent are born prematurely more than babies of other ethnicities. It's nothing that you have done wrong. There are still trials and investigations being done to find out why this is. Because you are of an African descent, your chances of having a premature baby is actually a bit higher than other ethnicities."

After offering words of comfort, she started to wrap up the meeting. She could tell we had heard enough for the day. The other doctors were just sitting there, exchanging glances, writing things on paper, and passing it between themselves. For a minute, it felt like I was alone in this room with this doctor. I couldn't take my eyes off her. Every word she said was accentuated like she had a loudspeaker. I can't explain why, but every word went through my ears and into my heart.

"That's all the investigation and the results we have today. I know we're going to have more as we go, and I'll update you as the information comes. Normally, it's every two weeks when all the doctors will decide the next cause of action. But in your case, I will do my best to make time when you have questions."

While she was finishing off the conversation, my baby's father spoke, "Is there anything we can do to help her for the next twenty four hours?"

I watched the doctor take a small deep breath as if she was trying to find hopeful words before saying, "You have done all you can do for her for now. We are all just waiting for her to pull through and get a little stronger so we can do what we need to on our end."

We were exhausted, and I think all the doctors knew it.

They looked at us both and one of the doctors said, "I think it's time for you guys to go and register her name. Do you have a name for her?"

The main doctor picked up this pamphlet which gave us directions to the nearest government house, where we could register the birth of the child. She also handed us another pamphlet, which was a funeral home. The moment she handed those over, I couldn't stop crying. She was giving us hope by telling us to go register the child's birth. That should have been a happy occasion for everybody. Giving her a name would provide a sense of an identity and belonging to us before the inevitable happens. She saw us both freeze when we flipped open the funeral parlor's pamphlet.

She avoided my glance, looking down at her hand cupping mine, and softly stated, "You might want to prepare yourself just in case you need this. I'm not saying you will, but just in case you do, these are all the documents we have to give you to help you."

In my mind, it just showed just how much they thought she wasn't going to make it.

I blinked away my tears and forced out a weak, "Thank you."

That was all I could say. One thing I knew I was going to do was register her birth. She deserved to be registered. She was fighting for her life. The least I could do was to make sure that she was in the system and that everybody recognized the fact that she was born.

We got up and turned to leave the room. We weren't the same two people that came into the room. Our shoulders were slouched, as devastation and hopelessness was written on our faces. What we heard was absolutely abysmal to the natural mind. Our child was suffering and we could do nothing but stand and watch. I had never felt so helpless and so useless in all my life. My mind replayed the doctor's statement. *If she makes it, due to all of these conditions, her quality of life could still be affected severely.* There was nothing she could do. My heart was already shattered. My baby was twenty-four weeks old, and she had only twenty-four hours to make a turn around.

We needed a miracle.

10
THE GOD OF THE CHRISTIANS

When we came out of the room, I couldn't even explain what I felt. I looked over at her dad and said, "Can you go and be with her for a minute? I'll be there soon." I couldn't stop the flow of the tears. It felt like all I was doing was crying. It was as if it was the only comfort I found. When I cried I was letting out what I felt on the inside, which no one knew or understood. It felt like it was the only way I could communicate. I had no control over it.

Before this, I wouldn't cry in front of people. I considered myself to be very strong and emotionally sound. I wasn't the type of person to break down, but at this point I didn't care.

I knew I needed to collect myself, because it would be a whole different scenario to see her again, knowing what I knew now. I remember turning away and walking briskly; it still wasn't enough. I needed to get out of there to collect my thoughts. I started running down the long hallway, and as I ran down the hall, my eyes were clouded with tears. My mind was doing a three sixty turn. I didn't even realize I was bumping into people, because I wasn't looking where I was going. All of a sudden, I came down the stairs and became immediately captivated, as the place I had landed in demanded my attention.

There was a room for people of the Muslim faith to go and have their time of prayer, and there was a Christian room as well. There was a third room for anybody who wanted to go and seek some spiritual guidance or counsel. I stood there for a minute and looked at these rooms, and all I could hear in my head were the voices of clients and friends who had in the past been telling me about the God of the Christians. They spoke boldly of Jesus who was a miracle worker. He was the only God I knew of that performed miracles with signs and wonders. All of these thoughts were in my head and without further ado, I charged straight into the room for the Christians. Up until today, I still don't know why I didn't go to the Muslim room, because that would have been the one that was calling out to me. But the Christians were adamant about their God being a miracle worker, and I hoped they were right.

When I walked into the room for the Christians, there were women bent low in prayer. I looked at them, but I knew I wasn't there for them. I walked straight down to the altar. Right there, I knelt to pray. I have never been more honest, more authentic and desperate in all my life. I was helpless and in dire need of aid.

I threw my hands up in the air and said, "My name is Rose Cox, [my maiden name], and Rose was the name that family and friends called me. You do not know me and I don't know you. But I need you. Your people have told me you are the God of miracles. You are the God who heals. You are the God who saves."

I was talking to the God of the Christians as I was balling from the depth of my soul. I continued to Him, "I need you to come and save my child. I need you to do a miracle for me. I know I'm not deserving, because I haven't lived for you. I don't acknowledge you as God, but I am desperate right now. I would do anything you want me to do."

Desperate times called for desperate measures, and I found myself standing there making so many promises to this unknown God.

Among those promises, I remember very candidly saying, "If you come and do a miracle, if you come and save her, I will give both of our lives to you. I just need you to come."

I spoke to the God of the Christians with every fiber of my being. When I finished making all these promises, I just fell down on the altar and continued to cry.

I've always heard of peace, but I suppose my first experience of true peace was right there. This calming feeling overcame me, one that I couldn't even put into words. I didn't even know it was called peace. All I know is that this calming sensation came over me. As I was laying on the altar, pouring my heart out to the God of the Christians, I called out to him.

"Jesus, you need to come and help me since you've helped other people."

As I laid there, this feeling took me over; it felt like I went to sleep. I just relinquished everything. I felt this lightness of my heart. I do not remember for how long. But when I came back to my senses, these ladies that I had met in the room came over and were praying for me. They had their hands on me. This time, I welcomed their prayers with an open heart, letting it touch the deepest part of my heart as they called upon the same God I was petitioning to. They didn't know me or my situation but they were interceding on my behalf. It seemed like they prayed forever taking turns.

While one was agreeing in prayer, the other was calling out and speaking in a language I didn't understand. It was just all so new and so weird to me to be so open right then. A part of me knew that there was nothing I or the doctors could do. The next twenty four hours was a touch and go kind of situation. The only person that could do something was the God of the Christians. So while they prayed, while they petitioned for me, all I could do was lay there and allow them to.

In the midst of their prayers I was drawn into this bubble; it was a sensation of peace and calmness where everything just seemed to have stood still. I didn't know it then, but I had just invited the supernatural into my natural state of life. That was the Genesis of my walk with the God of the Christians, the almighty God. The creator of this world, the God of Israel. The God of Abraham, Isaac, and Jacob was about to turn my life upside down with his presence. He was about to do what no man could do. He was about to do what no doctors were qualified to do. He was about to do a miracle that I had begged and asked him for. On that day, my spiritual life began, to the glory of God.

After that time at the altar, I went back upstairs. I felt a little bit guilty about the way my heart was so much lighter after leaving the Christian prayer room. On the walk to the NICU, all kinds of thoughts went through my head. *How can you even feel this much peace and tranquility when your child is up there fighting for her life?* That was among the first of my thoughts. What was this sensation that I was feeling? It was so alien to me. How could I be feeling this? I entered the room where my child was. By now her dad had left, which made me happy because it gave me the opportunity to be alone with her. I needed to spend some time alone taking her in. It was different this time, as now I knew what was wrong with her. I looked at her little head and prayed asking the God of the Christians to help make her brain start functioning correctly. I wondered what was going on in her little mind. I watched her heart beat, rising steadily up and down, and wondered how big the hole inside it was. I wondered exactly what part of the lungs were affected. When I looked at her belly, I wondered how much liquid was collected from her bladder. I looked at every part of my child, taking in all her features and all that was wrong with her.

It was a different feeling this time. I prayed for her while remembering the words that I had spoken on the altar and repeated them over her. I spoke to my child and petitioned for her.

Eventually, the nurse came and said, "It's been a long day for you emotionally. Why don't you go home and get some rest?" As she said this she looked down and smiled while saying, "Oh, you're producing milk."

Unbeknownst to me, as I was standing there, my breast had started lactating. I was so into my own head and feelings that I had even didn't realized that the medication had kicked in. It was as if it was happening to somebody else, because I didn't even acknowledge the fact that my shirt was stained with breast milk.

"Now before you go home, do you mind coming with me so we can collect some of the milk? The first milk is very good for a child. It will help her grow. It's got good fatty acids in there that we need."

I gladly agreed because I felt like I was starting to do something in my own ability to help her. I wasn't going to go home regardless of how tired or emotionally drained I was. I followed the nurse out into the mother's extracting room.

We went in, and she set me up. As she was getting things in order for me, she was telling me to have faith and that God is able. A part of me wanted to share with her that I had visited the God of the Christians, but I held that back. It was too personal. It felt like it was just me and Him that needed to know. Even though she was talking to me about Him, I wasn't ready to share that with anybody. For me, that was a big deal. I had just literally left my God and went to the God of the Christians to ask for help and petition for my child's life.

I listened to her as she encouraged my heart and prepared everything for me to help my child with the milk. She took the electric machine they had in the hospital. She got me all covered and put a pillow behind me to support my back. Then she took this suctioning tool that had a baby's bottle at the end of it and placed it on my breast, making sure it was positioned right on my nipples.

She looked up at me and said, "Brace yourself. It's going to hurt, because it's your first time. Remember why you're doing it and who you're doing it for. That actually helps," she paused, as if having a great revelation, then resumed, "Wait a minute, let me go get you a magazine. That should take your mind off things while you're doing it."

I thanked God that she had brought the magazine because when she turned the machine on, I felt this yank. My breasts were very tender. The pull of the machine was so painful, I screamed.

She quickly started reassuring me, "I'm sorry. I know it's painful, but you will get used to it at some point. Right now just breathe, and let the machine go to work. We can collect enough for today, very soon."

I listened for a moment then said, "Why don't you just do the other one at the same time? Let me go through the pain once rather than do one breast and then another."

It was excruciatingly painful, but when I remembered that my child was in that incubator fighting for her life, I thought, *What pain is she going through? What discomfort is she having at this moment?* When I looked at it from that perspective I was ashamed that I was trying to make a big deal out of suctioning and extracting some milk for her. That quickly made me gain my composure and want to extract as much as I could. She got another machine ready quickly and did the same application on my left breast.

And all of a sudden, after a few pulls and tugs, I saw this white liquid, gushing out of me into the bottle. It was one of the weirdest feelings I ever had, because that was another indication that I had given birth. This was milk. My body was producing for my child.

It was as if somebody had woken up my milk reproductive system and said, "Hey, get up. It's time to produce milk now that the baby's born." I sat there looking like a cow that was being milked with a breast pump to each breast. My pain was no longer significant, and I was grateful for the milk she was receiving from her mother. It was very special to know that very soon, my child was going to be feeding from the breast of her mother. I was told that it would be a long time before she could even learn how to suckle my breasts. But knowing that it was my milk that would help her in this fight was personal to me.

The nurse left the room as I pumped and popped back in occasionally asking, "Are you okay? Do you think it's enough?"

I responded, "No, I can go on."

I had milk. It felt like the more that it extracted, the more I had. It was just flowing. I think I filled about four bottles in one sitting. My pain, fatigue, and emotional distress were gone. I was just happily sitting there, extracting milk for my child. Eventually, I ran out of milk.

She came, took off the machine, closed the baby's milk and said, "Follow me."

We went to another room where they labeled and tagged everything. She proceeded to take the tags and wrote my name and my baby's incubator number.

She said to me, "Are you going to have a name for her?"

"Yes, I'm registering her tomorrow."

"We will need the name to tag all her food. It would be safer to use the name than the numbers. We don't want to have any complications."

She showed me how to write my name, date of birth of my child with her incubator number, and put the tag on under specified milk bottles that were going to be frozen for future use. Once she showed me all I needed to know, she opened a huge freezer. It had two of the biggest doors I've ever seen. It was one of the industrial ones. On one side it held thousands of little milk bottles that were frozen with names and tags.

My mouth dropped. "Is this all milk?"

"Yeah, this is all milk for our precious babies. Some of them were extracted by the mothers, and some were donated by other lactating mothers who are actually producing more milk than normal."

It looked like this yellow liquid. Cow's milk was normally white. The milk here was so rich in color, especially when they're frozen and concentrated. I was taken aback by the thought that these women were coming in to extract milk and storing it for their babies, but also giving some to other mothers that didn't have enough for their children. It was one of the most selfless acts.

The nurse showed me exactly where mine was going to be and she said to me, "Whenever you finish, this is where you tag and put your baby's milk. One thing I have to tell you, please don't let it go empty. We need more than enough rather than the lack of it."

That was my first time doing something that was considered normal for a mother. The first thing you wanted to do was feed your child according to the baby books. It's one of those beautiful experiences that every mother looks forward to after the birth of their child. Until then, no one had mentioned anything else about my milk, because we were all just waiting for it to kick in. But now I was being introduced to another part of the hospital. There was a waiting room and some relaxing music playing. There were magazines around. The TV was on, and there were two ladies in a chair. One of them was asleep. The other one was just kind of rocking herself. It looked like she was praying and murmuring things underneath her breath.

I asked the nurse, "Can I sit here for a while before I go home?"

"Of course you can," she said, "Your baby's sleeping. Let her rest. You can stay here if you want, but I recommend going home to get some sleep. You've been through enough today. Tomorrow is another day."

As she walked away, I took my seat in one of the chairs. It was nice, and very comfortable. I grabbed one of the covers and sat there listening to the soft calming music. It did great for my senses. I was having a Zen moment. I hadn't realized how emotionally drained I was. Not only had the information and the meeting with the doctors really drained me, but extracting that much milk literally did a number on me. I was absolutely shattered. I quickly reached into my bag, remembering that I hadn't taken my pills for the night. I reached into my bag and excitedly looked at my medication. My body was producing milk, and I needed it to continue. I grabbed a bottle of water from the fridge that was in the room, and I took my medication. I returned back to my chair, and I covered myself again and got into my relaxed position. I didn't even realize I had fallen asleep. I was so tired. I woke up to somebody tapping my shoulders.

It was nearly four in the morning. It was the same nurse.

She said, "You fell asleep. Do you want to get up and go home?"

I looked at her and I said, "I am so tired and I live about twenty five to thirty minutes away. I really don't want to go home now, do you mind if I sleep?"

"Are you sure?" she asked.

"Yeah, I don't mind. I will just sleep here and see my baby in the morning before I leave."

"Okay, I'd rather you be safe here than driving in this condition."

She helped me get tucked back in and then she left the room. I snuggled right back and went right off to sleep. I wasn't in my own bed but sleep literally took me over. It was about seven o'clock in the morning when I was forced to wake up to the sounds of footsteps and people talking. It was early in the morning, and fathers were coming to see their babies.

I went to the toilet, washed my face, straightened myself up, and then I went to see my baby. I was still very tired. I felt like I hadn't slept enough. You could look at my face and know I was tired. As I approached the door one of the nurses realized that I hadn't changed my clothes.

She came over and said, "I saw you here yesterday. You still haven't been home?"

"No, I slept in the mother and baby's room."

"Okay, do you want to see her like this? I would highly suggest you go home, take a shower, have a bit of rest, and then come back."

Ignoring her, I said, "How did she do last night?"

"Well, you can come in and see her. The doctors haven't done the rounds yet so we really do not know."

She opened the door, and I went in to see her. I didn't want to leave. I didn't want to go home and get that phone call. I wanted to be with her for those twenty four hours. Even though I wasn't in the same room with her, she was on my mind, especially when I was extracting the milk. But my baby occupied my thoughts every minute of every hour.

I stood there and watched her, and it didn't look like much changed. She was still in the same position. But just knowing that I was there with her, I wasn't far away. It felt like I was with her in spirit, even if not in the same room.

I sat down on the chair, just staring at her, and the nurse came over.

"The doctors aren't going to do the rounds until around ten o'clock. I would say, take this opportunity to go home, shower, have a little bit of a nap, and then come back. I'm sure they will be ready to tell you exactly what's happening."

I looked at my child and knew the nurse had a point. I didn't want to be sick or suffer from lack of sleep and be of no help to my child. I got up, turned my back, headed out the door, and my breasts started leaking again. I forgot I was about to go home. I went straight into the mother and baby's room. I got a machine already. I sat there and milked for my child. I was so happy that my body was finally doing something right. I felt like it had kind of betrayed me by letting my baby out so early and not caring if she was going to live or die. Shortly after I had extracted, it was as if that was my body's way of saying I'm trying to do right. I tagged them, put them in the freezer, and cleaned up the place. Then I grabbed my bag and went home.

When I got home, all I wanted to do was have a shower and go to bed. I stood under the shower, letting the water run on my face and my body. I cried again because of everything that had happened the night before that came flashing back in my mind.

I cried in the shower for a while before I dragged myself out, climbed into my bed, and fell asleep.

I slept for so long. I didn't hear my phone ring. I didn't hear a knock on the door. Apparently, my friend had knocked on the door, and I didn't even hear it. I was just in this lull of sleep.

Eventually hours later, I woke up. It was mid-afternoon. I slept over five hours. I quickly looked at my phone and saw several missed calls. I scanned them all to make sure they weren't from the hospital. They were from friends and loved ones, wanting to inquire about my child. Then I remembered that I still hadn't told my family. I knew it wouldn't be nice if they found out from somebody else.

So I returned the calls, and then I called my mother. I told her that I'd had my daughter.

"What?" she said loudly and in a voice that conveyed her shock, "Tell me you're joking."

"No, the baby came."

"So where are you now?" she asked with a panic-filled voice.

"I am home, but the baby's in the hospital."

I relayed everything that had happened and all that the doctors had told me.

During my conversation with her I burst out crying again as I said, "They don't know if she's going to make it or not. The twenty-four hours ends today, so we shall see what the doctors are going to say later on."

She inquired about the father, whether he was being supportive. And I told her that he was there. He was doing the best that he could do.

She felt my burden, I knew it. She said, "I will be praying for you and I'll be praying for her every single day."

My mom reminded me of something that I had forgotten. Apparently, I was born at seven months myself. I was a premature baby. My mom told me how I was very little as well, but I was big enough to come home. I also needed some special care as a premature baby.

My mind replayed the conversation and one part rang out, "Look at you now. You're perfect. So do not worry too much. I know it's daunting seeing your child like that, but you will get through this and she will make it."

My mom gave me much hope; I guess having dealt with me as a preemie baby gave her the confidence to believe.

I got up, got dressed, and left the house. I needed to pass by the shop to see how they were doing. When I entered, the questions started. Everybody was so concerned, attentive, and caring. I was so glad for the people that were in my life at that point in time, because they understood the burden that I carried. I realized they had everything in order in the shop. They were quite busy that day, and I just didn't feel like talking to a lot of people. I didn't feel like being around people; my whole heart yearned to be with my child. Knowing that the twenty four hours were coming to an end, I quickly sorted whatever needed to be sorted and was out of there. On the way out, I called my baby's father back, as he had left messages on my phone. He was kind of worried after not being able to reach me. I relayed the events of the night: how I was producing milk and that I slept in the hospital. I was sure to update him on everything before telling him that I would see him later. I hung up the phone, jumped in my car, and went straight back to the hospital.

On the way, I called him and said, "We need to get to the place where the birth of our child will be registered."

"I'll be there."

We set a time. I told him that I was going to go into the hospital to check up on my child, and I would meet him there.

As I approached the hospital door, fear gripped my heart because I saw a woman and a husband leaving the NICU. The expressions on their faces quickly brought back the fact that my baby was on twenty-four-hour surveillance. I ran in there; my baby was just lying there and not doing too much.

I spent some time with her, and the doctors came and filled me in, saying, "There's been no progress. There's been no change."

They told me they were making plans now to have a definite day to start doing the procedures that she needed. The longer they left it, the worse it could become. I listened and signed a few papers to allow them to do more investigations that could give more answers as to what to do. Then, I left to go meet her father.

As I drove through the traffic, I was thinking of how we were about to register a child that we weren't even sure was going to make it. But I knew I wanted to do it. It was as if I was solidifying the fact that she was born into this world. Even in the worst-case scenario, I didn't want people to forget her. I didn't want to forget her myself. I didn't want her fight for life to be forgotten. The least I could do was register her.

As I pulled up outside of the building, I saw her father. We walked in together, and we told the lady at the desk exactly what we had come to do. We sat down for a few minutes. Our name was called, and we went into this room. The lady gestured for us to sit down and face her.

"We have a baby at the hospital who is seriously ill. We were advised to come and register her birth, since it had already been forty-eight hours."

She proceeded to bring out the documents. She asked us for some government issued IDs to prove identities, which we did. And so we filled out all the necessary paperwork. Her dad put his name as the father and gave us an address in America. Everything was just perfect. Then he came to a bit where you have to sign the child's name.

When I was pregnant, he thought it was going to be a boy, but I had always said it was going to be a girl. We had a deal that if it was a girl I would get to name her. If it was a boy, he got to name him.

As we were sitting there he asked, "Do have you got a name? Because if you don't, maybe we can call her Yvonne?"

That was his mother's name.

"No, we had an agreement, and you're going to honor it."

"Okay, that's fine," he said, and didn't even try to fight me on it. Thank God.

The lady asked me, "What name will you give your child?"

I took the pen, and I wrote *Tatiana Alexandra Brooks*. The name meant a lot to me. I gave her this name that was of Russian origin, after a friend that I had years before. As I wrote her name down on this birth certificate and entry of birth date, I realized that Tatiana Alexandra Brooks fit my baby so perfectly. She was Tatiana. She was a beautiful one. She was the apple of her mother's eyes. She was her mother's world. She was her mother's heart on the outside. As I wrote that, a sense of duty for my child overtook me. The fact that I was a mother really laid heavy on my heart. I signed her name and handed the documents back to the lady to be notarized. We sat in the room as she went out to do her necessary paperwork.

Her dad looked at me, smiling, "I think it suits her. I think it's a pretty name."

Thank God, I thought because we weren't changing it. The lady came back with an envelope with all the necessary paperwork in it and handed it to us. The originals were going to be sent to us at a later date. We paid the fees, thanked her, and we left. As we came out into the afternoon sunshine, it dawned on me just what we had done. I got into my car and drove right back to the hospital. When I went to the hospital this time, I was quick to go in and give them a full name so she wouldn't be known as a number anymore. She'd be known as a person now. I gave the paperwork to the receptionist, and she logged it all in the computer. I went to the mother and baby room, extracted some milk, and it felt so good to write my baby's name on the tags. They had already put her name on her incubator. My baby had a name. My baby had an identity. Now she was my child. She was my own flesh and blood.

I couldn't tell you how much those little things meant to me; I held onto everything like a promise. That day with her felt different. I kept saying her name. I couldn't stop. It felt like for the first time I was identifying with her in a different way. She was my child. I was a mother, and I had given her a name that she was going to be known by for the rest of her life. It was twenty-four hours later, and she was still alive. I was producing milk and my baby had a name.

The God of the Christians was already favoring me!

11
The Power of A Name

The following day I went to the salon. I don't know what made me do this, but I left word in the salon that they should ask my clients to keep Tiana in their prayers. I think it was because with some of them, whenever they came to do their hair or to have any service done in the salon, they had to share their faith. And we all knew them.

And there was a point in time when we had actually ridiculed them for it and called them all kinds of names. You know, we called them Bible bashers and thought they were street side brainwashers. We laughed about it and made jokes, all in jest. But now, I was going back on everything I once thought to be true, knowing I needed a miracle in my life. So I sent word for them to pray for her and went back to the hospital to pump some more milk and see her.

Around this time, I was praying generic prayers, like, "Help me, Lord. I am coming to you, asking you in the name of the God of the Christians."

On this particular day, I prayed with her and left. I was so exhausted, and I must've fallen into a really deep sleep because that's when everything began. I went to sleep, and had a very bizarre dream where I was on the beach, one of my favorite places in the world. I've always been very fascinated with the sea, maybe it was because I couldn't swim. I was on the beach and all of a sudden I took off, hearing this voice.

I didn't see anything, not a single human form, yet I heard the voice saying, "Stop. Stop running."

I turned around, yelling, "Leave me alone, just leave me alone."

Then I continued running. I felt the fear gripping my heart, because I realized it was weird to hear a voice with no figure of a human body.

The voice said, "Why are you running?"

And again I replied, "Why don't you leave me alone? Why are you chasing me? What have I done to you?"

During this conversation, I was still running. I even picked up speed at one point, but the voice wouldn't relent. It was in my ear telling me to stop.

I felt the sweat dripping down the side of my face as I ran until I couldn't any more.

"Who are you? Stop following me."

I was looking around for help, scanning the beach. There was no one there to call out to, no one to cry out to for help.

When I reached my point of exhaustion, I turned around and yelled out at the open space, "Why are you chasing me? Leave me alone. Who are you?"

A part of me expected to see someone when I turned around, but there was nothing. It was an ordinary beach, and everything was normal except the voice in my head.

I asked again, "Who are you? Why are you chasing me?"

And he replied, "You asked me to come."

"No! I don't know who you are. I don't know what you are. I never asked for anything like this. Who are you anyway? Why would you be chasing me? If I say let go, will you leave me alone?"

I can still remember that voice as if it happened yesterday. It was as if time stood still, and everything on that beach was quiet for me to clearly hear him with no disruption.

The voice said to me, "I am the way, the truth, and the life."

Then I woke up drenched in sweat.

It all felt so vivid, it didn't feel like a dream. It felt like I'd actually taken a jog down the beach before coming home. I looked around my room, feeling terrified, because I knew the dream sounded like more of a reality than any dream I had ever had. The statement was on replay in my mind like a broken record: *I am the way, the truth, and the life. I am the way, the truth, and the life.* I had heard that somewhere, but I didn't know where. I laid there recalling the conversation in my head.

All of a sudden, I felt it quietly in the middle of my heart. It went off like a lightbulb in my mind. I knew without a shadow of a doubt that the one that I had gone to, asking Him to come and do what no one could do, was there in that dream with me. It was the God of the Christians. I burst into tears, because I honestly didn't know what else to do. I didn't know how to deal with all these emotions and feelings that were going through me. I was so scared; I couldn't go back to sleep like that. It was around 3 AM when I picked up my phone and started calling everyone who I thought could help, but no one answered. Everybody was in bed. Out of desperation I called a few of my clients that I knew were committed to the God of the Christians. I didn't explain to them what happened.

I just asked them to call me back, ending each message with, "I need to speak to you. It's urgent."

I needed to know exactly what was going on and who better to ask than my clients who knew me well?

Before I went back to sleep, I said, "If you are who you say you are, and that dream was you telling me who you are, help me to understand."

I easily drifted off to sleep and had a really lovely and peaceful rest.

The next day, I woke up late and rushed to the shop to make sure everything was good there. None of the phone calls I made came back to me. Then, I remembered a lady that was a client. We had hit it off so well. She was always preaching and sharing her faith, and she was one of the most persistent ones. Out of nowhere, I thought, *Why not give her a call?* She lived around the corner from my shop, and the dream was so present in my mind that I wanted to share it with somebody before I forgot any part of it.

I didn't call her right then; instead, I remember calling one of my friends saying, "Listen, I'm having some strange dreams that I don't understand."

But my friends weren't spiritual. We were the true definition of the statement "birds of the same feather, flock together."

My best friend at the time was actually a Muslim girl from the same country who had no idea about the God of the Christians. I knew it was tomfoolery to even think she would have any advice for me regarding this in our phone call. I remember telling her; however, there was no help there, because she didn't even have a clue what to say.

Her response was, "You know, you're in London. You're under a lot of stress right now, and your mind might be—"

I interrupted her saying, "Listen, I know this isn't a coincidence or another meaningless dream. This happened."

I let it rest for a moment, and I went to the hospital that day with the dream locked in my mind. I attended to my child and knew for a fact that something was about to change. I had to do something about it.

Finally, I called my client who I thought of earlier and left her the same message. As fate would have it, I received no answers from anybody, at least not until in the evening. I went home and my phone rang, and it was one of my clients, not even the one that lived near the shop.

I said, "I need to tell you something, but I need you to keep it in confidence. I don't want anybody to know. This is just between you and I."

She became frantic and worried, asking, "Roza, what's going on? What's going on?"

I told her about the dream.

When I finished, she said, "Oh my God, Roza, what have you done?"

"I'm like, what do you mean? What have I done?"

"Did you call upon the name of the Lord Jesus Christ?"

I was quiet for a minute before saying, "I think I did more than that. I went down to the hospital prayer room, went to the altar, and just called out to Him. I poured my heart out and told Him I needed Him."

"Well, let's just say you have opened the door to the spiritual. You have called unto Him, and He answered. God is faithful. When we call upon His name, He answers, so you'd better get ready. I truly believe that was Him in the dream, and I believe He will be speaking to you again. If you would, please write your dreams down so you don't forget them. But I do think he will pay you another visit."

When she said that I was scared and queried, "But why does He have to visit in my dreams? Why can't He just do what He has to do?"

She went on to explain, "The God of the Christians works in mysterious ways. He works in signs, wonders, miracles, breakthroughs, and victories."

As she said that, I was thinking, *There's more to come*. I knew exactly how I had felt in that dream. So vulnerable, alone, and scared. Everything and everyone was taken away, and it was just an audience between Him and I. I thanked her and put the phone down. I couldn't escape it. I prayed before I went to bed; this time, I asked Him to tell me whether it was Him or not.

I went to sleep and the same dream happened again. This was the second time, a replay of the first one. Exactly like how it happened on the beach, running away. The second time, I woke up and was drenched in sweat. I jumped out of the bed, took my clothes off, and started crying again thinking. *What is happening to me? This can't be real.*

I wasn't ready for this spirituality. I wasn't ready for God to enter my natural state of mind and living. I was a helpless mother in the most desperate time of my life, and I made promises. I asked for help so sincerely out of the depth of my heart, but I really wasn't ready for what was happening. Again, I felt like I needed to reach out for help.

I knew my clients and their numbers, but I didn't know their homes. I wanted to just drive to somebody and have them explain to me in detail what was happening and what I was to expect. I had so much going on as I was worrying about my child who wasn't out of the woods yet. On top of that, I was running a business and still trying to keep my head above water. I had too much on my plate, but I knew I couldn't just ignore this part of my life. I wanted to ignore the dream and continue taking care of my child, while doing everything in my power to keep the business and my life afloat. The thought crossed my mind to just pretend this never happened.

For a minute, that thought stuck in my head. I replayed the thought, *I'm going to push this out of my head.* I was torn, a part of me wanted to know what it was, but the other part wanted to deny it and disbelieve exactly what was happening. I went about my day's routine and did everything I'd done the previous day before returning home to rest.

Well, on the third day, the same dream happened. When I woke up this time from the same dream, I was like, *Okay, that's it. I cannot do this anymore.* I wasn't only irritated; I was angry. I felt out of control. I ran my business and personal life the way I saw fit, so anything I couldn't control became an intrusion. The rebellious part of me wanted to pretend like it didn't happen and put it all back in that box, lock it, put it away and be done with it all. But it wouldn't on that day.

I remember I was in the shop checking things out.

I got a phone call from a client of mine and she said, "I was praying this morning, and the Lord put you in my heart, He told me to tell you that He will do miracles."

"Okay," I said, brushing it off like I'd done after the third dream.

But something in me snapped. I just burst out crying.

"What are you crying about?" she asked.

I told her how bad things were with Tiana, how I had this dream for the third time, and how it was freaking me out.

She listened and then said, "You need to meet with a pastor or somebody who knows the Lord intimately and has a relationship with Him. I have a very strong feeling that He's at work right now. You can't stop it. The easiest thing for you to do is to actually accept the fact that He has come to answer your prayer."

She was clearly excited for me, but truth be told, I wasn't. I felt this dread coming over me. I couldn't let myself be happy about it, because even though I'd asked for it, I really didn't think He would answer. I really didn't even think He would listen, because I had never served Him. I lived the life I wanted. I partied hard. I had fun. I drank, I tried some things that I shouldn't have. The life I lived wasn't pleasing to Him. I saw myself as filthy rags. To think someone so sovereign and holy as the God of the Christians would even want to have anything to do with me seemed impossible. But I had come to Him in my time of need.

As I put the phone down, I promised myself that I was definitely going to see a pastor, but there was a problem. I didn't know any pastors. The only time I had visited church really was for a wedding, an engagement, christening, or whatever precious occasion that my clients would invite me to. I asked a few people if they knew a reputable God-fearing pastor. Because if I'm being honest, I did hear some stories about pastors and preachers doing "certain things" outside the will of God that made me have a certain perception of pastors. They weren't the most trustworthy people. There was a priest of the Catholic church that was less than a five minute walk from my shop.

One of the girls recommended him and said, "You know, he is very well known in our community. He's a very humanitarian priest and is very involved in the lives of the parishioners. You would bump into him at the supermarket; you see him at christening parties; you'll see him go into people's houses to pray for them. He was a very relational kind of pastor."

I made a mental note that if I didn't have any other suggestions, he would be the one I would go to. I was going by his reputation, because I didn't really know the guy personally.

I went about my day at the shop before going to see Tiana as usual, and she wasn't making much progress or moving that much. We were just waiting for her to make a change. The twenty four hours were over and done with, but she hadn't gotten any worse or any better. I went about doing things that I had to do just to maintain the normalcy of our lives.

A few days passed, but I still couldn't get the dream out of my head and I was having others as well.

In the dream the voice said, "I will not share my glory with anyone."

And I was thinking to myself, *What does that mean?* I remember one day walking into the shop, and there was this particular client of mine who was always coming over to have her hair done. I was doing her daughter's hair, and we just clicked. Before having Tiana, she would invite me to church nearly every week, but I'd politely decline. Or she would ask if I wanted to come for a prayer meeting. She had always been one of those relentless and borderline annoying ones before now. While doing her hair I thought to myself, *Oh God, I'm going to get it today.* I didn't even want to tell her right there in the shop, because I was very private. I was guarding it very close to my heart, and it wouldn't have even made sense to have the discussion in the shop. They all knew what faith I was.

As I was doing her hair, the thoughts were running through my head. She asked about how the baby was doing. She asked about what was going on and everything. Without even meaning to, I filled her in. Then I said to her, "When I finish your hair, do you mind if we have a word?"

"Of course, what's going on?"

"I just need some advice on something."

"Okay."

I finished doing her hair and I remember asking her to step outside. We went out right in front of the shop very close to the carwash that was next door, and then it felt like a tidal wave of water broke shore within me. I found myself telling her everything about the dreams I was having and what happened at the hospital.

Then I said to her, "I need a pastor. I really need to speak to someone about it."

While I was speaking, she grew so excited and her eyes widened.

She agreed that I needed to speak to a pastor; then she said, "We need to start calling upon the name of the Lord for this because clearly He's involved. He's reaching out for you. You cannot turn this down. This doesn't happen every day," she was repeating what the other ladies had said, "I have been praying for your salvation ever since I met you and you became my hairdresser. It was as if God put you into my heart and gave me the burden to pray for you."

I was shocked. It had never occurred to me that not only did she share her faith to me in public, but in private, she was praying for me. I could see from the genuineness in her eyes and her words that this was true.

She said, "Why do you think I keep inviting you to church and all these spiritual functions? It was because I'm always stepping out in faith, asking you and believing that one day God would work into your heart enough for you to want to come. I couldn't force you. God doesn't force Himself on people. He will give you an open door of salvation, and then it's up to you to take it or reject it."

That made sense to me because it felt like even though He had appeared to me in the dream, it was an answer to a prayer. It was the answer to the call at the altar; He didn't just come to me out of nowhere. He wasn't imposing Himself on me. To hear her say that made me kind of reflect back to the words I had spoken at the altar. I begged Him to come. I pleaded and said everything I could in my desperate moment. And there He was.

I listened to her speak, and eventually she said to me, "I have a man of God. He is my pastor, his name is Tony King and he is the senior pastor at New Hope revival church international. That is the church I attend. It is a Bible believing Pentecostal church. It is a church where we love, honor, praise and worship in the name of the Lord, Jesus Christ. He shepherds the flock that the Lord has put in his care in a way that is absolutely commendable. I trust him, and I know you can trust him too."

As she said this I was thinking, *I told her I was going to go down to the Catholic church and speak to the priest. But if she can arrange a meeting, I would love to meet the pastor.* She was so excited.

I remember her saying, "I'm going to go home and pray some more about this. I'm excited to see what God is about to do."

It was a wonderful conversation, and I felt so relieved after I spoke to her. This was someone I had known for some time. I could vouch for her relationship with the Lord, because nearly every week she would pop in —not even to get her hair done— but to invite me to go out with her to church or a spiritual function. Her persistence, generosity, character, and her love for people struck me that day. I knew I had made the right choice by talking to her. I knew that this man of God that she trusted in was somebody I could actually talk to. Before she left, she promised to call me back with a day and a time for us to go see pastor Tony. And so I went back in the shop, relieved that things had gone really well.

I left the shop after that encounter and ran right back to my child. At the hospital, they were putting together a timeframe of when to do some of the operations we discussed. They didn't know which one to do first, because all of them were connected. Fixing one thing could affect another. When I went to the hospital that day, I had a brief encounter with Tiana's consultant at the door. She asked me to pop into her office before I left.

I went into her office and asked, "How are you doing?"

A part of me wanted to share what was happening in my personal life, but I think I wanted to know exactly what her faith was first so I said, "I'm fine."

She explained, "We're thinking of doing the operation to close the heart murmur; then to give her a laser for her eyes; and then move on from there."

We discussed all of that but I was so distracted, because there was a question that burned in my heart, to ask her if she believed in this God who was introducing Himself to me now.

When she finished speaking, I said, "Can I ask you a question?"

"Yes."

"Well, this is nothing medical, and feel free not to answer. I'm just wondering."

"Okay, go on."

"Are you a Christian?"

She looked at me curiously and said, "Why do you ask?"

I said, "Well, no reason. I just want to know."

She looked at me right there and said, "Nope, I am not into spirituality at all. I am what you would call an agnostic or an atheist, because I really do not live my life in accordance with any spiritual law, principle, or regulations. I totally believe in science, because it's what I see in my work as a doctor that gives me the answers to the questions that I seek. I was born into a spiritual family, but that is what my family was. I do not practice."

She basically told me she was not the right person to even share this information with. Maybe if her response was different, I would have shared it and gotten her perspective of things. But I admired the fact that she was very honest.

So she asked me in return, "You're Muslim, aren't you?"

"Yeah, I was born into a very pious Muslim background, like my family. My grandparents are very well-known for their religious views back home in Africa."

We chatted about it, and she ended with, "To each their own. If you want to pray for your daughter, according to your beliefs, feel free to do that."

She went on to remind me that they had prayer rooms down the hall. I finished that conversation with her and thanked her for everything she was doing for my daughter. Then, I went back to the room and looked at my daughter. She wasn't growing, but she was feeding on my milk, which was amazing. I was producing so much, and I couldn't see any change in her body.

I was told that very soon, hopefully, she would start putting on weight, and we would be on the road to recovery.

A few days later, I got a phone call that Pastor Tony would see me at a certain time. Getting that information was awesome. I took the address and went to meet with him. My friend who referred me to him was with me. When we sat down, I told him about what was happening. I told him this would be very difficult for me because of the repercussions that would happen. I really don't think I would have willingly just accepted Christ under any other circumstances. I guess this was the only way that I was going to open my heart up to Him.

Pastor Tony listened for a while, and then said, "I'm so glad you came. I'm so glad you're doing something about it and not just trying to ignore it. Because things like this don't go away. God has given you an open invitation, and you would be foolish not to take it," he continued sincerely, "Before we go any further I want to ask you something. Are you ready to accept the God of the Christians as your God? Are you ready to commit your life and that of your child to Him? Are you ready for Him to be a part of your life? It is a big decision that one has to make in order to be a part of the Christian faith."

That was shocking to me. I didn't know any of that, because in the Muslim faith, there was no reciting of any acceptance prayer or creed to join the religion. It was just a case of, if you believed you read the Quran and prayed five times daily. I didn't know anything about the Sinner's Prayer that was recited in Christianity. I wasn't expecting that.

He said, "This is something you have to really think about. It's not something you take lightly, because once you confess it with your mouth, it's very serious. The Lord does honor that."

I remember saying to him, "Can I just think about it until tomorrow?" I wanted to know what I was getting myself into.

That didn't deter the pastor, who simply said, "Okay, I'm going to be praying for you tonight. I'm going to seek the Lord for you. You can call me tomorrow and tell me the decision that you've made, but I will tell you this first..."

I had a feeling that He was going to do something amazing this week. I knew He was sending me out into someone else's world. I just didn't know it was going to be a case like this.

"...I can tell you right now, right here, that if you were to give your life to the Lord Jesus Christ, it would be the best decision you would ever make. Not many have the testimony of calling upon the name of the Lord and he came."

I could hear him talking and saw the seriousness in his face, but I had questions.

I told him about the other dreams and he said, "You must make a decision."

I remember saying to him, "Keep me and my child in prayer and I'll definitely call you and let you know."

I thanked him and my friend who came along with me. Then I left with his number in my phone.

The conversation replayed in my mind on the way to the hospital. I sat there looking at my child, thinking, *Oh my God, I have a decision to make for the both of us*. I had this gut feeling in my heart that it was going to make such a huge difference in our lives. As I stood there, I prayed. I remember the prayer Pastor Tony spoke before I left the meeting. He asked God to speak to me and reveal Himself more. He ended the call asking for God's will to be done.

I found myself repeating those words to my child that night, and then I left. When I went home, I knew I needed to spend time with God. I'll never forget.

I sat in the middle of my bed and said, "God, if you can hear me... You know everything I have done today. I have embarked on this journey of knowing who You are, and I've been told that I have to recite the Sinner's Prayer to be a part of your kingdom. I need You to help me make the right choice. If You want me as part of Your family, let me know."

When I went to sleep, it wasn't peaceful. I was tossing and turning. I think it was because my mind was so fixated on this big decision that I had to make. I'd woken a few times in the night and then gone back to sleep.

The weirdest thing happened in the morning.

As soon as I opened my eyes, it was as if somebody just spoke to me from the depth of my heart and said, "Yes, you will accept the God of the Christians as your God."

It was so clear and simple; then a peace came over me. It was an absence of worry, burden, or unrest. I felt relaxed and lightweight after that thought entered my heart. It made me feel like I was making the right choice. I remember picking up my phone and leaving a message for Pastor Tony. I wanted to see him as soon as possible. He agreed to meet on a Friday at my house.

That evening when Pastor Tony came to my house with my client and friend, they came into my room, sat down and said to me, "You made a choice."

"I've made my decisions. I am ready to accept the God of the Christians as my God. I am ready."

When I said that, it was as if this peace was taking hold again.

The pastor held my hands and prayed before telling me to repeat after him.

I followed his instructions and repeated, "Lord Jesus, I come to you with all of that. I am asking you to forgive me, Lord, forgive me of my sins. Lord, wash me clean. Lord, bring me into your family. Lord, today I profess with my mouth and sincerely with my heart that you are God. You, the one true living God. Thank you for making yourself known to me. Thank you for all that you have done for me from today on, I will serve you. I will worship you. I will give all the glory to you for being the God of my life. Amen."

Every word was falling into fertile ground in my heart, because I wasn't taking this lightly.

I meant every word of it.

I was always that kind of person who gave a hundred percent of myself in everything I did. I was that kind of person. That was how God made me. I knew in my heart that if I was to give my life and my heart to him, that was it. The pastor prayed again, committing my child to the Lord. He then told me it was time to seek the Lord, to get to know Him. I didn't even have a Bible. He told me if I didn't have one, he could get me one at church. He also invited me to come to church that Sunday. It was unbelievable.

After the prayer I looked around and took in the fact that I had just accepted the God of the Christians into my life. It felt surreal. It felt different. I was happy. I felt like I had done something right. The first right thing I'd done, probably ever. It just felt so good. There was a joy in my heart that came with it. Now I needed to read the Bible to get to know God and His word. I'd have to memorize scripture, because that would help with my prayer life. The pastor was telling me all these things. He was encouraging me to engage in the gathering of the saints at church, because that was what God wanted us to do. He was just running me through all the things that were expected of a Christian. As he was speaking, I was thinking, *Yeah, my life is about to drastically change.*

Sunday was like my recuperating day for rest and shopping. Sunday was a day when I did whatever I wanted. It was my day off. He was sitting there, telling me I have to go to church on Sunday and pray. They have prayer meetings. I think it was on a Friday or a Tuesday night. But it didn't matter. The joy in my heart was just absolutely amazing. I went to sleep that night with a smile. There was power in the God of the Christians, and He was now my God. This was soothing to my troubled soul.

The next day, I wanted a Bible. I knew I wanted to know more about him. I was already curious. I wanted to read the word and find out what I had gotten myself into. I had all these questions so I went and purchased a Bible that was broken down into the simplest terms. At the Bible shop, I was looking at all these other Bibles, and they were just so confusing. Especially the King James version.

What type of English is this? I was thinking.

I think the guy in the shop realized that I didn't have a clue, because he approached me and said, "You're looking for a new Bible."

"Yes, I am. But I haven't got a clue what to buy. And they all seem so hard to understand."

"Are you a new believer?"

"Yes, I am. I actually just accepted the Lord yesterday."

His face broke into a grin as he said, "Praise God, hallelujah."

I stood there thinking, *Okay, calm down, dude. Like really is it that much of a big deal.* I wasn't used to the response that I was getting. To be honest, it was all lovely and encouraging, looking back at it now.

After he took a moment to glorify God, he said, "Okay, this is what I would suggest. Do not buy anything too complicated that you don't understand. You're taking baby steps right now."

He helped me choose the right Bible. As I held it and walked out of the place, I was thinking, *Oh my God, this is just amazing.* I didn't even own a Quran. I was grateful for that, because I don't think I'd be able to handle seeing the Quran *and* seeing the Bible without feeling guilty. Actually, there was no guilt at choosing this part. I was going to see it through, because this was my choice. No one forced me into it. If anything, I wanted it. I asked for it, and the God of the Christians —being so awesome— came to me. Now that He was my God, I was going to give Him all of my time.

I took that Bible with me everywhere. It was in my car. It was in my bag. It was everywhere. Anytime I had a spare moment, I picked it up and started reading it. The stories were fascinating. All through the years, you hear this story or that one, but holding the book in my hand and actually starting from Genesis was different. I would start from page one and go all the way, right down to the last page. I refused to rush it. I wanted to take it in. I wanted to understand what it said. I wanted to understand the contents of what it was.

I remember the pastor telling me, when you begin on this journey, you have to ask God questions. You have to ask Him to give you the knowledge and seek the wisdom. He was still faithful to answer every question that you had. I started reading the Bible that same afternoon I bought it. I even called and told the pastor that I purchased a Bible. I told him that I had already started reading it. It was eye-opening.

And he said, "I've prayed for you, and now I need you to stand in prayer."

In my head, I was thinking, *Okay, how many times do I have to pray? In the Muslim world, I know it's five times a day. But how many times am I expected to pray as a Christian?*

The pastor must have read my mind through the phone because he said, " You pray when you can, but sometimes you do get the urging of the Holy Spirit who actually helps you and gives you the nudging's to pray."

I was thinking, *Who is the Holy spirit?*

Again I think he read my mind and said, "There's a whole lot you need to know. I will help you understand all of this. My God is a triune God; He is one God made of three co-equal persons called God the Father, God the Son, and God the Holy spirit. The Holy Spirit is the spirit of the wisdom and truth of God that dwells in us. The Holy Spirit helps us to live the lives that God wants us to live."

I was actually very excited to learn this. The pastor wanted me to start praying earnestly, not only for me and my salvation, but to trust God and pray about my child. My heart leapt for joy to hear the pastor say God would answer the prayers of my mouth. That was very encouraging.

He even went on further to say, " During his time in prayer, the Lord revealed to me that we have to be very prayerful because this isn't only a physical battle. It's a spiritual one. And the life of your child will be impacted by your prayers."

He gave me so much hope speaking like that.

And he said to me, "We're going to start a prayer meeting in your house every Tuesday night. I'm going to get some of the people at church to come and be a part of it. We will be praying for the general need and the requests of other people. But we will make sure that we center it around Tiana as well. Because in corporate prayer, when the children of God come together and cry out to Him, it's powerful."

He was taking every word that he heard from the Lord and trying to make it happen.

Meanwhile, I'm thinking, *Okay, I've never had a prayer meeting or Bible study in my house.*

So I asked him, "What will they need, and what will they expect?"

His reply shocked me, "Nothing, we are just coming with our Bibles to pray and see what the Lord wants us to discuss, but it will be all centered around prayer."

I agreed, with a simple, "Okay."

I went back to the hospital and this time when I arrived, I wasn't flipping through magazines and newspapers, trying to amuse myself. I had a book that needed me. I would dive right back into my Bible and start reading. Church day came on Sunday, and, as she promised, my friend came with me. She wasn't much into spirituality, but she saw something happening in me. She said she would go with me so I wouldn't be alone.

As we were driving, I thought, *Oh my God, I am actually going to church to worship God.* I woke up that morning and reviewed some of the passages I had read the day before. Some of the sentences just jumped out at me. It felt like my heart knew them. I found myself literally reading, wanting to take in the knowledge, and absorb it all.

When we arrived, the church service was about to start. Everybody was just so lovely; when we walked in they all introduced themselves. My friend and client from the salon came over and hugged us. She was so excited. I didn't understand what it meant for another Christian to win another soul to the Kingdom. Maybe Pastor Tony had told them about us coming. I don't know, but the hospitality they showed us was lovely.

We sat down and at the beginning of the service, Pastor Tony turned around and said to them, "Today, we have the honor of welcoming two people. One is a former Muslim who has just accepted the Lord a few days ago."

The room erupted into applause; everyone was praising God saying hallelujah and glory. Then he asked me to stand up and introduced my friend.

He said, "She came to support Roza, who right now has accepted the Lord. She has a premature baby in the hospital. I would like to ask each and every one of you to remember them in your daily prayers."

I stood there in awe as he asked the entire congregation to pray for me and my child. I couldn't believe that people would love and care enough to want to add you on their prayer list every single day when they were crying out to the Lord.

He ended the call for prayer saying, "In fact, they are going to start now. Please stretch out your hands. Pray for Roza, Tiana, and the journey they are on."

The whole church literally stretched out their arms toward me; the pastor also laid his hands on me and prayed. As he prayed I was thinking, *Oh my God, this guy can pray.* It was so effortless. The words just poured out of his mouth from a very deep place inside him. I was listening to him and thinking, *I want to be able to pray. I want to be able to call upon God like that. I want to be able to know God in a way that I know what to say to Him.* They prayed for some time for me and Tiana. They prayed for my walk with the Lord; then, he asked me to sit down after they said 'Amen.'

The sermon that day really struck my heart; he spoke on the love and faithfulness of God. I couldn't be distracted, because I was so hungry for the Word. I think that was my favorite part of the service. He was such an eloquent preacher, and he simplified everything to the point that you understood. Sitting there and listening to this man of God go on about the love of God, the faithfulness, and the mercy of God in our lives was life-changing. It felt like the whole sermon was tailor made for me. I didn't want it to end, because he was talking about something I could relate to. He finished the sermon. He prayed for the congregation and dismissed us.

After leaving church that day I wanted to share the whole experience with my child. I found myself standing there at the incubator and just telling her how I had been to church. I told her that everybody had prayed for her, and I'm going to start praying. I'm going to learn how to pray. I told her how the Lord said he was going to perform miracles. I was updating my child on what was happening in my life, whether she heard it or not, because it would impact hers as well.

I opened my Bible and read some passages loudly to her. I don't know why. I just felt like I wanted to share this with her. It was absolutely amazing.

I called out my daughter's name to God that day. I think it was one of the first times I actually realized the true power in a name.

When you call the right one, miracles happen.

Roza Perry

12
HOSPITAL MIRACLES

I started to find a new routine as I got settled into church, prayer meetings, and reading my bible. I went back to the hospital shortly after we started the prayer meetings, and they had made the decision to start the operations and procedures. They presented me with a schedule which explained each operation and when they were going to have everything done. There were about five or six major ones that they were planning. They didn't even know how they would turn out. They had predictions based on other babies, but they couldn't give me a definite answer as to how Tiana was going to respond to it. I was very fearful looking at the paper and not knowing what was in store for my child. I gave Tiana's father a call and I told him about everything. I just wanted him to know the dates and the time so he could be there. They were meant to start in a couple of days.

Initially, in my heart, I thought I could just keep the Lord to myself. I didn't feel that it was her father's business, because he never once mentioned God or spirituality. I understood how hard it was for people to embrace it when someone changes as drastically as I had. It felt like God knew exactly the people he was entrusting me and Tatiana to, by sending my client who introduced me to Pastor Tony. She later became a close friend. I called him and my friend along with a few others from the church to update them about what was going on with Tiana. I told them to keep praying because she was about to go through really major surgeries, especially her heart murmur that needed to be closed.

I was so deflated when the consultant handed me this paperwork outlining all these surgeries that they had planned to do. The poor child was barely breathing, and she had to have a heart procedure.

Pastor Tony was very strong in his faith.

No matter what, he would reply, "I trust in God. I believe in God. And I truly do believe he will come through for us. We just need to stand in prayer.

We just need to believe. We know that He is able to do exceedingly abundantly, far above everything we could ever hope, ask, or imagine, according to his power at work within us."

He would speak faith like that. He told me to seek the Lord and pray about it, and I did that night.

I went to read my Bible, and it happened to fall open to the Psalms of David. I could relate to this section a lot because some of the Psalms of David showed the position of need that he was in that no one could deliver him. Nobody in human form could save him but God. Those were the songs that I started pouring myself into, declaring the word of God. I spent a whole part of that night seeking the Lord about Tiana when I received that information. It felt like every time I seek the Lord in prayer, a peace and tranquility fell upon me when I was done. So much so, that I started yearning for more. I started memorizing scripture. I started remembering some of the scriptures and letting them literally sing deep into my heart. When I thought about it, God gave me some form of comfort. One day, Pastor Tony called me saying he would come to the hospital to pray for Tiana. So we arranged a time, and we met at the hospital. He wanted to pray for her and lay hands on her before all these operations were to take place. I was so excited about that, because I needed this good faith before she started this journey of all these procedures.

I met Pastor Tony in hospital; unfortunately, they wouldn't let him into the room. These babies were so delicate that they were only allowing the mother and father of the baby to go inside. The nurse in charge didn't want to budge, because she wasn't in a position to alter the rules. I was just about to lose it, because my child needed the prayers.

The pastor could see how heated I was getting and said, "It's okay. I can still pray from out here."

I stood there thinking to myself, *That isn't the same as you being present and seeing her with your own eyes.*

He clearly sensed my hesitation, and we had the discussion of the omnipresent God.

I didn't understand that until he broke it down, saying, "God is everywhere at the same time. It really doesn't matter that I cannot go in the room. I can pray for each and every child in that premature ward in the hallway, and it will be the same."

I didn't want that. I wanted him to physically lay his hands on my child, but that couldn't happen. I had to accept that.

We stood outside the NICU ward, and I watched this man lay hands on the wall and pray for every child in the room. He called upon the name of God. I stood there agreeing and standing in prayer with him.

When he was finished he said, "God heard that prayer; don't be disheartened. When the time is right they will let me in."

There was nothing I could do, but I was glad that he had prayed. Then he left. This was the effort this man had made. It felt like my whole life was now centered around prayer, not only for myself and my child, but for the other babies. I was sharing these mothers' pain, anxiety, and fear of what tomorrow would bring. Some of them started looking forward to seeing each other, because we met in the mother's rooms. There we would exchange stories about our baby's developments. There was nothing that brought you closer than the pain of a baby that you couldn't heal.

There were a couple of mothers that I started building a bond with. They would check up on my child when I wasn't there, and I would do the same for them. I was spending so much time at the hospital that it felt like I lived there. I was there nearly every single day, and I wouldn't leave until late at night. I'd sit in the chair, pray, read my Bible with my child, then go home, and read and pray some more.

A few days later, I realized my fridge was empty. I had lost a lot of weight and wasn't eating right. Even though I loved cooking, the passion seemed to have dwindled away. As I looked at it, I thought to myself, *If I don't eat well, it will affect my child.* So much was happening that I even forgot to take care of myself. I would go the whole day with barely eating anything. I was literally skin and bones. That day I thought to myself, *I need to start looking after me for her sake.* I decided to go shopping to stock my fridge up; I planned to start cooking and taking food to the hospital.

It felt urgent so I packed my purse and went to the supermarket right away. I bought everything I needed at the store and then decided I wanted to go to the local market for some fresh beef, lamb, and chicken. When I arrived, it was like the ethnic market where literally everything you needed was there, but they also catered for all races. It was very busy; people were everywhere. As I got out of my car, I thought, *I am not ready to be in crowds. What if I saw someone I knew?* They would ask about my baby, since I shopped there so much when I was pregnant and before then, too. Some of them didn't even know I had given birth. I was thinking that I would do my best to make it a quick stop. No window shopping; just get what I need and get out. For some reason, I had turned into this hermit that wanted to either be in the hospital or at home. Even being at work wasn't as exciting as it used to be. It felt like I had to do it to keep the business afloat.

But all I wanted to do was be with my child in the hospital or be with God at home. Those were the primal needs of my life at that time. So, as I got to the bushes, I thanked God in my mind that I'd made it through all those people without stopping. I walked in and found a long queue going all the way out to the door. I'd made the effort to drive all the way there, so I decided to stay. So I was standing there impatiently, tapping my feet on the ground. You could tell I didn't want to be there. I looked at my phone, checked my messages, and made a few phone calls. I put it back in my bag and continued standing there.

As I was taking in all of my surroundings, this lady came to stand behind me. Instead of taking her place in the queue after the two people behind me, she wanted to talk to me.

"Hi. How are you doing?"

She had an African accent and I looked up thinking, *Here we go. One of those Africans that just wants to talk and talk and talk. I am not in the mood. I don't even want to be here right now.* It was one of those days. I didn't join the queue to start a conversation. I came to get my meat, and I was going to be out ASAP.

The lady addressed me again, proclaiming, "I have a word from the Lord for you."

"You do? But lady, you don't even know me."

I was very ignorant. No one had ever told me about a word of knowledge or wisdom coming from somebody else. I hadn't gotten to that part yet. I was still on baby steps in my journey.

She could clearly tell from my face that I was very dubious of a word from the Lord because she said, "Yeah, you are going through a very difficult time in your life right now. But it's also a very beautiful time because the Lord is all over you. I saw you when you came into the shop. And the Lord said to come and tell you—"

"Tell me what, exactly," I rushed her.

"The Lord told me to tell you not to let anybody touch her."

"Excuse me?"

"You heard me, the Lord said to tell you not to let anybody touch her or do anything to her. Do you understand that or should I go on?" When I didn't reply, she added, "God is about to do amazing things in her life. Miracles are going to be performed, and He will not share His glory with anyone."

Her words took me right back to the dream I had experienced.

"Do you understand the meaning behind my words?" she stood there, waiting for an answer.

"Yes, ma'am I think I do."

My eyes began welling up with tears.

"It is well with you. God is with you."

I fished around in my bag for a tissue.

She quickly weaved her way into the busy market, so I couldn't see her anymore. I stood on my tiptoes to see if I could see her, the tip of her head, or anything. But she was gone. I didn't even get a chance to question her. *Who are you with? What's your name? Where'd you come from? What's your relationship with the Lord? Why would He use you to come and talk to me?* I had so many questions to ask, but she was gone.

Only a few people knew that my child was about to undergo some surgeries. I stood there with my heart so full, beating so fast in my chest. I just couldn't understand it anymore. Gone was the need for the meat. Whatever reason I came to the market in the first place felt so minuscule that I left my place in the queue and started walking back to my car. That experience freaked me out. I sat in my car, thinking, *Oh my God, how can this be? Is this another side of spirituality that I don't know?*

I picked up my phone quickly and called Pastor Tony. I left him a message to call me back. I was driving to the house to unload my shopping. I couldn't get this woman out of my head. I just started thinking, *Did someone tell her something? Was she related to somebody in the shop, or someone at church, or somebody that was in my circle now? How did she know this?*

I got home, unloaded my shopping, and went straight to pray. I took it back to the Lord. I told Him what happened, as if He didn't send the lady to me.

"God, if that is You speaking, tell me. She mentioned something that I had dreamt about weeks ago, but I didn't even think it was important. But now that somebody has mentioned it, Lord, will You speak to me? I'm praying that You will show me what to do. Please let it be known before they do anything. You can see that they are literally going full steam and booking days for all of these operations to happen. I need you to speak to me."

I called my friend from the church and left a message for her to call me back. Everybody was at work at this point. From the house, I went straight over to the hospital and just wanted to see my child. I took out the paperwork with all the operations listed and looked at it, thinking, *She needs it. Without this operation she might not make it. How can You say the doctors shouldn't even do anything with her life? It doesn't make sense to me. I don't understand it.* The supernatural God I now believed in knew the past, the present, and the future. He had given His word, even though it didn't make sense to me.

That night I asked Him again to speak to me and give me confirmation. I had the same dream as before but this time I didn't freak out. A part of me expected it.

Before going to sleep, I remember saying aloud to God, "If you want me to go ahead with this and tell the doctors not to do it, you will have to tell me. Because they won't understand it. They will come down on me like a ton of bricks."

I woke from the dream and knew God had spoken this time. He did what I asked in a way I could understand.

When I got out of bed, there were messages from Pastor Tony.

I returned the call and told him what happened and he said, "We will trust in Him, period."

Well, that seems like it's very simple to him, I thought.

"If you believe that God sent a word, and he confirmed it to you, trust in Him, period. That's it."

He didn't leave room for any doubt.

So now, how would I return to the hospital and tell them not to operate on my child, because God sent word to me that this is the wrong choice? My heart raced when I realized I would also have to tell her father. Surely he would think I had lost my mind.

I went to the hospital and made an appointment at a desk to speak to Tiana's consultant ASAP. I told him it was urgent and that I needed to speak to her. They told me to wait for a while.

They passed on the message, and when I'd been sitting in the chair beside my child's incubator for an hour or so, she walked in.

"You wanted to see me?"

"Yes, I do. Do you have a few minutes?"

"Yeah, come with me."

I picked up my bag and followed her into the office.

She could clearly see I was feeling very jittery, because once I sat down she said, "What is it? How can I help you? What's going on?"

I could have just come out and said what was happening. However, because of the conversation I had with her in the past, I didn't trust that she would understand. So I took another route.

"Do you have to do all of these operations listed on this paperwork?" I pulled out the paperwork holding it in my hand.

"Yes, remember we had the meeting. She really needs to have these to have a chance at making it without operations, or we don't even know what quality of life she would live."

I didn't know what else to say. I think my words just burst from my lips, and it felt like I wasn't really in control of them. My emotions took over.

"Well, she's just too little. She's just so tiny right now. I don't think she can take anything right now, because she hasn't put on any weight. Nothing has really changed. So I want to wait. I don't want to do anything right now. I just want to give her the time to get stronger before we do it."

A part of me wanted to say, "You will never touch her to do the operation."

That was how I felt inside. But I couldn't say that to her. How would she understand? It didn't even make sense saying it to myself, let alone to this medical doctor who had over twenty five years of experience. She trusted nothing but the work that she did and the reward of seeing her patients.

There I was, someone not acclimated to the medical field at all.

But I reminded myself of what God was telling me to do, stared her straight in the eye, and said, "I don't think she's ready for it."

"Now, she needs these operations. We don't have time to wait around. We have booked the dates and we're going to proceed. I'm just waiting on the team to know who's going to be there."

"I'm not going to sign for her to have anything, because I do not think she should have it now. That's my decision."

"Well, I cannot do anything without your consent or her father's. Have you spoken to her father about this?"

"No, I am the one in charge of her. We're not even in a relationship, and he often travels back and forth to America."

She was looking at me like I was a crazy mother.

Then she said, "Roza, you've been through so much. This is a drastic life change. I do understand that, so I'm going to give you some time to think about it, but my professional opinion is that you're not making the right choice. Take some time; go home, eat, rest, and think about this properly.

"Okay, I will do that. But while I'm gone, please do not proceed in taking my child for any of these operations."

As I was talking to her, I became emotional.

She threw her hands up and said, "Okay, I will back off a few days, and give you time to collect yourself. Think about this, and hopefully come to your senses very quickly so we can proceed from where we left off."

At least she'd given me her word that she wasn't going to push anything. As I walked out of her office, I saw the concerned look on her face. I was thinking that I needed to speak to the Lord right now. I went back, checked on my child, and then jumped into my car to head home. I showered and sat down on the floor. *God, have you seen what I've just done? Well, Lord, I have asked them to stop, but I'm asking you to quickly perform a miracle. I need you.*

I remembered the Psalms where David had implored the Lord, sought the Lord, and asked Him to answer his prayers. If it worked for him, I could ask the same of Him. And so I prayed at night; I sought the Lord and beseeched Him.

The next morning, I prayed some more. I ran to the hospital to make sure that she was doing okay and that they hadn't done anything. They were doing the necessary daily checks, like checking her blood and oxygen levels. I was dreading to see this chart that they had put up on the baby's incubator to tell the parents exactly what time the operations would be done. That didn't happen that day, which I was very happy for. I spent some time with my child, pumped some milk, put it in the refrigerator and left. I received texts from Pastor Tony so I updated him on what had just happened. The next day came, and there was no operation paper. I was very happy about that.

On the fourth or fifth day after the meeting with the consultant, I was at work with a client. And now, whenever I had a phone call from the hospital, I became instantly afraid. I excused myself, went to the back of the shop, and answered.

"Roza?"

"Yes, I can hear you. What's going on?"

It was clear that she had heard the fear in my voice when she said, "Calm down, Roza."

"What's going on?" I asked her again, with my heart pounding hard inside my chest.

"Well, I just thought we should let you know something. If you can get yourself over here, we would appreciate it. But this is actually good news."

Relief flowed through me.

"Okay, what's going on, please?"

"Well, Tiana just urinated all over the incubator."

"What?" I was full of questions.

It shouldn't have been possible. They had a tube that was collecting the urine from her body, because it was putting too much pressure on her bladder and her opening. Her female opening wasn't even big enough to release anything.

"What are you talking about?"

"Roza, I don't know. All I can tell you is that you should get here right now. We've got a new set of Pampers on her, but I thought you'd want to take the sheets home and hold on to them."

"I'm coming straight away."

So I went and explained to my client that I was needed at the hospital. I grabbed my bag and washed my hands. I don't know how quick that journey was. I must have weaved through traffic. All I wanted to do was get there.

I ran through the corridor and down the stairs onto the other side of the building. As I came towards the reception, she recognized when she knew what happened.

She said, "Oh my God, Roza. Oh my God. This is great news."

"What? Wait, where is the consultant? Please tell her I'm around."

I ran right into the room to put on my protective covering and then went into the room. When I got in there, my child was laying on the new bed sheets. You could tell they were new; they were nice, white, and crisp. And she had Pampers on her. Something just looked different about her, and her belly wasn't swollen anymore.

You see, even though the urine was being collected, I think there was a residue of it. So her belly was protruding the night before.

I looked around for the nurse, who approached and I asked, "What happened? Did you guys try to do something?"

"No, actually, we didn't do anything. I was working on another child when I heard that gush. And it came from Tiana. Thank God I was just nearby. I looked and there was urine everywhere."

I started crying. The nurse explained that my baby was growing and developing. In my head I was thinking, *Thank you, Jesus. Thank you, Lord. This has to be You.*

I started texting and letting everybody know that Tiana improved. She wouldn't need any operations down there. They will have to remove the tube now and allow her to urinate by herself. I was just so excited.

The consultant said, "You are happy, aren't you?"

"I'm ecstatic. How can this happen?"

She told me they didn't even know. It was just one of those things that happened. And just like the nurse said, things are developing slowly. Her body is slowly going to come to realize it has certain functions to perform.

I had to hold it all in me. I couldn't wait to share the news with the church and tell them exactly what was going on. We were still meeting up for prayers. This would encourage their hearts to know that their prayers have been answered. One hurdle was gone!

I went home, entered the privacy of my room, and let it run out. I was so happy. I put on praise and worship music and thanked God for what He had done. In my mind, I replayed a moment before I left. It was the moment when the consultant told me that her belly had gone down and there wasn't too much pressure on her belly or lungs because of the water retention.

They were so backed up with all these operations because they were having more babies coming in. It started feeling good to call Him my God. I was seeing the fruits of my prayers. I prayed to him and he answered.

There was nothing more beautiful than knowing that the Lord of the universe —Creator of all mankind— heard and responded to my prayers. It gave me a high that I could never explain or put into words. The next few days flew by. I told my church and everybody at the prayer meeting; we were all so encouraged to stand in prayer some more. God was amazing.

My routine continued between Tiana, church, Bible studies, and work. And she eventually started gaining a pound here and there. They would weigh them every few days. And even though her progress was slow, I was just happy to know that my milk was doing its job.

The nurse told me one day that the consultant wanted to see me. I wasn't ready to have that conversation again.

And so I tried to avoid her. But I walked into Tiana's room one afternoon, and there were three nurses standing around my child and a consultant who I had never met before. Fear gripped my heart. As I walked into the ward, I thought to myself, *What's happening? Why are they all over my child?*

"What is going on right now?"

My heart was beating too fast. I couldn't focus.

"Calm down. Well, we've done the test again. And we didn't want to tell you quite yet, but we're doing a second one for a second opinion."

"Second opinion on what?"

"Well, we did the first scan, and it looks like her heart murmur is actually closed up."

"What?"

I should've known God was at work; I should have expected this. But I don't think I was expecting it to happen at that point. I was like, *What?*

"Yes, we did a test this morning. The scan came back, and it showed that the murmur had closed up. Her stats have been improving more than they were for the past how many weeks?"

This was one of the major ones that they were pushing to have done, because this would improve her blood and oxygen levels. It was the main reason why she was intubated anyway, because the air just wasn't reaching her lungs.

"Somebody needs to explain it. If you don't mind, can I see the scan and all that?"

"Of course, we've just had it done. This is the heart doctor. And we've just had another scan done. So we're going to be waiting for that to come before we can finalize and tell you everything."

"What do you want me to do?" I asked.

"Well, you can go; we won't get it right now. Because they're quite busy. But you can come back in a little while."

There is no way I was going to go back, at all. So I went downstairs, got myself some tea, sat down on my chair, and opened up my Bible. I started praying since it hadn't been confirmed a hundred percent, but my God was at work again. I delved into the Psalms. I started praising Him with Psalms of thanksgiving. I started worshipping him.

I wanted to scream and shout for joy. But I couldn't do that. Why? Because I felt like it was too soon. They were doing a second opinion. I already knew.

It was as if God spoke to my heart and said, "It's done." I just had a peace about it. I went into praise and thanksgiving even before they came back with the second opinion. They didn't call me to tell me about this because they were not sure and didn't want to give me false hope. They were trying to avoid giving me misinformation that would impact my emotional state.

And so I sat. It must have been hours before I saw Tiana's consultant walking towards me with a piece of paper in her hand. I was thinking, *Oh God.* And then behind that consultant was the heart doctor.

"Roza, we have some more great news," said the consultant.

I started smiling. I said, "It's confirmed."

"Yes. Her murmur has closed up all on its own."

Praise God.

I was so happy. I had to respect the fact that the other mothers weren't in my situation right now. And so I had to contain myself, but my heart leaped out of my chest.

And I said to her, "Oh my God, I can't believe this."

"I know. With the size of her murmur, normally you need the operation to close it. It doesn't just close up by itself."

I thanked them, and they said they were going to do a scan in a few more days just to confirm it.

God has closed it, period, I was thinking. It was so beautiful having a relationship with the Lord that no one knew about. In the physical, they look at you; they put you in a corner. They put you in a box of their own understanding while you're operating on a dimension unknown to a whole lot of people including me. I started calling everybody and texting again. Everybody was jubilating and thanking God. That was a great day because out of all the operations, that was the one that worried me the most. I was on cloud nine. I left her, went home, and had a party with the Lord. He had granted us another miracle. *I am your God. And I will forever be your God. And that's how I feel,* I continued thinking. Oh, it was beautiful. The routine continued again. Now I was beginning to see a little bit of light at the end of the tunnel. And slowly by surely, her heart started getting better. Her oxygen levels started improving drastically. Even though she had jaundice, her complexion was progressing because the oxygen was flowing in the right directions. Now they were talking about giving her some time to see if they could take the intubation off and put her on C-PAP instead. It was less invasive than the intubation.

It was amazing. I continued seeking the Lord.

And sometimes, people from the shop would come and say, "Oh, God woke me up last night and told me to pray for you."

It would always blow my mind that God loved me so much. He would put me in their minds and ask them to pray for my needs. Some of them were so spot on, because there were days when I was running on empty. There were days I didn't have any strength left. I wasn't eating well. And because I had gone to get the meat but didn't pick it up, I still wasn't cooking or eating right.

When the pastor realized it, he said, "You've got to start taking better care of yourself. She's going to need you. God is doing what He's doing. You are going to have to do what you can do. And part of that is eating and taking care of your mental health. That's all part of your wellness and it matters, too."

And so for the first time since having my child, I was actually taking care of myself. That was the second miracle.

The third one happened with her eyes.

One day, the consultant said to me, "I know you said we shouldn't do an operation. But now we're going to move on to the next one. We're going to be working on her eyes in a day or two. So right now we're going to do a scan just to see how the cornea and the retina have developed."

"Do you have to do it now? Can't you see that her body is working?"

I was very close to telling her consultant, "See what's happening here. Do you think this is all a coincidence? How many babies have you had that this has happened to? God is good."

But I caught myself in time, not wanting to push.

"Nope, Roza, I'm sorry. We have a timeline with this. I've tried to push things back. And I know she managed to escape those other operations, but it's time that we start doing what we have to. So we're doing the scan tomorrow morning. We can call you afterwards."

I checked my schedule and said, "I have booked a client in the morning. But I'm going to call her and make it earlier. So I will try to be here."

"I'm afraid you might not be allowed in the room. They might be doing it over there. Or they might be wheeling her incubator into the theater room to do it, because it's normally too emotional and stressful for the parents."

I didn't care. I just wanted to be with my child.

"It's not a problem. I will be here."

I called her dad and filled him in on today's events. I didn't explain anything other than that. I don't think he took me seriously.

I said, "You know, God did this."

I'm sure he was shocked that I was even mentioning God, because we had never had that conversation. And all of a sudden, now I was giving all of the praise and glory to God.

He never mentioned anything.

He just said, "What happened to the operations being done? They gave us a timeframe that they haven't even followed through with."

"Listen, I've got it all handled. I'm just calling to let you know they're going to be scanning her eyes. And if you want to be there, God is doing it again."

Whenever I would mention God's name, there would be a silence on the other end. I didn't know whether he wanted to believe it or not. I don't know, but he didn't make his feelings known. Anyway, he arrived at the hospital before I did. And then the consultant must have told him that I was giving them the cold shoulder on doing the operations.

While they were scanning her eyes, he was like, "So what is this about you not wanting her to have the operation?"

"Listen. I just think that she doesn't need some of the operations, and that her body will actually start growing and developing. Her body will perform the functions that it should."

I was sitting there, trying to make him understand my reasons.

I continued, "God is working in her life. You think all that has happened is just a coincidence?"

I felt like I was defending myself, but also defending what God had done. He couldn't see it.

"You know, she needs all of this."

"Listen, I'm not even having this conversation right now."

How can I explain this? I couldn't. So they came out and the scan was good. And now they would receive the results in a few hours.

Again, we sat there waiting, and his phone rang. It was important, so he had to leave.

"You go and do whatever you have to do with your father. When I get any information, I'll call you."

So they did the scan, and hours later, I was told that they wanted to see me in the consultant's office. *Oh God, here we go*. I entered, and my heart was beating so fast. I thought I was going to pass out.

So she sat me down and said she needed to have a doctor with her.

"Well, we were going through the scans, and I had to let him come and check it out with me. We haven't had a second opinion, but we're pretty sure our conclusion is actually right."

"So what's happened?"

"Honestly, it doesn't look too bad. It seems like her eyes are developing. We are very happy with her progress. There is development in the cornea, so this is good news. She will not need to have the operation."

I was sitting there clutching at the chair.

"What?"

"We're very happy with the progress. We will have to wait and see when she is fully developed. But for now, she is okay."

I burst into tears. I didn't know what to do, say, or even think.

"Thank you, God! Thank you, God!"

"Well, she's a fighter. You know, she's doing it. She's fighting."

With her every answer, I said, "Yes, she's fighting. I believe that. But guess who's fighting for her all the more?"

"Who?"

"God."

I didn't say, *Allah*, I said, *God*.

And then she looked at me in a way so as to say, *Yep, that's your guy*.

"Jesus has got us. Jesus is doing all of these things," I said, "Do you think all of these things are natural?"

She looked at me and said, "Well, I believe in miracles." She was clearly trying to lightheartedly play off what I believed. "I have seen some in my line of work in all these years I've been practicing."

"Miracles are supernatural. They are beyond any human capability or comprehension. They will happen in this hospital, because Jesus is at work. Jesus has his hand on my child, and her life wouldn't be the same. Her journey won't be the same."

As I was sitting there, I didn't know where these words were coming from. I just thought that if someone was listening to me, it was as if I was prophesying into my child's future. She looked at me and got up from her chair. I guess she had had enough of the conversation.

She said, "Well, let's continue to hope for the best. We'll follow up again in a few days. But I'm pretty happy with what we've seen on the scan."

Again, I was ecstatic. The emotions I had gone through every time, I couldn't even put into words. No one would understand. I called her dad, and I told him. I called pastor Tony. I told everybody, and it was just amazing. That's the only way I can describe it, because of everything that I had been through with her. I remember standing in church and them asking how she was doing. And I would tell them she's doing so much better. It was one hurdle after another, and they would praise God with me. The Bible studies were getting stronger. More people were joining in. It was as if God was getting people in it literally to come join us for prayer.

They didn't have to, but everybody came to my house for prayer. Tiana was doing so well. So, the weeks passed by, and the major medical issues were resolved. The jaundice was gone. She was able to urinate. The heart murmur had closed up. Her eyes were doing well. Now, they wanted to take out her breathing tube and use the C-PAP, which was a less invasive form of oxygen supply. This was a big step, because they didn't know whether she was able to breathe on her own or not. This was monumental.

So on the day that they were doing this, I wanted to be there; her dad was there, and they finally proceeded to remove the tubes. Everyone was so anxious, you could cut the tension in the room with scissors. It was crazy. The nurses were wishing us well; the consultants were hoping for the best; we, the parents, were standing on high alert. As they extubated her, a long pipe dragged all the way out of her mouth. It felt so invasive to see how deep it must have been in her throat; it must have been painful for her. As they pulled it out, she coughed. And hearing my child cough for the first time during this ordeal was surreal. Because of all the air that was trapped on the sides, she coughed and then she sneezed and then she started struggling to catch her breath. And we were all standing there thinking, *What's next?*

They had to give her a few minutes to see whether she would catch her breath and start breathing on her own or not. As it so happened, she breathed for a few minutes, and then her coloring started changing. She started turning dark blue. Her lips started changing color as well.

And then the doctor said, "Okay, I think this is enough for today. She's managed for a few minutes, but she's struggling now. We need to intubate her again."

Then they wheeled her away and put the tube back. That was a bit of a disappointment, because I had a hope that they would just take the tube out and she would start breathing on her own. But no. If that was a test, I passed it. I wasn't about to let go of my faith in Jesus after all I had seen him do. I thought to myself, *No, this is just a hurdle we will get across. She's not ready for it yet.*

She's doing everything that she should be doing. The only thing that is wrong now is her lungs are a little too weak for her to breathe on her own.

We were still on the road to recovery.

When the consultant came back, she said, "I'm sorry. I don't want you to be disheartened; just think of how far she's come already. And honestly, she's doing so much better. Now, we actually have enough hope to say she looks like she's going to make a full recovery. I don't know about her future speech, mobility, or neurological state of affairs right now, but we'll cross that bridge when we get to it. For now, she's doing really, really well."

I needed to hear that. So again, I reported back to the prayer warriors, I went home, and I prayed. I sought the Lord some more. And at this time, my family members didn't have a clue. I never shared any of this with my family. They would call to find out how she was doing, but I just kept it on medical terms with them. I told them the progress of what was happening, but I never mentioned the Lord Jesus Christ to them. I wasn't ready to deal with that yet. At this point, everybody wanted to know how she was doing. By now, nearly all my customers at work knew she was doing better and was on the road to recovery. I would receive cards in the mail from coworkers. I think prior to her heart murmur being resolved, they were too scared to even presume that she was going to make it. However, once they felt she was out of the woods, I would arrive at work to find flowers and cards at the front desk for us. People were just so lovely, and I kept updating them on her progress. The support was unbelievable.

Another week came and passed by. There came a day when I was at work and received a phone call.

The voice on the other end stated, "Tiana's doctor needs you to get here right now."

I thought, *This does not sound good.* So, I called Pastor Tony, and I called Tiana's dad, who had left for America. I couldn't reach him; he wouldn't be back for several days, so I left him a message. I told everyone I would update them once I found out what was happening. I got to the hospital, and the NICU ward was busier than I expected. There usually wasn't much going on there. Generally, only parents and nurses were allowed in the ward to make for a peaceful environment. I had never seen it so busy. They were cleaning up and disinfecting everywhere.

I wondered, *What's going on?*

I saw a mother with her baby in the corridor and I asked her, "What is all this commotion about?"

"There has been an outbreak of MRSA."

Astonished, I replied, "What?"

"Yes, a couple of babies tested positive for it, and now they're checking every parent that's come into contact with their baby. They're also going to be checking all the nurses. Even the doctors will be checked."

I thought, *Oh my God.* I knew what MRSA was; I was very familiar with some clients and their children who had contracted it. MRSA is very serious. It stands for methicillin-resistant staphylococcus aureus, and it can cause a staph infection that is very difficult to treat because of its resistance to some antibiotics. I also knew it was highly contagious. I knew that if any of these babies contracted it from the two infected babies, it would be very hard to get rid of in the ward. I thought, *Oh my God, these babies can't take much more.*

The mother went on, "The two babies who tested positive for MRSA have already been quarantined on the other side of the ward to give the other babies a chance to fight it."

After this news, I assumed the hospital asked me to come in to discuss the MRSA outbreak. But apparently, they had called me before it was even confirmed. They called me to tell me that Tiana's vitals weren't doing very well. They didn't know exactly what was wrong, but they suspected that she had some sort of infection. So I ran straight over to the consultant's office, but she wasn't there.

As I was walking out, I saw one of the other doctors that I knew had worked with Tiana.

"Listen, I need some information, and I need it right now. I was told to come. But now that I'm here, I'm not getting any answers. What is going on?"

She shoe her words cautiously, "We just got the test results back. We had to do some tests."

She assured me that they would come and speak to me in a little while.

None of us were allowed into the rooms to see our babies, because they were protecting them and disinfecting surfaces since they didn't know the full extent of the infection.

I was sitting in the mother and baby's room when the nurse came to get me and said, "They need you to come over and speak to the consultant."

I made it quickly to her office, and I could see the concern in her face.

She looked at me and said, "I'm sorry, Roza. It's not great news."

My heart dropped.

"Tiana has contracted MRSA as well as a couple of other kids. We are going to have to start treatment ASAP, and we will have to test everybody that she has been in contact with."

I just burst out crying, "How did this happen?"

"Well, we don't know where the source is. We don't know who's infected or not. So you will not be able to see her until you are tested. The nurses and I will be tested as well."

I felt like we had taken ten steps forward, and this obstacle was going to drag us back twenty. I was just so tired and depleted. I was absolutely overwhelmed. I needed to be with the Lord. I wanted to seek him. Running to Jesus was my new habit. I saw how he always answered me, so I wanted and needed to seek him out about this issue. When the consultant was speaking to me, all I could think was that I needed to see my child.

Oblivious to what the consultant was reporting, I interrupted, "I'm here now. Do you want to do the test?"

"Sure, go into the other room and the nurses will assist you."

I did as she said. There were other mothers whose babies had contracted it and even the mothers whose babies had not. They just wanted to test everybody to make sure. All of us were waiting to have an MRSA test done, and eventually it was my turn. It wasn't painful. The nasal swab was just uncomfortable. They put the swab deep into my nasal cavity to collect secretions. Then they took it to the lab to test it. It took about forty-eight hours to get the results. Tiana's positive test results were a complete shock to all of us. They started working on finding the best form of treatment for her. When they told me, I was going to have to wait for about forty-eight hours before I could have contact with my child, it was tough.

It wasn't only for me; it was the rule for everybody. They were trying to decrease the likelihood of uninfected babies becoming infected and to keep those who had it alive. I went home. That was a very hard night because it felt like all the hope, confidence, and faith I had was being pulled away from me. But I wasn't about to let it go that easily. I needed to seek the Lord. I had a good talk with Him and asked Him what was going on. I felt like He was leading me to passages in scripture where it was all about trusting in Him. That was all I could get from what I was reading.

So, I went back to the hospital the next day. As expected, they told me the results weren't in. I just wanted to stay in the mother and baby's room to be close to my child; that was enough for me.

I called everybody again to update them, encouraging them to stay in prayer, because MRSA was very serious. If only they could have seen the precautions that were being taken; the hospital's disinfecting was painstakingly fastidious. Seeing everything they were doing made me feel a whole lot better. They started Tiana on some antibiotics because the oxygen levels in her blood were much too low. She had gone through so much with the MRSA infection.

Her body was just too tired and weak to fight it quickly. Those were trying days because her body had been through the ringer, and we were so close to completing all the important procedures that she was meant to have.

But now we were dealing with a whole different ball game. I was absolutely devastated. The churches rallied around me again. Everybody was so supportive, standing alongside me in prayer. We spent countless hours crying out to the Lord during our Tuesday prayer meetings.

And because MRSA is so resistant to antibiotics, she didn't respond to treatment immediately. Her body was just not fighting it quickly or effectively as we had so desperately hoped. Week after week, she wasn't getting any better.

During this time, all I had was my faith. I had believed in Jesus too fiercely and had come too far to give up now. And if I decided to let go of Jesus, what would I have held onto? I'd rather hold onto God and lose, than not hold onto God and lose. Not holding on would be a devastation. And every time I prayed, the peace I felt and the way He spoke to my heart was incomparable. At this time, worry had filled my mind so much that I was dreaming, but I would forget most of my dreams before I woke. That's how clogged up my mind was. I continued seeking the Lord, asking him to give me a word to hang onto. Through wisdom, I understood that only God could do this.

And without fail, in prayer meetings or at church, somebody would come up to me and say, "God wants me to tell you that this is going to be a hard week, but He's got you. He's got you, and He's got Tiana in the palm of his hand."

And those were the days that kept me going. Everything they said was so on point. There were days when we were so close to losing Tiana that I would sleep in the hospital overnight so I wouldn't have to leave her. I was too scared to go, even for a moment.

A few weeks later, once we had all been tested, we found out that two nurses who were working on Tiana's ward had contracted MRSA. They were given some time off from work. The doctors were tested as well; thank God they didn't have it. However, they continuously tested people because the fact was, you may not have it this week, but you could contract it next week.

There was ongoing testing that we had to go through, and whenever somebody contracted it, they would get sick leave. And eventually they got it all under control. All the babies were on medication. There were no new cases, and the nurses that were infected were already quarantined at home and taking antibiotics. Nonetheless, it was a very difficult time. Those few days when I couldn't see my child were very hard. The good news was because Tiana's dad and I tested negative, we were able to go right back to taking turns sitting with her. Those were very scary days, because she had lost all the weight that she had previously gained from breastfeeding over the past month.

My sweet baby was skin and bones. It felt like we had come so far, and now we were right back to square one. But God wouldn't leave us alone. He kept refreshing us with His word and with people around us who were standing and praying for us. He would literally give a word of wisdom to our church family, in order that they might minister to us. I was seeking it more than I had ever sought Him before. It was astonishing. It was as if the more her illness progressed, the more my faith grew. Every time I was faced with a difficult task, God showed his faithfulness, thereby increasing my faith. In Him, I found strength to get up every single day and handle my business. I would go sit at the hospital and watch over my child. My whole existence revolved around these three things: God, my child, and the church. Literally, that was all I did.

It was nearly six weeks later before Tiana really started showing signs of improvement. And it took so much longer than we thought, because her body was already so weak; it had gone through too much.

But I will never forget the day when they did a test and the consultant came back and said, "She's doing better. She actually is responding to treatment. The antibiotics have kicked in. It's going to be a slow recovery, but she's going to get there eventually."

Because the MRSA infection had taken so much out of her, they postponed extubating her. The MRSA had made it impossible to even attempt putting her on a C-PAP. It wouldn't have made sense to do that. So they left her breathing tube in as she gradually began responding to the MRSA antibiotics.

That was a very hard time, even though she was recovering. It was as if whatever she was going through affected me, because I was exhausted, emotionally spent, and not eating well. I did not realize the extent to which the stress was physically draining me until a random day when I was visiting Tiana in the hospital, per my daily routine.

Her doctor turned to me and said, "Roza, I'm really worried about you. Now, you appear to have lost a drastic amount of weight, and you have bags under your eyes. I'd like to make a suggestion to help you take care of yourself."

I stared at her blankly, wondering, *What do you mean?*

She continued, "I'm going to ask you not to come to the hospital for a few days. I need you to go home, eat, and sleep. Don't even go to work. If you can delegate tasks in the shop and let someone else take over, I would advise you to do that. I do not want you to get ill, and you will if you go on like this. You're literally one step away from collapsing. I need you to do this for me. This is for your own good. Imagine if you were ill, how would you be able to be there for your baby? Don't fret, I will have a word with Tiana's father and ask him to come in more often to allow you time to stay at home. You're running on empty right now. I'm seriously worried about you," before I could even reply, she continued, "but I've got something for you."

She returned with some multivitamins and asked me to have a blood test. I knew I was anemic during my pregnancy, as it had said so in my file; but she thought I needed some iron tablets as well. So she sent me over to the lab to do a blood test.

I went to get the blood test done; they told me that I was so dehydrated that I needed to do an IV right away to help my system. I wasn't doing too well. Those six weeks were taking such a toll on me and I didn't even realize it. After the IV, they gave me the iron tablets and told me I was still seriously anemic. My blood count was so much lower than normal.

I told the doctor, and she advised me, "After you have had these few days of rest and come back, I'm going to put in a request for you to see a counselor so you can sit down and talk about how you feel."

I didn't want to argue; I didn't have the strength to. She was right about me needing to take care of myself like I was previously. I was running so low on water and blood, it kind of made me want to get healthier for my child.

I said to her, "If it helps, I will go."

I made sure I had the papers listing everything that I needed. Then, I went to see my child, said goodbye for a couple of days, and told her I'd be back. It was hard to think that I wouldn't see her for that long, but I knew her dad would be there. I'd ask him to call me if anything changed. Everybody knew I needed to rest, and they encouraged me to take it. I went home, called the shop, and delegated all the duties. I told them my doctor's orders. That night I cooked something, ate a good meal, and took my pills before grabbing my Bible and going to bed.

In the middle of the night, I woke up. I wasn't even that hungry, but I was on a mission to put my weight back. I sipped on some tea and water, and then I went back to sleep.

I called the next day to find out about Tiana, and the consultant said, "I know I said two days but make it three. She's doing okay. She's improving. She's out of the woods. Please just take the next three days to eat, sleep, and rest. That's all I want from you, do you think you can do that for me?"

I had no choice but to do as she said. It was hard, but God knows I needed it. I nurtured myself those three days. I watched movies, relaxed, and delved into the Bible. I listened to sermons and worship music. It felt like I was being refreshed. Everyone at church was just being so amazing and keeping me in prayer. The pastor decided I was too tired to host the Bible study and that they would do it at my friend's house instead. I was told to follow the doctor's orders, and that's surprisingly what I did. I have to tell you, it felt like God

Himself came down and touched me. I felt refreshed. I had slept. I was rested. I think I had three meals every day in those three days. I was feeling so much better than I had in a very long time.

When I walked into the hospital, I appeared rejuvenated. The consultant was pleased with how I looked this time, compared to the raggedy state I was in a few days ago. Everybody was commenting on how much better I looked. I couldn't wait to see my child. When I saw her this time, she was so much better. Thank God. The next major thing was to move from the intubation to the C-PAP, an oxygen support machine that was less invasive compared to the intubation. Since the first attempt with the C-PAP didn't work out, I started seeking the Lord about it more. Faith started pouring out of me. My Bible would fall open scriptures that confirmed how God was so faithful. Whatever He started, He was going to finish. Those scriptures gave me hope that I held onto in the darkest of hours. It was God's word that got me through, as well as the people He sent to surround me.

My family didn't go through any of this with me. My mother at the time was in Africa with some of my siblings. Some of my siblings were in London as well, but they were never part of this journey with me. I don't even think any one of them came to the hospital to see my child. It wasn't a problem, because God had provided whatever I needed. I decided I wouldn't let them in too much, because then I would have to explain the fact that I wasn't a Muslim anymore. I could only imagine their reactions. I needed this space that they gave me, and I didn't resent them for it.

People are very quick to judge what they don't know. I am very guilty of that myself. There was a time I judged Christians, not only for their belief, but also because it was so different from what I knew. I believe we always criticize what we don't know. It gives us this cushion of ignorance that we can fall back on when we don't understand exactly what's going on in someone's life. My walk with God was a beautiful time, and I held it with that same regard and tenacity. I wasn't going to let anyone destroy that.

They were ready to try again and see if she would start breathing with the C-PAP a few hours a day, instead of the intubation. That day came and we stood in the room alert and waiting. Just like before, they took the breathing tube out. Then, she was gasping, then coughing, then sneezing. She was breathing again and trying to catch her breath. My daughter had every ounce of her mother in her. She was a fighter and wasn't going to give up easily. I saw her struggling to catch her breath, trying with all of her might to let out air and take it back in again. In my mind, I was praying for God to breathe into her lungs. It's amazing how you can be standing and say nothing, but your whole being is crying out to the Lord in a silent prayer. That was what happened that day. It felt like God responded, because she breathed on her own for more than three minutes. Then they gave her another three minutes and pumped her chest a little bit. Then the doctors were happy enough to get her on C-PAP and let it help her. We started using the C-PAP 12 hours a day. The C-PAP was a whole different ball game. After they put it on the first time, I sat there and I waited for hours until she fell asleep.

The MRSA was gone and she was on the C-PAP, so I could finally have skin to skin contact with her. Until then, I had never had a chance to hold my child. I touched her toes and fingers but had never felt her in my arms. I was kind of scared to even touch her, because I didn't want to harm her in any way. Fear would have to leave, because I longed to feel her skin on mine. On the C-PAP there was a way they could get her out of the incubator with the machine still attached and put her on me. The nurse advised me to give it a few days so that she could get used to the C-PAP. Then I would have the first skin on skin contact. I waited for the day like it was Christmas. I held onto that hope. I remember going home and praising the Lord, texting everybody to tell them she was off the support system and on the C-PAP. It was beautiful.

She was doing so well on the C-PAP. Soon, they let her breathe on her own for an hour, then they put her right back on it. The next day, they tried for two hours before putting it back on. They had to do it step-by-step, because they didn't want to give her too much to deal with. Two weeks later when they felt like her body had really adjusted to the C-PAP and she was responding well, it was time for our first skin to skin contact. Oh my God. I remember that day.

That morning in the shower, I scrubbed myself a little more than I usually did. I just didn't want to transfer any germs, so I scrubbed my body knowing that, very soon, I was going to feel my baby's heartbeat on top of my chest. Her dad was excited for it as well, and we met there later that afternoon.

I arrived at the hospital and anxiously told the nurse I was ready, "Please let me hold my baby."

She took me to the chair, arranged it, and said, "Take your top off and your bra. Please take everything off and disinfect your skin. First wipe down all the moisture. Then, I'll bring her out and lay her on top of your chest."

I cleansed everything, under my armpits, both of my breasts, and anywhere I thought Tiana might be. When I was done, I sat there eagerly waiting for them to bring my baby to me. The anticipation was killing me, but I knew there were steps to be followed. The nurse carefully detached some of the wires that were on Tiana and then opened up the incubator. She picked her up out of the incubator and placed her right on my chest. Her body felt so warm, and her skin was paper thin. It was so surreal. She put my baby on my chest and covered us with a blanket.

Then she said, "When you're comfortable, she can feel that. If you are edgy and agitated, she can feel that energy too. Try to relax and enjoy this first cuddle with your baby."

For the very first time, I felt a heartbeat right on top of my chest. One of her tiny hands was laying on my breast. One of the most surreal things happened. It was as if somebody had told my body that this was the initial first contact between my child and I; my breast started filling up with milk. When God designed the body, He designed it to perfection. Everything worked in order, according to His plan. Even though I was on medication to help me produce more milk, I would have some dry days. But this wasn't one of them. After around twenty minutes of holding her, I didn't want to give her back.

The nurse came and checked. I was there stroking her hair, singing softly, and telling her about Jesus. I sat there telling her about all the things we were going to do together; I felt like I truly was a mother. Nothing brought it home more than having my child laying on my chest.

All of a sudden, I felt some liquid dripping. I called out to the nurse saying, "I think she just peed on me."

The nurse joked, "Well, that would be a nice welcome package for you. Wouldn't it?"

She hurried over to me and lifted the blanket, and my breasts were oozing milk like never before.

At that moment her dad came in and the nurse said, "I think this is enough for today. Or if you can wait for a little bit more, before allowing dad to have the same experience. These little babies get exhausted, very easy. Let's wait a few hours."

I didn't have a choice. I had to let the nurse take Tiana away from me because I was becoming drenched in my own milk. The nurse told me that I could have that every day, if all was well. That night I didn't even want to leave. I just wanted to hold her again.

On the ride home, I cried and praised God. I didn't want to bathe when I got home because I didn't want to lose the scent of her on me. I could still smell it when I got home so I just got into bed, said my prayers and laid there replaying that day. That was a very special day.

That was an absolute milestone. And the next day I was there early in the morning, because I wanted more of what I had felt. I knew that the nurse on duty completely understood. After she completed her rotations and fed the babies, she placed my baby on my chest and gently covered her. I was somewhat hesitant, worried that I might begin lactating due to our attunement. Thankfully, that didn't happen. I stayed there with my child on my chest, soaking the moment in as I silently praised and thanked God for that moment. I was rocking her, talking to her, singing to her, simply being Mommy. It was absolutely brilliant. I held her for over an hour, and then they put her back on the C-PAP. By this point in treatment, she was using it for a few hours during the day. She was being given medications to help her organs strengthen, develop, and mature properly, so it would have been too much to stress on her lungs to not use the C-PAP. Her breathing still was not where doctors wanted it to be. However, her lungs were improving due to the consistent treatment she was being given. Through it all, everybody was in prayer with me. They all wanted an update. Everybody was amazingly supportive.

Her dad would come later on in the day to have his own skin to skin contact. It was now real. I was able to cuddle my child in limited positions; but for now, that was enough. Just knowing that she was fighting made me so proud. She was pulling through; she was getting stronger and better every single day, and that was the joy of my life. Now, they began to do more rigorous brain functioning tests. We received the news that the most recent brain scan determined that her brain function was actually doing better than before. The waves were moving at a quicker pace. This news made our hearts soar, because initially, tests weren't indicating strong functional activity.

Then, the doctor pulled us aside, gently reminding us that despite these favorable brain scan results, she might have developmental issues down the line.

She handled us with care, softly saying, "We've seen good improvement with the brain scans, but we will not know how much the illness has affected her development until she's older. It is possible it could leave her with a residual speech impediment or mobility deficits. This is not to scare you all; we just can't promise there will be no future difficulties. We just don't know."

Oddly enough, that was fine by me; that wasn't a problem as long as I had my baby. We would roll with the punches, like we had thus far.

They went on to check for hearing. The issue was, the cochlea grows as baby does. So, they couldn't detect deficits extremely early or reach a definite conclusion as to how much hearing she had left. They didn't know if she was completely deaf, partially deaf, or hard of hearing. They didn't have a clue.

Three weeks after we started skin to skin contact, they determined that she had some hearing. However, they were unsure of how much. They assured us they would know more later on and that, for now, everything was looking good. Things were starting to work right now. Her body was responding to treatment. God was doing miracles in that place.

It felt like God just tackled every obstacle that was placed before us with the greatest strength. It was amazing to see. Little by little, I started sharing with people that I was praying. I would casually mention it when having conversation with consultants.

I would say things like, "God is in control. Jesus is faithful."

People saw a difference from the girl that delivered her baby on September 15, 2009 to a prayer warrior who was testifying about God's faithfulness six months later.

It was amazing to have come that far with the Lord. The other thing that I was really looking forward to was breastfeeding. That couldn't happen with the CPAP mask on her face. They wanted to wait until she was one hundred percent able to breathe with no outside assistance or oxygen. At that point, they couldn't teach her how to suckle, because before a baby is full-term, the infant doesn't instinctively know how to latch onto the nipple and suck. Because I was unable to breastfeed my baby, all this time I was pumping the milk and having them feed it through a tube. And I was so looking forward to bonding with my child in this way; I couldn't wait. I knew the benefits of breastfeeding. I knew it was beneficial to her, so I couldn't deny her that.

I was anticipating it to no end. There was a day when they said they could try it out to see if she would know how to suck. I was waiting for this day with such excitement that I took my pills; they told me not to extract the milk for that day, because they wanted my breasts full of milk. That way, it wouldn't be too much effort for her to suck it. I was just so happy sitting there as they removed the C-PAP for some time. They put her in my arms and helped her to latch onto my breast. She tried, but the whole motion of sucking a nipple or even having the milk come out was too much effort for her. She would stop and breathe and then try to latch on again. It lasted just a few minutes, but I was grateful for the experience. The doctors told me to be prepared that she might never want to latch on. That didn't crush me as much as I thought it would. I didn't want to do anything that would make her struggle or be painful for her. It was way too much effort for her. The decision was to continue feeding her the way we'd been doing with the tubes and give her some time to grow stronger. Eventually, I would try again. That was okay with me.

During my first experience with breastfeeding, I just had this feeling that she could see me. Maybe just in black and white, but I didn't care what they said. I just had a feeling that my child could see my face. For a long time, her eyes were covered to protect them from the light when she had jaundice. Afterwards, it was to protect her from the light that was shining on her from the incubator. Most of the time, she would have her eyes closed. I think the light might have been affecting her eyes. However, the few minutes during which she opened them, I had the feeling that she could see me.

I would talk to her saying, "I am your mother. I'm your mommy."

Even if she wasn't sleeping, her eyes were closed. That was okay with me, because I never stopped talking to my child.

I celebrated any improvement or milestone in the NICU, because only God understood what we mothers were going through emotionally. There was one baby that was so ill, they had to be transported to another hospital for emergency treatment. I never saw that mom or baby again. There were new babies coming constantly as well. So, any improvement on your child was a blessing, and you treated it as such.

The second week after my breastfeeding, I was so happy because there was another mother going through the same experience.

I remember we met in the extraction room and she stated, "I can't wait to just stop pumping manually like this and just breastfeed my child."

She hated the pump, just like I did. We joked about it and spoke about what we wished would happen. By now, I was in a much better place to give God the glory and be comfortable saying it to people. I had spent months with this lady in the hospital; so when she needed support and encouragement, I was there. I would encourage her by saying God was faithful and would look after her and her baby. I didn't even know what her faith was. I was just sharing mine to encourage her heart when she was having a difficult day.

About a week after that conversation, I came to the hospital to see my child. That mother and her baby were gone. I wondered what happened and asked the nurse on the way out. She told me that they had lost the baby during the night. That crushed me. The child had the same heart defect and many of the same issues as my baby. I had heard of the babies passing but I didn't have a relationship with the mother. This one was different; we would check on each other's babies. I thought back to the conversation that we'd had about her plans with her baby.

I remember her saying, "We're pumping like cows. I mean, look at us. We're lactating cows sitting over here."

I could hear her voice in my head. Her baby was no more. I never saw that woman again. I didn't realize how much I was going to be affected by that news, but I cried that day. And it made me fall back on God in gratefulness for his mercy over me. There was another baby next to her who had one arm fully developed and the other arm that stopped halfway. Every child had their own challenges and their own birth defects.

I kept telling myself that my baby was here. God was so faithful to us. God moved heaven and earth. God did miracles in that hospital. It was like one after the other one just to show His might and power. I listened. I saw, believed, and trusted. Every time He did something more, my heart picked up on it. My faith grew stronger. It was unbelievable. One day, the pastor came to the hospital and prayed for Tiana, as he often would. This time, they let him into the room to see Tiana. He stood there and prayed for her and the other children. He didn't personally touch them, because that would have been invading people's personal space. But he prayed for them. Then he left.

I needed him that day. I needed someone to come and pray and I was still so deflated and really hurting over this child and her mother. I was so grateful for the support and the comfort I had in the pastor's prayers. That was a difficult night. I think that made me want to hold on more.

All of a sudden I was scared to go home. I was thinking, *What if it happens to me? What if I go home and something happens during the night?* I was spending more and more time in the hospital. Day by day, she became stronger. She was getting much better.

One day the consultant found me by Tiana's bedside and said, "It's looking really good. Her lungs are developing, and she's breathing more effortlessly now. So we're thinking of weaning her off this C-PAP altogether."

We had come such a long way from day one up to now.

At one point it felt like she had at least fifteen wires everywhere coming from every part of her body. Now we were at a point where she had only the feeding tube, the C-PAP, and another one that took her temperature. Just to hear her say that she wouldn't have to use the C-PAP at all was absolutely amazing. She also mentioned that because these premature babies were so prone to Apneas and relapsing, that it was wise for them to put some oxygen tanks in my house. That way, if she needed it while at home, I could always help her out. We looked forward to the day she would be able to be without the C-PAP. I told everybody; we prayed and trusted in the Lord.

Eventually, the day came. I cried that day. The C-PAP was gone. It was good to know that she wasn't in discomfort anymore. They had already started feeding her this small feeding bottle, which was specially made for premature babies. She still was not able to suckle, and they didn't want to take the tube out. What they were doing was supplementing the feeding tube and the teeny-weeny bottle. She just couldn't take it all at once. Standing there and watching my child with nothing on her face for hours on end was just amazing. I thanked the Lord.

One day they asked, "While you're standing and she's got nothing on her face, do you want to feed her?"

They gave me this little feeding bottle. Now feeding her was very touchy. You had to be skillful at it, because she sucked so slowly. It took so much energy to suck the milk out of the bottle and swallow it. There was a way to do it so it would not overwhelm her, because she could either choke or have it come out of her nose. Breathing and eating at the same time was the technique she needed to learn. The nurse handed me the bottle as she walked me through it. All of a sudden we just heard a splutter, and she started coughing up the milk. She had tried to suck in the milk, but it went down the wrong way. I was so scared, because she was turning all shades of colors on me.

The nurse quickly took her out of my hands, laid her on the bed, and used a suction to remove the milk from her nose. After that, she put the C-PAP on for a while.

And she said, "Okay, this is why we are still on the feeding tube, it's too much for her right now. She can't suck and breathe at the same time."

We thought it was best not to try breastfeeding again. I think the smallest of her organs was definitely her lungs, She just couldn't do it fully right now. The nurse said, "We're going to just let her come to the point where she can do it, we're not going to rush her. We're going to try this and take the C-PAP away again tomorrow."

The next day, they tried again, and she was okay. She was alright after that, too. Very soon after that, the C-PAP went away. She only needed it sometimes when she had an Apnea or when she was sleeping so deeply and forgot to breathe. Things started changing slowly, and when I walked in to visit the first thing I saw was how her chest was going up and down; her cheeks were dented slightly from the tube pressing on her skin for so long. In my eyes everything about her was perfect. She was putting on weight, but she was still tiny. She weighed 630 grams when she was born.

Now she was under five pounds. Feeding was still something we needed to work on. About two weeks after that, I had another meeting with the consultant, and this time it was good news —great news actually. Now it was time for them to think about releasing her to the nearest hospital. You see, that wasn't even a specialty hospital. She was born at the Royal London hospital. They were going to move us over to Newark hospital, which was about a ten minute drive from our house. They only send the babies there after they are all healed and ready to go home. The consultant told me that was going to be the next step of action. She also told me that, before we left the hospital, they were going to have doctors come over to the house to check her out.

I still can remember the day we moved to the new general hospital. I was so excited, because this hospital was so much closer. This was a great sign, because that meant we were one step closer to going home. They were getting all of this stuff ready to move on the ambulance. They weren't taking any chances. She could get stressed out on the journey. For her safety, they made sure they had a C-PAP on board and that all of the necessary precautions she needed were available.

Before we left, I personally wanted to say thank you to the nurses. I wanted to say thank you to the consultants and everybody who had really helped her. It wasn't the end of the journey; it was just the end with them. I bought some thank you cards and a bouquet of flowers that I gave to the consultant to put in an office. I handed them all a card. I think there were four or five of them all. When I said my goodbye, I said thank you to them. I told them God was faithful and had done miracles there. Even Tatiana's consultant, who was agnostic, agreed that miracles were done in that place.

One of the nurses responded, "Absolutely, God is faithful. He's a God of miracles. They don't call Him that for nothing."

I thanked them all, and we moved on to our next journey in another hospital. I rode with my miracle baby, Tatiana Alexandra Books, in the back of the ambulance.

Roza Perry

13
TO GOD BE THE GLORY

Leaving that hospital was absolutely amazing, because there were times I feared we would never see that day. Others might see it as a continuation of the journey from one hospital to another, but I saw it as a victory. It meant she was on the way to recovery. That hospital was so much closer to my house, and it was where most of her therapy was scheduled to be done.

I was absolutely elated, praying over my child. I was sharing that part of the journey with the nurses that were in the ambulance that helped to make sure she was delivered to the other hospital safely. We were on the road. It was both amazing and bittersweet to say goodbye to all of these lovely people that had shared my pain through those horrible months. They were such a huge part of my journey, and I knew they would never forget what God had done in the hospital. Science may give a reason or antidote to a problem, but there were some things that you could never take the glory away from God. This was one of them; whether they believed in him or not, we all bore witness to what God had done for this child.

A lot of things were in my mind during the ride to the hospital. When we got there, we were assigned a room with a few more recovering babies. I met a whole set of different mothers, doctors, and nurses who were going to be there for the last part of our journey in the hospital. I started telling them exactly what my child had overcome. It was widely known around the ward that this was the child that was born at twenty-four weeks gestation and was on her way to full recovery. It was amazing. People would approach me and ask how she was doing. Everybody knew about her.

The church was still praying. We were still having Bible studies and prayer meetings for the life of my child. God showed his faithfulness in a way I couldn't ever doubt, because that journey truly changed me. It touched the deepest part of me and changed the whole trajectory of my life.

We did another few weeks in the hospital. During this time they booked us for all the therapy that we were meant to get, because they did believe that she was going to need help with her speech and mobility. They were holding on to some of the diagnoses that were made in the other hospital, but things were less strained in this hospital. The babies that came to this hospital were well on the way to living their lives with their parents. This thought gave me so much hope.

One day I came in to check on my child. By now, her dad had gone back to America but was meant to be back in a few weeks. I had a meeting with the doctors, and they were quite happy with her progress.

They said, "If everything goes well, we will release her in a week."

I couldn't believe it. I was absolutely ecstatic, again. I called all of my support group and friends to pray. Tiana actually had a date to come home.

Before she came home, they needed to do a few things in my house. They came over and put an oxygen tank into every room. Because premature babies had tendencies to actually forget to breathe, they didn't want to take any chances. They wanted that oxygen tank there for emergencies.

I started to prepare my home. It was cleaned and disinfected, because Tiana was still so susceptible to germs and infection. I was told that because of the weather being so cold, I would do well with not letting her go outside. Some of her appointments would even be done at home. That was the plan for the future, and I couldn't believe it. It felt like all of my Christmases had come at once. That was the best present that anyone could have given me. I went home, prayed, and thanked the Lord.

The day came, and I remember it was a Saturday. I went to the shop, because I knew it was going to be such a long journey. I'd have to stay home permanently and hand over the running of the shop to my manager. I had everything in order to speak to her about things concerning the day-to-day running of the shop. Then I went over to the hospital. When I arrived, she was sleeping, and I was so scared to touch her. It was like I had come to accept that we couldn't do some things with her just yet. It was going to take time, and breastfeeding was out of the whole equation. It took so much energy out of her. They suggested that I continue extracting the milk and feeding it to her slowly through the premature bottle that they had provided. I was taught how to feed her, as well as how to insert a feeding tube. They showed me everything concerning taking care of my child.

On the day I arrived to take her home. It was a bit more exciting, because they were going to show me how to wipe her down and give her a mini bed bath.

The nurse came and found me standing there staring at her, but I was scared as well. I had never had a child before. Now this little baby would be dependent on me for everything. I was standing there looking at her, wondering, *How am I going to bathe her? How am I going to feed her?*

The day I longed for was here, and there was fear in my heart.

It was as if the nurse could read my thoughts, because she approached me and said, "You're going to be fine. Anytime you need help, just make sure you call the numbers that we're going to provide. Somebody will help you. We do understand that it's your first child, and it's going to be very hard. Just know there's a whole system backing you. Reach out whenever you feel overwhelmed, and don't think you need to do this on your own."

I watched as the nurse picked Tiana up. She weighed just under six pounds, which was still small. However, that was a long way from where we had started. She was growing stronger each day. I was still apprehensive about picking her up and thinking I'm going to hurt her. I watched the nurse handle my child with care. She showed me how to take off her clothes and get the bath bucket to give her a wet towel bath. I stood there thinking, *Oh my God, tomorrow or the following day, I'm going to have to do all of this on my own.* The nurse showed me everything that she needed to. Then, the doctors came in and checked her out thoroughly from head to toe to make sure everything was good before they said it was time to go home.

It was a beautiful time. We put my child into my brand-new car seat, and they gave me a bag that contained some of the memorabilia from the hospital. They gave me a file that contained everything about her.

The consultant looked me in the eye and said, "It gives me the ultimate pleasure to tell you that your child can be turned over to your care. You will be leaving to go and build a safe, protective home for her. We're just so proud to be part of these few weeks of her life in the hospital. This has been an absolute miracle after reading her file and coming to understand the journey."

That was all I needed to hear.

I burst out crying, looked at the doctor, and said, "It was God that did it. The miracles all came from God. He deserves all the glory because He did this."

I thanked each and every one of them for all that they had done in helping us. They presented me with a release form of mother and baby. I signed it, and my friend picked up the bags and the car seat. The nurses walked behind me with the consultant. It was like a sendoff party; there was a whole group with me leading the way with the car seat walking right out of the door. It was a very pivotal moment of my life that I will never forget.

Once we came out of the hospital, I felt this need to get down on my knees and say, "Thank you, Jesus."

I didn't care what they thought of me. It was a very cold day, and it was actually snowing. One of the male nurses came over and said, "You know what? I will walk you guys to the car; I will help you from here."

I stepped out into the cold, put the car seat down. I got down on my knees and touched my head to the ground.

I lifted my hands up and said, "Lord, thank you. Thank you, Jesus, for everything you have done. This journey has come to an end now, but Lord, I give you all the glory. I honor you. I praise your Holy name."

Then I got up, and everybody was just staring as if to say she's gone crazy. Those that knew the Lord knew exactly what I was doing. When I finished, we picked up the car seat and headed into my car. He strapped the baby in, and we said our goodbyes with everybody watching from the doorway of the hospital.

On our way home I felt a sense of relief. Every bump in the road, I would turn around and look at my child. I couldn't believe it. It didn't feel real. If it was a normal day and not that cold, I would probably have sung all the way home without concentrating so much on the road. But the weather conditions were terrible. I clutched the steering wheel harder than I ever had, and I was much more careful driving, knowing there was a little tiny human in my car who meant the world to me, whom I loved with every fiber of my being.

I looked at her, sleeping in the car seat, and my heart swelled with love. Not only for her but with love for God also. This part of my life was going to be amazing because it would be me and God at home with our miracle baby. I was so looking forward to it. We arrived home, and it was time to settle into life as a mother for the first time ever. I truly felt like a mother after so many months, because now it was just her and I. Phone calls had been received; texts had been sent. With the worship music softly playing in the background, I felt a sense of calm and peace.

The Lord was reassuring me, "I'm on this journey with you."

I couldn't sleep that night. I spent most of the time watching her, scared that something bad might happen to her.

That first night was the hardest. After that, it felt like my motherly instincts just took over. We settled into a life of routine. She would wake up in the morning, eat and go right back to sleep. She slept a lot. It was the only thing premature babies could do. My baby didn't even know she cried because she had the intubation for so long. She didn't know she had a voice.

I remember a few days after we came home, she literally let out a scream. I ran from the kitchen to her because I couldn't believe that she could actually make this sound. Even hearing her scream and cry was beautiful because it showed the normality of her being my baby It let me know that she needed me. I followed the instructions I saw in the book until I found out what was wrong with her, whether it was a full nappy or she had gas and needed to be burped. It was amazing. I was a mother and I was loving every moment.

We were out of the hospital for about two weeks. One day, I was in the kitchen cooking and I heard what sounded like a hiccup. But it wasn't just a hiccup. She was struggling to breathe. I started screaming, because I saw her face turning blue. I knew that wasn't good. So I ran for the oxygen, but I screamed so loudly that my neighbor heard me and he came running through the door, picked her up and started doing the compressions on her tiny chest while I was on the phone calling the ambulance. Because she was a premature baby, she was on priority, which meant she was in special needs care. So within a few minutes, the ambulance was there.

She was sleeping, forgot to breathe, and went into an Apnea. That was one of several to come. It was what was expected. I knew it was going to happen, but even then, it was one of the most frightening things to watch. We went back home, and this time we were told not to allow anybody into our home. She was still susceptible to germs, and infection after that episode she would need time to heal. We stayed for two or three days, and then they let us go. When we came back, we decided to move the prayer meeting to somebody else's house, just so they wouldn't be as much of a risk of transferring anything to her that could be dangerous.

Everything was fine, but the best part of my life was just seeking the Lord and falling in love with him in a way that I didn't even expect. My family didn't know what had happened in the hospital. Some of my friends didn't know. Only people around me and the people in the shop knew something was happening in my life. Something spiritual, something beautiful that no one could explain.

I remember one day I was watching a sermon, and the pastor said, "If you're denying me before all men, I will deny you before my father."

I didn't understand that so I rewound it and listened to it again.

I was thinking, *Lord, what do you mean?* All of a sudden he spoke to my heart in the same way I could hear his voice on the beach when I was running away from him. "You're ashamed of me. You're not ashamed of me."

I knew the Christian faith wasn't one to be held inside; it was for everybody, Jews, Hebrews Jews, Gentiles. I felt like it was so beautiful so I kept telling myself that was the reason why I was holding it so close to my heart. But then when he said that to me, I knew God saw the truth. I was scared of what was to come. I didn't want to give too much time to think about that, but I knew it was going to happen. I think that was what kept me from sharing him to the people that really mattered the most like my family, and close friends. I sat there and the tears just started pouring down my face. I felt ashamed.

He was saying I was ashamed of him, but actually, I was ashamed of myself. He didn't care about the past I had or the messed up life I lived.

When I called, He opened His arms to me and did miracles for my child. Yet here I was not sharing my faith in Him out of fear. I felt like an ingrate. He had done his part, and now it was mine. My heart was very heavy that day. I remember making a phone call and talking to a few of the ladies at church. I explained exactly how scared I was about it.

One of the ladies who had become my friend said, "He knows exactly how you feel even before you feel it. Go before the Lord, repent, ask for forgiveness, and ask Him to help you to declare your faith to the world. I don't know how He's going to do it, but He'll tell you exactly how."

And so I did.

I went before the Lord and repented for hiding Him. I repented for being so scared to do the right thing. I repented for wanting to keep Him hidden when He didn't hide me. In the presence of all who could see, He had healed my child.

When I went to bed that night, it wasn't a peaceful sleep, because it was as if I knew what was to come. I did the normal routine. When it was time to do my daily prayer and worship, I found myself thinking, *I can't do this. I have to let the world know.* I could've called my family first but I wasn't ready to put anybody in charge of my faith. My faith was God's. He gave it to me. The gift of salvation came from Him. I wasn't about to let everybody be in the driver's seat of that. At the time, Facebook was only a few years old; I didn't have the time to join Facebook and share my life's journey. I thought, *What a beautiful way to tell the world that I had given my life to the Lord, Jesus Christ.* If I put it on there, it would be hard to miss, because people were so into Facebook. It was growing so quickly and was a platform that everybody wanted to be on.

I prayed to the Lord for courage and protection. I prayed for Him to stand with me just like He had in the hospital. I knew what was to come. I wasn't gullible. I wasn't going to pretend like it was all going to be hunky-dory. I grabbed my laptop, signed up on Facebook, and created a profile. I put my picture so everybody knew it was me, and I spoke right there. It's amazing when fear leaves; faith, courage, and the power of God kick in. I wrote words that I knew would please the Lord. I declared to the whole world that I had given my life to the Lord Jesus Christ and would serve Him with all the strength in my being.

That was it. I was done. I made my announcement and slowly closed the laptop.

I went back to my day. As I was doing my daily tasks, there was a thought in the back of my mind that something was happening. It was as if I could feel the attention my post was generating, because my family was very well known in Africa. My mom came from a very strong Muslim family. My dad converted to faith, and I knew people would have a lot to say about it, especially from family. Whatever impact I expected was tripled. It was as if everybody decided they had a say in my affairs, and it was absolutely mind-blowing. I remember before I opened the laptop, I prayed, *God, we're in this together;* that thought helped me to remember that.

I did not personally tell anybody in my family. I just didn't want people to think they could tell me what to do. This was my life. I was very hardworking person and never depended on anyone. When you say my name, people will remind you of how hardworking I am and what a party girl I am, as well. Those were the two things people associated with me. But my life was mine to create. That was my comeback defense. I didn't care what anybody was going to say. This was between God and me. I didn't even want to touch the laptop that day, because I knew something was going on.

The next day I thought, *Okay, let me check and see what is going on.*

It was absolutely mind-blowing. People that I knew and people that I didn't know felt like I was a traitor. I could understand my family having a say and my loved ones. These were my design, my family, but I didn't understand the backlash from a total stranger who literally just knew me by name and never had any relationship with me whatsoever. I wasn't a pushover, so going through these horrible unpleasant messages in which I was being called all kinds of names was a true test of my faith. I responded to a few and defended myself. I felt like I wasn't going to explain myself anymore. I was tempted to just shut the page and forget about it, but it was too late to go back. This was the beginning. A lot of people were coming to follow what was going on.

Family members wanted me to know how they felt personally; some called, some texted, and some sent direct messages on Facebook. There was no way I could respond to each and every one of them, that would take every minute of every day.

Up until today, I handled this part of the story with care, because it caused so much hurt, rejection and abandonment. Many words were spoken that stuck with me for a very long time. It left me feeling lonelier than I've ever felt in my life; I was way out there on my own with nobody but God and my child. Looking back now, I was so full of anger towards these people. There was no support whatsoever. It was as if the whole world turned against me.

This experience showed me that God would never send you where his grace won't find you, because I found solace and peace in Him. He knew what was to come. Every time somebody rejected me, I would run to Him. Every time I found out what a loved one said, it was painful; but I ran to him. I fell out with so many people in that period of my life.

One day I remember telling God, *It's okay. Everybody can walk away. That's fine. I can't take this anymore. I'm not fighting. I'm not explaining. I'm not trying to win anyone over anyone, because it doesn't matter what story I tell them. Their minds are already made up.* As far as they were concerned, I had crossed that line.

Some even went to the extent of questioning my mental state of mind and sanity, saying I was brainwashed. They thought there had to be another power at work that coerced me into doing this. When the people that are meant to love you the most are the people throwing stones —when you're already on the floor— it leaves you in a state that only a few people will understand.

God was there every minute of the way. That's when He pulled me a whole lot closer. It was as if every time a word was used to describe me, His word would come forward to remind me exactly who He said I was in Him. Every time somebody threatened that my life was going to go bad, because I have now switched sides, God said, *I've got you.*

It took years and years for God to work through their hearts to bring about healing, forgiveness, and reconciliation. I would never forget some of the things that were said to me or the treatment that I received from them. I have forgiven, but I haven't forgotten. Forgetting means that part of your life didn't exist and it did. It was very real to me. God healed me from that part of my life, even though the wounds remained. It was my journey, not theirs, so I had to forgive for my freedom. The Lord Himself had forgiven me so much for all the wrong I had done, and I could do the same for others. To say it was easy would be an absolute lie on my part.

Through all of this, I was still having to look after my child. I would spend two or three nights here and there in the hospital with her when her lungs would flare up. When she caught a cold, we had to go to the hospital. When she had an apnea attack, we went to the hospital. When the weather changed, we went to the hospital. Then we went to physical therapy to help her ligaments and joints. She was having neurological appointments to check on her brainwaves. At some point they decided she should have started speaking, but she wasn't making a sound. So, we started speech therapy as well. We came to the point where a child would start crawling, but she wasn't doing that; so, we had to get more therapy. My journey didn't stop when I was getting all that hate about my faith. That hate came as part of the journey, but the journey was still continuing with the Lord. He saw me through all of that with so much strength that I didn't even know I had.

Some days, I was running on fumes. I didn't have the energy to even get up and do it. I had a child to take care of. Tiana needed my attention, my time, my efforts, and I also had a business that I was struggling to keep afloat.

I remember praying aloud, "God, I cannot do this.."

I was fighting back, and it was exhausting. That day, I wrote all the names down of the important people that I felt had hurt me, said horrible stuff, and had made me realize their displeasure in the route taken.

I said to God, "I give it back to you. You will work this out. You will take care of this because this is way above what I can deal with."

I left it there, and that was it. I deleted some of their phone numbers and blocked others from my social media page. I wasn't going to open that door and give them access to me to be hurt, rejected, to be called names, to be abandoned again. It gave me an opportunity to realize I was the black sheep. They always have to remind me that I had done something wrong by making a choice about my faith. I was done with all of this.

Time passed, and my child was growing stronger. I was also getting healthier. I started going back to work. My life slowly became more normalized. I would drop my child at the daycare center for special needs. It was a lovely nursery, not too far from where we lived. In the morning, I was working about three or four days in a week. It was work. My child, home, and church were my priorities. I hadn't partied in so long, I wouldn't have known what to do if you put me in a club.

After Tiana had turned two years old and still wasn't able to walk or speak, everything she did was very slow. I wanted to take the next step, which was to dedicate her childhood to God. I promised the Lord at the altar that I would give my child to Him. It's amazing how when they were rejecting me, God was pulling me closer. That was the beauty of it all. He was the sustainer. He was the one holding me together. Without Him I would have fallen apart. The memories of the promises I made in the past started coming back. If I was going to do it, I wasn't going to do it in a grand way.

I thought to myself, I'm going to give her time. I wanted to wait until she was stronger, walking or talking. I wanted her to be a part of the celebration; I didn't want her just lying there. I wanted this child to be part of the celebration of her life.

The week that she took her first step was the week we started planning for a celebration. I told everybody I was about to dedicate my child to the Lord. My church was right behind me needless to say, I had over two hundred and fifty guests on my guest list. I wanted to throw a dedication party that they hadn't seen in my area for a very long time. There were no expenses to be spared at all. I wanted to not only glorify God, but I also wanted people to realize what God had done. I wasn't going to do just a small little dingy party. My God was not dingy. What He did in Tiana's life wasn't a small thing. When I looked at it that way, I wanted to give the party of a lifetime. That was exactly what I did.

On the day of her dedication, I woke up excited that this was the day when my child would be officially given to God. This public declaration wasn't only for her, but for me as well. I gave a sincere prayer that came from my heart because I felt like this meant so much more to me than people understood. This was the stamp of ownership, to let Him and others know that we belonged to Him.

When I came out of my bedroom after the prayer, my house was already filling up as we prepared to go to the party location. People were coming over to my house to help with the arrangements. I rented out a local sports center hall in the area that held at least four to five hundred people. The decorator turned up as well to gather a few things before she headed to the hall to go and decorate it. Some of my workers were already in my house fixing breakfast for those that came early. It was an amazing atmosphere. My house was so full of people. Everybody was laughing, joking, and looking forward to a wonderful day. It was barely nine o'clock and already everything was in motion.

We were going to have a dedication service at the church first, before everybody proceeded to the hall where the entertainment and the food was going to happen. Some people were knocking on my door, wishing me good luck today if they couldn't make it. They expressed how they were so proud of me for the journey and the beauty of what that day meant for me and Tatiana. People knew this was a big deal to me.

Some of the people I invited were Muslims and wanted to go straight to the hall. But others came over to the church and witnessed the dedication service, which was the most important part of the day for me. My pastor, Pastor

Tony King, was going to be the one to officiate the dedication ceremony. There was a buzz in the air and a lightness of the heart. As I watched them walking around the room, going from person to person, I thought to myself, *This is what I wanted*. I wanted people to look at that child walking around and know that God is able, and God is faithful. I watched my child running around with the other kids, and I couldn't help but glorify God in my heart. This day was for her. I was so emotional.

Her father had flown in from the United States; he and his entourage were going to come straight to the church. Then from the church, they would proceed to go down the hall where the party was happening. It was one of the happiest days of my life. Before we left for the dedication, I had a mixture of everybody in my home which was beautiful. We got all dolled up to the nines and piled into our cars to drive over to the church in Greenwich, London.

When we got to the church, so many people attended that there were hardly any parking spaces left. I hadn't seen my church full like that before. Everybody that could make it turned up to the church. We got out of the car, and everybody was congratulating Tatiana. My daughter looked absolutely gorgeous in her white gown. I had packed whatever little hair she had into two ponytails. I wanted the white to represent the purity of her life and her. I was going to be changing that child all through the day. I think she had about three or four outfits to change into throughout the day. As we entered the church, it hit me. It was finally happening. I couldn't believe it. I was so ecstatic. The pastor gave a sermon about dedicating our children to the Lord. He spoke of how our children were a gift from the Lord. He went on to describe how we were meant to raise them up in the ways of the Lord so when they grew up, they wouldn't depart from it. Those words kept ringing in my mind, how this was just the start of her journey. As she grew up, I was to make sure that she knew who the Lord was. I sat there with every word that he was saying finding a place for it in my heart.

After the sermon, he called her father and I in front. He called the godparents on both sides to come up to the altar as well. He picked Tiana up, held her in his arms, and then he prayed. It was like God Himself was present on that day to see that it went to plan. The pastor prayed fervently over her, then over me, and over the father. Then he dedicated my child to the Lord. He asked the Lord to be with my child all the days of her life; to never leave or forsake; to never have his hand taken away from her; to watch and guide her wherever she went. But most importantly, to be glorified in the child's life for all who had eyes to see and ears to listen; for all to hear the testimony of this child's life.

The whole room erupted in applause; everybody started congratulating her and taking pictures with her. The service was done, and the pastor released us all to go into the second part of the day. Before we left, the pastor called me to the side to congratulate me. He told me God was pleased with this, because this is exactly what God wanted us to do where our kids were concerned. I thanked him for being with me through the journey. I thanked him and his wife, Evelyn, for being there. After saying, "Thank you," where it was necessary, I made a joke that we were going to have a fabulous time at the party.

I had hired caterers for the food and ordered double the amount for the people I invited. I wanted people to have a fantastic time. I wanted people to not forget this day for a very long time, if ever. The musicians were already there. Photographers and the videographer were already there. Everything was perfect. The stage was set, and I had told them we were on our way over. I was going to have fun today; oh, how I was going to dance. It had been a long time since I was so giddy and happy.

Everybody was talking about the party, but I didn't realize there would be so many people actually turning up. It was jammed. We couldn't even park. I swear to God, for the rest of my life, I wouldn't forget it. God had to be the one who made it possible. The whole day exceeded my expectations.

There was a special area set up for us to sit down. And the whole enterprise started taking up their place, and the music was playing and the DJ announced that we'd arrived.

He asked if there was anything special that I wanted him to do, and I said, "Yes, I wanted my pastor to bless this day before we even started eating, drinking, or having fun."

My pastor took the mic, and he prayed over everybody, blessing the food. Then, the celebration began.

I'm someone that could be described as "extra." I don't half do anything; if something's worth doing, it's worth doing right. I'm very passionate about a lot of things, and it shows in the things that I love. I love food, décor, and everything that signifies aesthetic beauty. You could see it in the party that I threw. On that day, there were so many cakes. It was absolutely ridiculous. But under the center of this cake was this princess cake with the princess standing right outside of Disney World. My child was obsessed with Disney and loved everything princess themed. That cake was the centerpiece of the table. It was absolutely stunning. It was one of the best parties I'd ever thrown or will ever throw, because I don't think I could ever handle a party of that magnitude again.

I watched my child weaving her way through the crowd and remembered the faithfulness of God. I remembered where God had been with us. Again. I remembered exactly how God found me. I looked at it all from the perspective of a mother who was absolutely desperate; who had come to her breaking point; who had been knocked down so low that there was only one way to go. That was to go seek the power that was beyond anything she'd ever known or heard. Most of the people in the room didn't know the details of the journey, but I knew deep in my heart.

I didn't know when, how, or where, but one day I was going to share the testimony of how faithful, loving, and merciful God is. God could have rejected me. God could have said a whole lot of things, but in His infinite mercy, He looked down and saw a broken vessel who needed Him. He saw someone he could glorify himself through. He saw a child laying there that needed the breath of life, who needed the wind of God in her lungs. A child that needed a mighty touch of heaven. Without it, there was no way she was going to make it. In His mercy, He decided to act.

I was never going to be the same.

God is faithful.

TO GOD BE THE GLORY
Fleming Island, Florida, United States, 2021

My journey with the Lord happened at twenty seven years of age. As I wrap up this book, I'm preparing to celebrate my thirty ninth year, and my daughter is now twelve years old. This book is long overdue. If I had my way, it would have been written a long time ago, but God had other plans.

Tatiana Alexandra Brooks is a happy, smart, intelligent, loving, kind, sensitive, introverted child. I call her my miracle, baby because that's exactly what she is. She is my only child, and I am very content with who she has already become.

The blessing of the Lord found me at a time when I wasn't ready for it, at a time when my life was in my own hands. When I least expected it, God —through his mercy— had a plan for my life to call me and give me the gift of salvation.

When I look back, it all happened in the United Kingdom, in England, and now here I am living in another country. This is all by the grace of God.

Concluding this story really makes me reflect back on how far the Lord has walked with us and how far we have come. Sometimes, it feels like I'm telling the story of somebody else in another time or era, because it's been that long.

I've had people ask me, "Why did it take you so long?"

The only answer I can give is that life happened. We propose and embark on plans, aspirations. and dreams. But it is the Lord who makes it happen. There was a lack of trying on my part, because I had attempted to write this book for years. The last time, I had three chapters left until I finished it completely, and my friend was typing the book as I wrote it. Her house burned down with the laptop, and all of my writing inside. I was absolutely devastated.

This was a sign that the timing was wrong; perhaps, it was too soon to begin writing it. That this story was really supposed to become focused on my Tiana, my baby girl, and everything that happened before she came along.

It wasn't easy moving over to America, but God has been faithful. It felt like every time I was close to writing the book, the enemy came at me, with distractions from all sides. I guess the enemy knew the impact this book was going to have. Even if this book only impacts one person and helps them to make the right choice in turning their life over to the Lord Jesus Christ, I will be ecstatic..

When I lost my book, I was devastated. I totally gave up on it. I mourned the loss of it for months. I didn't have the motivation to embark on trying to write it again. I woke up one day and it felt like God just said, "This is the time to write it." Now, my child is 12 years old. 12 is the, is the number of completion of perfection so I do want to believe that this was the right time that the Lord had, it might not be right to others because of the pandemic that we face with COVID-19. But to me, the Lord had a time of purpose for this book. It was meant to be written for a time like this.

God has been faithful through it all. It hasn't been an easy ride. When you sincerely repent and commit your life to the Lord, that's when Satan gives you his full attention. Over the years, he has done all he can to steer me away from the course. I even remember one of the hardest things that I went through was the loss of one of my best friends who had been with me through some really difficult times. He had been a godsend in my life and was there for me when most people walked away. He committed suicide on his birthday in 2013. I hit rock bottom, because I felt a lot of guilt there on my part. I didn't see this coming.

God came for me again. He raised me up from the pits of darkness to continue my journey.

I moved to America shortly after I visited Israel in 2013. Little did I know, after the death of my best friend, the Lord was going to call me out of England. When we commit your life to the Lord, you have no idea where He's going to lead you. But as long as you're faithful and as long as you're willing to follow his plans, things will work out. He said it in Jeremiah 29:11, *I know the plans I have for you, says the Lord. Plans of good and not evil; plans to give you a hope and a desired end.*

You have no idea of what the desired end contains from the start to the finish. But as long as you're obedient, God is forever faithful. The faithfulness of God is eternal. He can never go against Himself or go against who He is. It is part of His character to be faithful to us, even when we're not faithful to him. It's only been the faithfulness of God that has seen me through the years. There were so many changes, trials, and tribulations to get over. However, there was one thing that was constant and one thing that remained: that was the hand of the living God upon my life and my child. It felt like He was watching over us in a foreign land.

Sometimes I don't feel Him, and I ask, "God, where are you? Have you forsaken me?"

That's when I go right back to the Word; I go right back to the basics and fill my heart with what He said.

"I will never leave or forsake you."

That is powerful. God is omnipresent so when He says He'll never leave nor forsake you, it means it doesn't matter where you will be in this world that He has created. It doesn't matter how out of your comfort zone or your support system you are. He will always be with you.

I have no immediate family here in America. When I moved over here in 2013, after the death of my best friend, it was not something I planned or something I wanted. I knew God had called me out of England. My time there was over, it was time to start fresh in another new place, in a new country, in a new continent. It came with its challenges, but my God remains faithful. God's love for his creation is more than we can ever fathom because through the years, I've come to truly realize that God loves me. He doesn't see me like I see myself. He doesn't see my past mistakes and hold them against me. The blood of Christ has washed me white as snow. The blood of Christ has covered every sin at the cross of Calvary. He took it upon Himself to pay a debt I could never repay, and my life in its entirety belongs to Him. He sees what He says I am, which is loved, blessed, and highly favored. I am an overcomer, made in the image of my Creator. I am given the precious gift that He gave me in the form of my child.

It can be easy to allow the trials and the tribulations we've faced to shape our idea of who God is. But if we are just able to throw our faith out there to just take Him at His word, God will exalt His word because it is eternal.

The Bible says it, *Plans may wither, flowers may fade, but the word of the Lord abides forever.* When God makes promises, he keeps them. As long as we believe and stand on his word and His promise, He will fulfill them.

A few days before I left England, I felt this urge to visit a church outside of my home church, at which I used to attend prayer meetings on Friday night. During that service, the pastor prophesied over me and my child, that he knew I was leaving. He said God showed him exactly what He had done and what He was about to do in the land where I was going. It was phenomenal. God made it known that He would be with me every step of the way; He made and kept promises that I hold very close to my heart today. I will never let go of those promises, because I know he's faithful. I know his word will come to pass and nothing —not even the worst days— can threaten the plans that He has for me. That keeps me going.

Sometimes when things get hard, it makes me reflect back to my journey with the Lord, how it started, and how far we've come. He started a good work in us and is so faithful to finish it to completion. When I think back to what He brought me from it gives me the hope and the confidence to trust Him for the future. I live with the living proof of the miraculous hand of God.

When I look at my child, it reminds me of what God has done. I remember everything that they had diagnosed her with and how none of it has come to pass. There's nothing wrong with her speech. There's nothing wrong with her brain. There's nothing wrong with her mobility. My child is absolutely perfect with wisdom and intelligence that I know could have only come from the Lord. The doctors predicted, but God had the final say. That's why I had to write this book. That's why I know I owed it not only to the Lord, but to myself and my daughter.

I want my grandchildren and my great-great-grandchildren to hold this book and say, "Look at what God did for my great-grandma's life and in Tiana's life. If the same God can do this for them, he can do this for me."

If this book helps to turn anybody back from a path of destruction onto the path of life in Jesus Christ, it will have achieved its purpose. If this book gives hope to somebody that is struggling right now in the pits of it all with nothing but darkness around them, I pray that this book will give them the ability to see the light that is in Christ Jesus. He is the light that is able to overcome the darkness, the power that is able to move mountains. If God can resurrect the dead, what else can he do in our lives?

I couldn't sit on this book and testimony any longer. I couldn't leave this world and go home to be with the Lord without testifying to what He has done.

I am a living witness that when you seek God in all sincerity, from the depth of your being, He will respond. He will listen, just like the Bible says.

Getting pregnant by someone I barely knew was my mistake, but God took this situation and turned it into something beautiful. He put a testimony in my mouth, and a love for Him in my heart. Nobody could take that away. That is what God can do with your mess. He takes it and cleanses you. He literally rewrites the story according to his plan, his will, and his purpose. Even if I wanted to run away from the Lord, I knew I couldn't get any further.

He found me in London, one of the most beautiful cities in the world where most people live for self and have very little time and care for the Lord. I lived in that society and I loved it. If God can come for me in that situation and turn my life around, he can do it for anybody. The Bible says the hand of the Lord is long and mighty to save. Nobody is beyond his reach. He is the God that can do the unimaginable. He can do the impossible. He is the God that can go far above everything we could ever hope for, ask, or imagine, according to his power, that worketh in us.

Every time I am faced with a new trial, I face it with the knowledge of the past, very close to my heart. He is the same yesterday, today, and forevermore. If He can deliver me yesterday and overcome my frailties and unbelief, I can trust Him for all that comes my way. That's exactly where I am with Him. There are times when I sit down and reflect on the past. I feel all kinds of emotions, because, as much as I have gone so far from it, I am still the same person who feels like I've lived nine different lives. A lot of changes. A lot of changes go along with a lot of uncertainty.

He's been the only constant in my life. If you don't know how much I love my Lord and savior, then you truly do not know me at all. He is the center of my being, and that's what I've asked Him to do from day one. He's honored that thus far.

Twelve years later; twelve years of good mountain top moments; twelve years of valleys in the low. He's always there. I haven't yet been overcome, and I will not ever be. In the completion of this book, I faced an unexpected and very difficult obstacle. It now comes in as one of the most difficult times of my life, but the grace of God has kicked in to enable me to write it. Just like before He comes in like a mighty rushing wind, He comes in to do what only He can do. He comes in to do what he is known for, which is miracles. I'll be writing another book to share that testimony of what God has done. But for now, if you're reading this book and you don't know the Lord Jesus Christ, go to Him in prayer. If you don't know how to pray, just talk to Him. He doesn't need fancy words. He doesn't need the lingo. He doesn't need the perfection of speech. Just go to Him as you are, because there's nothing you're going to tell Him that He doesn't already know.

The compassion, mercy, and the love of God is something human beings don't totally fully comprehend or understand, myself included. If we understood the Father's love for his children, it would start to make sense just how much He longs for us to come home to Him. Just how much He longs for to protect, guide, provide, and heal us. He has a Father's heart, and that heart won't let Him rest until His children come home to Him. That's why the word says that our Lord Jesus Christ wouldn't come back until the gospel had been preached to the four corners of this world, until all had come to the saving knowledge of Jesus Christ of Nazareth.

God literally moved heaven and earth to get to this African girl who needed Him. This girl who cried out for Him from the depths of her being. I am so grateful. I am so thankful that He heard my prayers. He easily could have turned a blind eye. He easily could have not responded.

It makes me want to encourage and share my testimony to all who have ears to listen so that they would know that God loves them.

God loves you. God is absolutely crazy about you.

For the rest of my life, until that day when he calls me home, I will never ever forget how the God of the Christians; the Lord, God Almighty; God of Israel; God of Abraham, Isaac, and Jacob found me broken at a crossroad.

Broken at a Crossroad

www.ingramcontent.com/pod-product-compliance
Lightning Source LLC
Chambersburg PA
CBHW071958070526
44583CB00015B/1242